African Foreign Policy
and Diplomacy from Antiquity
to the 21st Century

African Foreign Policy and Diplomacy from Antiquity to the 21st Century

Volume 1

DANIEL DON NANJIRA

Praeger Security International

PRAEGER

AN IMPRINT OF ABC-CLIO, LLC
Santa Barbara, California • Denver, Colorado • Oxford, England

Library of Congress Cataloging-in-Publication Data

Don Nanjira, Daniel.
  African foreign policy and diplomacy : from antiquity to the 21st century / Daniel Don
Nanjira.
    2 v. cm.
  Includes bibliographical references and index.
  ISBN 978-0-313-37982-6 (hard copy : alk. paper) — ISBN 978-0-313-
37983-3 (ebook)
  1. Africa—Foreign relations. I. Title.
  DT31.D625   2010
  327.6—dc22   2010015498

ISBN: 978-0-313-37982-6
EISBN: 978-0-313-37983-3

14 13 12   2 3 4 5

This book is also available on the World Wide Web as an eBook.
Visit www.abc-clio.com for details.

Praeger
An Imprint of ABC-CLIO, LLC

ABC-CLIO, LLC
130 Cremona Drive, P.O. Box 1911
Santa Barbara, California 93116-1911

This book is printed on acid-free paper ∞

Manufactured in the United States of America

Contents

VOLUME 2

Preface

African Foreign Policy and Diplomacy from Antiquity to the 21st Century has grown from my experience in lecturing to undergraduate and graduate students and in talking to a wide variety of audiences on the subjects of African diplomacy, foreign policy, and international relations. These lectures have been given to academia and United Nations system organizations; provided at global conferences on trade and development, international business, politics, economics, and similar topics; and delivered to diplomats and members of government institutions as well.

I have been constantly amazed at the way in which African international relations, foreign policy, and diplomacy have been misunderstood or taken out of perspective. A clear and coherent explanation African conditions—and even performance in the world—has been strikingly lacking. Also lacking is an authoritative reference list of readings that could facilitate the study and informed interpretation of African issues in the context of African international relations, foreign policy, and diplomacy. This deficiency results, for example, in cumbersome research problems for many students who must consult an extensive reading list before they can comprehend the gist of what they would wish to know about Africa.

In addition to having been a student of international relations, development law, and diplomacy for many years, I also have been a diplomat, serving as an ambassador of the Republic of Kenya. As Kenyan ambassador, I spent more than a quarter of a century serving that African nation in multilateral and bilateral diplomacy, and participated both in the formulation and execution of African foreign policy and diplomacy. With this perspective, I have felt challenged and obligated to explain in simple terms not only the processes, procedures, and outcomes of African foreign policymaking, but also to detail how this policy is *actually made* and implemented with clear indications of the makers and modes of implementation that drive African foreign policy and diplomacy.

Thus, this book seeks to facilitate an understanding of the making and execution of African foreign policy and diplomacy. These are the main directors and managers of African international relations. In turn, African international relations legitimize the presence of Africa in global international relations, and project, propagate, promulgate, protect, and promote Africa's national interests in, and contributions to, the global system of politics and geopolitics, sustainable development, trade, international business, economics, and the environment.

African Foreign Policy and Diplomacy from Antiquity to the 21st Century further seeks to achieve this goal through critical analyses and explanations of the origins and development of African international relations, foreign policy, and diplomacy as manifested in the roots and foundations of these constituent disciplines of Africa's domestic and external conditions from the most remote reaches of antiquity to the present.

The milestones that exist in the events, history, issues, and dictates of the processes and procedures highlighting the determinants of Africa's foreign policies and diplomacy also are examined. It should be noted that the terms *foreign policy* and *diplomacy* actually are pluralitantums— although used in the singular, they actually have plural meanings. Thus, every time the expression *African foreign policy* is employed, in reality it means many African foreign policies. These distinctions and other conceptualizations are examined.

The history of African international relations, diplomacy, and foreign policy is addressed in this book in perspectives and periods stretching over the centuries and millennia, from the earliest times to the 21st century. As an expert in, and practitioner of, the making and execution of African foreign policy, as well as its management through diplomacy and foreign service, I am convinced that the details collected in this book's two volumes will be of considerable use to all readers interested in the topic of Africa, especially those at embassies and legations, researchers, students, teachers, and others.

First, *African Foreign Policy and Diplomacy from Antiquity to the 21st Century* presents information on, and analyses of, specific African study areas such as African economic development, the global economy, and international business in Africa, etc. This presentation of information is well suited to courses for students of African and comparative studies, as well as the related field of international relations and any courses that examine Africa dating back to antiquity that include the roots and foundations of these three disciplines—African international relations, diplomacy, and foreign policy—as a study area.

African Foreign Policy and Diplomacy from Antiquity to the 21st Century is a handy tool as a textbook that contains supplementary knowledge on various kinds of African challenges, problems, and issues, including adequately addressing the multidimensional challenges confronting contemporary Africa. As a professor who has been teaching African international relations, foreign policy, and diplomacy for a number of years, I am fully aware of the gravity of the problem of finding the most recent and accurate sources of information on these African topics and themes. There is nothing more useful to students, both undergraduate and graduate alike, than readily availing to them a source of information that is able to provide them with the fundamental knowledge and information that would suffice for their courses. I hope that this book meets this requirement by presenting analyses to enable readers to better understand the origins, development, maturation, and application of African international relations, foreign policy, and diplomacy from the perspectives of the makers of these policies, the processes and procedures that they follow, the roles that they continue to play, and the consequences of their decisions as of the policies that constitute African international relations, diplomacy, and foreign policy are implemented.

African studies, comparative studies, and international relations have, over the millennia, undergone a long and grand evolutionary process starting from the *Homo genus* stage of crude relations and interactions between and among family stocks to the *Homo Africanus-Africanus* stage we observe and know today in which Africans act as communicator, negotiator, aggressor, peacemaker, and participant in relations and partnerships from within, as well as from outside of, Africa.

Second, this book contains an extensive collection of readings and reference materials on Africa that will facilitate research efforts and supplement the knowledge and data that may be sought in specific African study areas. It will also explain the African international relations, foreign policy, and diplomacy issues and challenges that have faced Africa historically, and continue to face Africa in the new millennium. These are the aspects of the African Condition that legitimize Africa's presence in the global system, especially in terms of international politics and security, climate change and global warming, globalization and the law of nations, as well as many other issues. This book also provides a quick reference to useful and relevant information on African issues for readers and other interested individuals and institutions.

I would like to close with the following noteworthy thoughts:

- Africa is not a country or state—it is the second largest continent on Earth and a region of immense natural beauty and endowments. Africa is a huge paradox. For example, Africa is very rich in natural and human resources, yet it is the poorest continent on Earth. Africa was the cradle of humankind and civilization, yet it has been described as the "dark continent" of savages and primitive people. Africa has more than 2,000 African languages as well as countless dialects, and yet you need to speak in foreign languages—French, English, Portuguese, Arabic, etc.—in order to communicate.

- The writing of this book was necessitated by the serious and grave handicaps that are encountered in teaching African and comparative studies in universities and colleges. These deficiencies prompted the need for a comprehensive analysis and treatment of Africa as a study area.

- This book updates existing information relating to Africa's international relations, foreign policy, and diplomacy in a comprehensive manner to support the study of new and emerging issues and challenges facing Africa in the coming decades and beyond.

- There is a need to adopt a novel approach to African international relations and to the making and execution of African foreign policy and diplomacy that stresses the ignored or neglected side of the African coin. This need constitutes describing of acts of Africa to give a just and balanced analysis of the events, issues, and dictates shaping Africa; describing the conditions for the success of Africa as a subsystem of the global system, especially in the new millennium; and creating the impetus to make a contribution to knowledge about Africa as the second largest continent on Earth.

Acknowledgments

The writing of this book has been a formidable task. The effort for realizing it as a successful project has been enormous for, indeed, the subject matter covers a vast area consisting of events, issues, themes, and challenges that call for deep and prolonged research and analysis. I have been most fortunate to have wonderful help from a number of individuals whose positive attitudes toward my desire and efforts to produce a comprehensive study of African foreign policy, diplomacy, and international relations, have been most encouraging.

Let me, therefore, at the outset express my genuine thanks to Praeger Publishers for agreeing to publish this study. The book aims at making a constructive contribution to knowledge about Africa as an actor on the global stage. Tim Furnish of Praeger Security International was most helpful in furnishing me with ideas and suggestions that I found useful in preparing an outline for the study, and I am grateful to him for his guidance. I am further thankful to Anthony Chiffolo, director of Praeger Publishers, who showed readiness to help and to ensure that the work was neither delayed nor interrupted. My genuine thanks also go to Steve Catalano, senior editor at Praeger Security International, for his understanding, patience, and flexibility. These have been assets that any writer would find most encouraging. Africa is a huge and paradoxical continent with a complex history whose correct analysis and interpretations call for broad approaches This effort required the latitude to undertake deep research and create critical overviews of African situations before reaching any conclusive statements on the various aspects of the African Condition.

I realized the complexity and vastness of the subject matter of this book right from the beginning of the effort. All pointed to the need for a longer-than-usual writing period; but I was determined to accomplish this job at my earliest opportunity. This meant getting the work organized in such a manner as to assure competence and effectiveness in the preparation and completion of the project. For this, I owe a special debt of gratitude to Marietha C. Shete for her calm demeanor and professional composure, informed expertise, and tenacious assistance, as well as constructive and constant advice that she offered on how such a voluminous piece of work could be organized, and compiled for efficient completion of the project.

All of these individuals have played a role in shaping this work and helping me to attain my goal of creating a study of Africa that will create interest in, and support the study of, the African Condition. It is my sincere hope that this study will help Africanists and non-Africanists alike develop increased interest in being students of Africa for the sake of promoting the cause of Africa to reclaim her civilization, and reclaim her *Africanness* for the common good of humankind in the third millennium. This would be the best way of turning this two-volume offering on Africa into useful elaborations, explanations, and clarifications of the African Condition and the status of Africa as a subsystem of the global system in these and subsequent times.

The African Roots of
Continental Geopolitics:
Antiquity through the
18th Century

CHAPTER 1

Africa: The Natural Order—Africa Was First in the World

AFRICA AS A STUDY AREA

What is Africa? Why Africa? Why study Africa? Is it moral to study Africa? Often, one hears terrible "howlers" about Africa. For example, that Africa is a country; that Djibouti is in Nairobi; that Chad must be in Monrovia; that Niger is in Nigeria. These, and other similar blunders, are as alarming as they are intriguing and vexing—especially, when they are said in a country by educated people who should know better.

Not only has science and technology shrunk the world into one global village through the Information Revolution and international telecommunication technologies (ICTs), but the world has Plinyism on Africa—"ex Africa semper aliquid novi" (there is always something new out of Africa). Gaius Plinius Secundus, also known as Pliny the Elder, was a Roman officer, writer, philosopher, naturalist, marine expert, lawyer, natural historian, and encyclopedist. He became an important naval commander in the Bay of Naples. His fame made him known to Vespian (9–79 CE), who was a Roman emperor from 69 to 79 CE.

Born in 23 CE, Pliny attended good schools and later published a famous encyclopedia in Latin titled *Naturalis Historiae* (*Natural History*)[1] This was an encyclopedia of 37 books, 10 of which he himself published around 77 CE. This huge encyclopedic treatise examined natural and man-made objects, and described many natural phenomena. This vast contribution to knowledge has survived—but it is the only one of his works to do so.

Book 8 of Pliny's encyclopedia gives an elaborate analysis of land animals: elephants, snakes, lions, camels, giraffes, crocodiles, hippopotami, dogs, hedgehogs, cows, sheep, wolves, etc. The rest of Pliny's encyclopedia books were compiled and published by his nephew (the son of his sister), Gaius Plinius Caecilius Secundus (circa 62–115 CE) whom he adopted.

Pliny the Elder's *Naturalis Historiae* was one of the most important books in ancient Rome. It is in Book 8, that he wrote one of his famous sayings—and it was on Africa. "Ex Africa semper aliquid novi" is still a famous quote today. Pliny's book aims at interpreting and clarifying these complexities as they determine Africa's place in the world. Thus, by looking at the often neglected side of the African coin, an analysis of the African Condition not only confirms that practically all roads led "ex Africa," but also that many of the same roads had to, and must, lead "ad Africa," if any equitable balancing acts of Africa would be attained. The focus on Africa should not just be about the bad things all the time, such as corruption, primitive cultures, poverty, bad governance, etc. On the other side of the African coin, one finds rich cultures, natural beauty, and vast resources, which have been plundered by Europe for so many centuries. One must also say something about Africa's progressive initiatives and attainments. This is being done by African institutions as well as other well-intentioned international community organizations. Such balancing helps to better understand Africa, rather than just giving the dark side of the continent and its peoples.

As a naturalist, Pliny the Elder was aware of the presence of Africa as part of the Western Province of the Roman Empire, which had many zebras, elephants, and other kinds of unusual animals. There were so many events happening in Africa—wars being fought with barbarians and invaders of the Roman Empire—and there were so many stories coming from Africa, that it was considered impossible to manage the affairs that were shaping Africa daily.

ROOTS AND SOURCES OF AFRICAN INTERNATIONAL RELATIONS, AFRICAN FOREIGN POLICY, AND AFRICAN DIPLOMACY

African international relations (AIR), African foreign policy (AFP), and African diplomacy (AD) cannot be discussed in a vacuum. They are the instruments through which the nation states of Africa not only relate to one another endogenously, but also through which they engage other foreign political entities on the international stage.

Of vital importance, therefore, will be to indicate not only the origins and development of African international relations, African diplomacy, and foreign policy, but also their nature and function throughout the millennia as important disciplines for Africa and her nations, and their actions, interactions, reactions, proactions, and even inaction as members of the world community.

African foreign policy and diplomacy are the core of this book. Nonetheless, this study covers a much broader ground than the parameters of diplomacy and foreign policy. These two disciplines, together with African international relations, are the trio of pillars on which international Africa balances. They are the triangular protectors and defenders of Africa's Condition in the eyes of the world. They have the challenging and daunting duty of managing the determinants of the African Condition on the global stage for the common good of Africa, and of other nations, both individually and collectively. The diplomacy and foreign policy of African countries cannot be studied or pursued in a vacuum, but they must be appreciated in the context of a comprehensive understanding of African international relations from the remotest antiquity to the present.

This means that AD is implementer and enforcer of foreign policy, and manager of AIR. In turn, AFP is the director, guide, and promoter of Africa's decisions, desires, and interests in global international relations. This view requires the treatment of African international relations in a holistic, rather than fragmented, perspective of Africa as a continent and subsystem of the global system of sovereign states.

DEMOCRACY AND DIPLOMACY AS THE FOUNDATIONS OF AFRICAN FOREIGN POLICY, INTERNATIONAL RELATIONS, AND DIPLOMACY

The conceptual definitions of "democracy," "foreign policy," and "international relations" help to better understand the African Condition on the global stage. For now, it should be noted that the difference between African and Western values is as big as the difference between the concept and practice of democracy and diplomacy in Africa. The value system of a people, a nation, or a continent determines the kinds of relations that the continent, the nation, and the people will eventually adopt. This is applicable even in times and cases where the leaders of those nations decide to violate their country's value systems. The violation or suspension of the constitution of a country for personal, dictatorial, or corrupt reasons does not make that country anarchical. The constitution can be suspended, but that does not mean that the country has no legal code or constitution as the basic law of the land.

In like manner, democracy as conceived by the Western value of "one man, one vote," does not mean that it is ipso facto better than the African way of dealing with democracy through African Socialism, Ubuntu (an ancient African Bantu expression meaning "humanity to others," which is a Pax Africana idea that conveys the very essence of community or brotherhood), or Amana (a Hausa concept whose meaning includes faith, trust, and honesty, as integral elements of socioeconomic transactions) for example, or through the search for people's rights in Africa as distinct from individual human rights, or even through a collective resolution of the problems of famine and hunger, poverty and disease, education, and capacity building. In short, any argument that Western democracy or Western values are superior to African democratic value systems constitutes the highest degree of irrationality.

In traditional African society, decisions relating to matters of state or affecting the people (for example, the relationship of the people to their country) were extremely important. For example, the education of a child in a village was the responsibility of the whole village, people's rights (such as the collective right to a family or to clan land) had to be obeyed blindly, and the prohibition of inheritance of land by women was unquestionable.

THE CORE FUNDAMENTAL OBJECTIVES OF THIS STUDY

It is noteworthy that international law—the law of nations—recognizes sovereign states as the primary subjects of international law, and grants international legal personality to subjects of international law other than states that are also important actors as subjects and objects of diplomacy and foreign policy. In view of this, a comprehensive understanding of the foreign policies and diplomacy of Africa can best be arrived at by putting these disciplines in the overall context of the entire African continent as viewed and assessed from the perspective of Africa's history, evolutionary process, economy and economics, environment and geography, human and natural resources and endowments, as well as Africa's potential, business opportunities, trade and development possibilities, products, and social and legal structures. As foundations, sources, and determinants of African diplomacy and foreign policy, the above themes require that these disciplines be examined in an overall African context.

This book was based on four fundamental objectives. First, it aims to outline the themes, problems, and challenges that face Africa and determine the nature and function of Africa's diplomacy and foreign policy. Second, it aims to cram a comprehensive survey of information, knowledge, and critical analyses of the various aspects of the African events, issues, and dictates of life into two volumes that will examine each of these aspects extensively, each in its own compartment for the use of anyone or any institution that may be interested in a given aspect of African diplomacy, foreign policy, and international relations. This is a study of African international relations, politics, economics and related issues, and the global system in which Africa participates as a collection of states that are sovereign political units and subjects of international law. Third, this book endeavors to determine the roots, foundations, and sources of African international relations, African diplomacy, and foreign policy, and trace them to antiquity. The analyses deal with the various sources and backgrounds of physical, historical, political, social, cultural, economic, and environmental origin from which the theory and reality of African international relations, African diplomacy, and foreign policy are derived. Fourth, this book targets a broad audience, which is invited to use this book as a master text on African international relations, African diplomacy, and foreign policy that collects national, regional, and global perspectives on Africa.

The nature and function of contemporary African international relations, African diplomacy, and foreign policy are best understood if examined in the historical perspective of the events and dictates that have shaped, and continue to shape, Africa from remotest antiquity to the present. In this regard, the African journey begins with the story of the creation of the universe, through the formation, evolution, and peopling of Africa; the evolution of African populations and their cultures, customs, traditions, and civilizations, as well as their economic, business, political, and legal orders; the development of African societies and institutions (both state and private institutions) as the prototypes of government, governance, democracy, and democratization, as well as the foundations of justice and human dignity; and the internationalization of the standards of behavior and interactions within and beyond African state borders.

These structures demand protection, promotion, projection, promulgation, propagation, and provision to defend Africa's individual and collective image, the national and group interests of sovereign states, and other legal personalities that are empowered to address these issues and problems, and to find lasting solutions to them. This is what African—and any other—international relations, foreign policy, and diplomacy are all about.

AFRICA'S PLACE IN THE WORLD

Africa was *the first* in many respects. She was first the cradle of humankind, providing the habitat for *Homo genus*. Africa is the only continent to have been inhabited by humankind for at least 5 million years running. Africans were first in technology discovery and use, in governance and (collective) government, and in statehood, with the first city-state on Earth, known as Old Kingdom, which was in Egypt in 3100 BCE. Africa has one of the most diverse linguistic, cultural, and historical legacies on Earth, with more than 2,000 languages, and countless dialects, spoken on this continent.

Africa has the fastest growing population in the world; is the most poorly inhabited continent; and has the largest desert on Earth—the Great Sahara Desert. She is the most isolated, ignored, and marginalized continent, yet Africa also is the most exploited continent in history.

Africa is the most haunted continent, with endless conflicts, wars and civil strife, corruption, etc. She is also the most fragmented continent in the world with 53 states making up 54 sovereign units. (The Sahrawi Arab Democratic Republic (SADR) is still claimed by Morocco, but in August 1982 at the OAU Summit in Nairobi, it was recognized as a sovereign, independent state. Thus within Africa, there are 54 sovereign states, but outside of Africa, the SADR has not been recognized as a sovereign state, so globally, Africa has 53 states, i.e., members of the UN.) Africa hosts the largest number of the world's poorest or least developed countries (LDCs) with 34 of 50 total LDCs in the world having been in Africa for many years.

Africa is the world's most tropical continent, yet it is the only continent whose agricultural production and productivity have been deteriorating annually since 2000 CE.

Africa is also *second* in several significant ways. It is the second largest, second driest, and second most populous continent. Although it is after Asia (China with around 1.3 billion people, estimated July 2008 at 1,330,044,544, and India with about 1.1 billion, estimated in July 2008 at 1,147,995,904), Africa's population was estimated at 952,777,000 in 2008, and one billion in 2009.[2]

Africa is a subsystem of the international system. Her place or presence in the world does not, in the context of this chapter, refer to the power politics of the international community. "Place" here refers mainly to geopolitical, cultural, political, social, historical, and other aspects of Africa as a member of the world community, but not as a power in international politics.

The political abomination of cultural groupings in 54 national borders has produced endless conflicts, wars, and civil strife in Africa. Over the years, Africa has suffered many injustices, despite her innocence. For example, her children were captured and sold into slavery as objects. They were subjected to the worst, most dehumanizing conditions of the slave trade. As such, Africa became an innocent burden-bearer of Europe. Because she provided free and cheap labor, she was exploited, impoverished, and raped. She has been deprived of her natural resources, whether they have been minerals like diamonds, gold, and copper, or agricultural crops and commodities—the so-called cash crops—that include, or have included, cocoa, coffee, cotton, ivory, tea, sugar, pyrethrum, rubber, sisal, pineapples, and bananas. Africa also has suffered from European colonial policies and practices that succeeded in transforming and depriving her of her spirit, soul, and Africanness while turning her into a by-product of the European-Western value system at her own expense and at the expense of African values.

Africa's fate has made her matter a lot to the world. She has provided many gifts to the world, but especially to Europe and the Americas. Although Africa has been involved in diverse and numerous contributions to the world, she has not reaped the economic, trade, and financial benefits in a commensurate manner, especially in regard to the West. Here, reverse resource flows from Africa to the West, corrupt practices, plundering, and exploitation of Africa by leaders, governments, and certain international institutions—like Western banks—have greatly impoverished Africa.

Thus, Africa's presence in the world from remotest times to the present has been a huge paradox—of being the first and the last, poor in plenty, exploited and impoverished; rich in cultures and civilizations, and yet defined as primitive; the cradle of humankind and yet baptized as the Dark Continent; wealthy and yet vastly squandered; the first city-statehood on Earth, and yet the first to be described as a continent with bad governance and corrupt government leaders; innocent, and yet colonized and transformed. The comparisons are nearly limitless. The image of Africa on the international scene has been dismal, with vast acculturation, poverty, ignorance, illiteracy, disease occurance, and all of the negative attributes of these plights. The phonist system (the use of the foreign, ex-colonial language structures of Francophone, Anglophone, Lusophone [Portuguese], and Arabphone, meaning French, English, Portuguese, and Arabic languages, respectively) that was instituted in Africa as a result of colonization, and the overall colonial heritage in Africa, created living and working conditions that continue to haunt Africa and the African people 124 years after the imposition of colonial rule.

Thus, Africa may be isolated and marginalized; she may be impoverished, burdened, and exploited; she may suffer from neo-colonialism, corruption, and bad governance; and she may continue to suffer from many other consequences of the colonial legacy—like conflicts, economic, and sociocultural deprivation, environmental degradation, natural disaster devastation, pandemics, poverty, disease, and ignorance. But, Africa can no longer be ignored. Therefore, in the coming decade and beyond, Africa will continue to emerge as a strong economic, commercial, and political power on the global scene. This may take long before it is accomplished, but it shall be accomplished. Africa's place in the world shall not be ignored. Africa shall matter more than before once her paradoxes are resolved and her wealth is used for the benefit of her own people. Then, Africa shall make a difference. It is just a question of time.

AFRICA AND THE STORY OF CREATION: CREATION OR EVOLUTION OF THE UNIVERSE?

A considerable number of arguments, theories, and even doctrines have been advanced on the creation of the universe and the origins of humankind. The discussions have been quite controversial, but two dominant schools of thought have emerged: creationism and evolution. These arguments are explained in the ensuing analysis.

Creation of the Universe by Divine Command

It has been argued that the universe is probably 14 billion years old. How was the world created? Who created it? Two schools of thought have been advanced. According to one, the creation of the universe was the act of a supernatural being.

The book of Genesis in the Holy Bible explains how God created the universe and all of its inhabitants including man in six days, and rested on the seventh day. According to the story, God created the heavens and the earth on the first day. The earth was a dark, formless wasteland that received light on God's command. In the subsequent days of God's creation, light, the sky, the waters, the dry land called "the earth," the basin of the water called the sea, the vegetation—plants and fruit trees—as well as creatures living in water and on the earth were created at God's command.

On the sixth day, God created man in His own image and blessed him and commanded him to multiply and be in charge of all the things living and moving on the earth. On the seventh day, God rested.[3]

In the context of the divine creation, therefore, the universe comprises the heavens and earth. The term "universe" is used interchangeably with "the world." In like manner, the expression "the Earth" is used interchangeably with "the world", and "the universe." The common characteristic to all three is that they are said to have been commanded into existence by a supernatural being.

Evolution of the Universe, the Big Bang Theory, and Continental Pangaeism

The Big Bang Theory is a cosmological premise that the universe originated approximately 20 billion years ago from the violent explosion of a small point source of extremely high density and temperature. Some scientists have argued that the universe emerged 14 billion years ago. This cosmological model of the universe is supported by scientific evidence and observation. The term "Big Bang Theory" generally refers to the idea that the universe has expanded from a primordial explosion at some finite time in the past, and continues to expand to this day. The Big Bang Theory was proposed by Georges Lemaitre (1894–1966), a Belgian physicist and Roman Catholic priest/monsignor who called it a hypothesis of the primeval atom.[4] The model relies on Albert Einstein's (1879–1955) Theory of General Relativity as founded by Alexander Friedman (1888–1925), a Russian cosmologist and mathematician. It describes the general evolution of the universe. It was Fred Hoyle (1915–2001), however, who coined the phrase "Big Bang" during a 1949 radio broadcast as a derisive reference to a theory to which he did not actually subscribe.

The theory developed from observations of the structure of the universe and from theoretical considerations. The theory was advanced and tested between 1912 and 1950. The Big Bang is considered the birth of our universe and gives it the age of 13.73 ± 0.12 billion years old.

In this view, available scientific, archeological, and other evidence suggests that before and up to 200 million years ago, what some scientists, naturalists, and meteorologists describe as Pangaea, meaning all lands or all earth, was a vast landmass that evolved over the millennia into a single super continent on the planet.

The hypothesis of German scientist and meteorologist Alfred Wegener (1880–1930), simply explained, is that Pangaea was a giant supercontinent consisting of a single, huge landmass formed probably between 570 and 510 million years ago. Then, from about 200 million years ago, the structure of the continents began to change and break up. As millions of years passed, a continental drift or movement of the land occurred. Wegener's realization that similar fossils could be found on opposite continents helped to form his theory of plate tectonics that postulated that movement deep in the earth caused landmasses to drift and separate over the eons. This process of tectonic drift was heightened between 180 and 200 million years ago when a new ocean was formed. Today that ocean is known as the Atlantic Ocean, and it emerged between eastern North America and present-day northwestern Africa.

By 100 million years ago, the supercontinent had been split into two huge sections. One was called "Laurasia" in the northern hemisphere, north of the equator, and the other was called "Gondwana" in the southern hemisphere, south of the equator. These two sections of the supercontinent were actually two huge continents from which other continents emerged later along this long evolutionary process. Laurasia assumed another name of "Laurentia" and comprises present-day North America and Eurasia. Eurasia, in turn, comprises the Baltic and Siberia, Kazakhstan, and North and East China cratons, but excludes India and Arabia. Sixty million years ago, Europe separated from Greenland.

Gondwana remained named "Gondwana," but its keystone was present-day Africa as the main landmass. Gondwana housed Africa and what are now called South America, Antarctica, Madagascar, Australia, and India. When the continental drift advanced, Gondwana's landmasses separated, leaving Africa behind and creating South America, Antarctica, Madagascar, the Indian sub-continent, Australia, New Guinea, etc. It was as if the Mother of the Continents—Mater Continentium—was abandoned by her children when an enemy—the continental drift—struck and sent the kids into a panic. They had no alternative but to flee from their mother and settle elsewhere! Thus, Africa was part of Pangaea in its great evolutionary process. Africa was part of Gondwana—the southern keystone—in the southern landmass. Africa remained in Gondwana, but the continental drift prompted parts of Gondwana to part from Africa: these later became known as the Asia/Indian subcontinent, Australia, and the other "deserting children" of Africa. Africa, from the beginning of the formation of the continents, was the Mater Continentium—the Mother of the Continents.

The name "Gondwana" was derived from the Gondwana region of central-northern India. It is a Sanskrit term meaning "forest of the Gonds," after the Gondi people that inhabited this part of India. Scientists and meteorologists thought it appropriate to apply this term to the evolutionary process of the earth that took so many years to evolve.[5]

The evolutionary passage involving Africa had significant outcomes. These included a great evolutionary process that happened between 35,000 and 8000 BCE, and which caused considerable variations that transformed humankind. This transformation was especially noticeable in two areas: climate and human conditions, especially in terms of culture. Other radical changes involved the cooling down of climate and weather in northern Africa that made the sub-region dry. Those climatic changes led to the birth of the Great Sahara Desert, as well as the other deserts in Africa, including the Kalahari. The Sahara Desert was formed about 7,000 years ago and introduced a new order in Africa, for the desert divided Africa into two parts—North Africa and Sub-Saharan Africa.

The emergence of Africa as a continent—the second largest continent on earth—must be described in the context of the emergence of the universe as the world as we know it today. In this case, Africa was the first continent to be identified as such, as the first habitat of the first human society. In subsequent millennia, wide and even radical changes happened in Africa that would reshape the continent in such a multidimensional fashion as had never been known before. Natural, climatic, human, environmental, sociopolitical, historical, racial, linguistic, and other changes occurred, which will become clear in the course of this book. One of these orders, as hinted above, arose with the birth of the largest desert on Earth—the Great Sahara Desert.

COMPARISON OF CREATION AND EVOLUTION

The book of Genesis states that God created man in His image on the sixth day and said "Be fertile and multiply; fill the earth and subdue it. Have dominion over the fish of the sea, the birds of the air, and all the living things that move on the Earth." The narration further affirms that the same God "created all kinds of living creatures on Earth: cows, cattle, wild animals [and] creeping creatures on earth." Then, He rested on the seventh day.

Controversial interpretations of the story of creation are age-old and continue to present. How can the concept of evolution—sometimes also called Darwinism after English naturalist Charles Darwin, who formulated the theory of evolution in his 1859 book *On the Origin of Species*[6]—be reconciled with that of divine command? If, as will be argued in subsequent chapters, it is true that humankind had a common ancestor with the great apes (orangutans, gorillas, and chimpanzees), and that the two species separated about 6 million years ago, then how can one understand the story of creation by divine command? How can humankind evolve from animal-kind without separate creation and be created at the same time in the lineage and image of God? If Adam and Eve, the first humans, evolved from the great apes through an obviously long evolutionary process, then how could they have been created by God?

Neither reasoning nor scientific arguments alone can, or will, resolve the mystery of creation of the universe and of humankind. The clash between reasoning and faith is inevitable, since divine power and the existence of a supernatural being are beyond the intellectual comprehension of humankind. Thus, one deals here with a tabula rasa (unscribed tablet) situation where the smaller the ring O, the better it is for human reasoning; where the larger the ring O, the more complicated it becomes as the space outside of the ring, which represents ignorance, widens.

However, where faith and reasoning collide, faith should prevail. Therefore, arguments in favor of evolution become totally nonsensical if they insist that humankind evolved from the natural process of change. More importantly, evolution and creation do not necessarily oppose each other. They could be, and are, complementary. What if the spark that ignited the Big Bang was at the prompting of a supernatural being? Thus, if humankind and the hominids or "near-men" who walked on four feet and had hairy bodies with similar facial, arm, eye, or head features, but were only 4-foot 6-inches tall evolved over the millennia leading bipedal humans somewhere around 10 million years ago, then there would be no contradiction between creationism and evolution.

The school of thought pursued by the current author is one that calls attention to common sense and endorses the arguments supporting faith as the best resolution out of this messy and wishful argument.

For all practical purposes, therefore, whether one believes in scientific evolution, whereby the universe came into existence through the Big Bang—an abrupt appearance owing perhaps to cosmological mutations—or in biblical divine power through which Divine Providence wished and decided on the existence of the universe, one proposition seems to be self-evident: there were landmasses and other forms of material existence. These forms, through gradual but steady processes, started to split into small forces culminating in the continents, waters, and lands that we know today, and the creatures that inhabit them. Obviously, no human reasoning can fully and authoritatively comprehend or unravel the decisions, desires, and dictates of the supernatural. Therefore, in matters relating to the supernatural, one can only draw on faith, not on logic or reason. In this case, the universe is too vast to have happened by accident. Some divine hand must have been involved in its creation. The logical conclusion would be that Divine Providence brought the universe into being, and over millions of years, the cosmos, Earth, and her inhabitants, evolved into what we are today.

THE NAMING OF AFRICA

There is no evidence to suggest that a general name was applicable to the African continent as a whole before the alien invasions endured by the continent from 1200 to 145 BCE.

The Phoenicians: 1200–800 BCE

The first alien arrivals in Africa happened between 1200 and 800 BCE. The Phoenicians were a Semitic people, probably from the region of present-day Lebanon. They fought against the Berbers—original inhabitants of North Africa—and defeated the indigenous populations. They were excellent merchants and business people who invaded North Africa and settled along the Mediterranean Coast. They were known as the conquerors of ancient Carthage, which they occupied from its foundation in 814 BCE. By 800 BCE, they had created strong business contacts that made Carthage a very rich Mediterranean city-state and a flourishing business hub in what is now Tunisia.

Carthage, which means "new city," became known to foreigners for a number of reasons, including the proximity of the city to Europe and the Middle East—these being the areas of civilization in its earliest forms during this time in antiquity. This was a historical exposure of the vast African continent to the external world. Carthage became a business hub in the Mediterranean region and attracted traders from North Africa, Europe, and the Near East, including Egypt and that area of the Middle East—the Great Valley—called Mesopotamia. Carthage was established in what is now Tunisia. The Phoenicians founded other towns in North Africa, including Utica, in 1100 BCE.

Later, Carthage fought against the Romans under General Hannibal who defeated the Romans using an army that included 38 elephants he marched into Northern Italy where he was subsequently defeated and captured. Perhaps the greatest genius in military tactics of all time, Hannibal committed suicide while in a Roman jail rather than be tried by the Romans. By the 4th century BCE, Carthage was an important and historic city-state with its own colonial power along Africa's Atlantic coast.

The Greeks: 631 BCE–146 CE

As the years passed and civilization shifted to Greece where the city-state system flourished (as described later), interest in colonization of North Africa moved to the Greeks. Phoenician colonization had been well established by the time the Greeks became interested and created a colony in North Africa starting in 631 BCE. The Greeks first colonized those parts of North Africa that are located in present-day Libya. First, they settled in the city of Cyrene in Libya in 631 BCE, which later was known as Cyrenaica and became a flourishing Greek colony and vital business hub. Greek civilization expanded to settlements in Tripoli and Tripolitania. When Alexander the Great of Macedonia (356–323 BCE) decided to spread his power to North Africa, he went as far as Egypt, starting from around 334 BCE. He founded Alexandria in 332 BCE and gave the city his name. Alexandria became a very prosperous business hub in the ancient world in North Africa, and was a major city of Hellenistic and Roman times. Alexandria, like Carthage, grew in importance as a commercial hub and great center of learning where education and science thrived.

The Greeks believed that the world ended in Abyssinia—a very old country that was first to gain independence in Africa already in ancient times (982 BCE) long before many nation states existed. According to the Greeks, the known world could not exist beyond the country which one of the great Greek historians, Aeschylus, described as the end of the known world.

According to Aeschylus, Ethiopia was "the land of burned-faced peoples." In Greek, "ethio" means "burned," and "pia" means "face." The nation now known as Sudan was one of the factories of the early city-states in Africa. Sudan was connected to the west of the continent by the Sudan Belt, which ran from the east to the west (like a belt) just to the south of the Sahara Desert. These contacts endured throughout the centuries, even after the globalization of Christianity to Africa in the first century CE, and of Islam in the 7th century CE. The trade links and activities that ensued brought many foreigners to the north, east, and west of the vast African continent. The arrival of the Arabs introduced their culture, language, and religion especially in the north of the continent. In present-day Tunisia, the Arabs introduced the name of "Ifrikia," in the Middle Ages. The Sudan became Islamized and has remained Islamic since then. The inevitable culture clashes continue today. Currently, the Sudan has 597 tribes speaking more than 400 dialects, with Arabic and English as the official languages of the country.

Greek colonization was marked by the following milestones:

• A Greek mercantile colony was established in North Africa at Naucratis, 50 miles from what would later be Alexandria.

- The Greeks colonized Cyrenaica in Libya shortly before the Egyptian Pharaoh Amasis (570–526 BCE) ruled Egypt.
- Although in 513 BCE the Greeks attempted to create a Greek colony in between Cyrene (Cyrenaica) and Carthage, they did not succeed and were expelled from there two years later.

The Romans: 146 BCE–476 CE

What later became known as the Maghreb Region of Africa became part of the Western Province of the Roman Empire following the defeat of Carthage by Rome. The Western Provinces of the Roman Empire were a vast area. The Maghreb comprised present-day Tunisia and Carthage, Algeria, Morocco, Western Sahara, Libya (then consisting of Tripolitania and Cyrenaica), Egypt (Aegyptus), and Mauritania.

Between 150 and 146 BCE, the city-state of Carthage was at war with the Roman Empire during a period known as the Punic Wars. At first, the African General Hannibal (c. 247–184 BCE) won. Hannibal defeated the Romans before their conquest of Carthage by leading a Carthagian military army of 10,000 soldiers riding on elephants to Northern Italy where he met a very surprised Roman Army. As the world's best military strategist, he was able to command Carthage's army and its elephants.

The third and final Punic War was a fierce fight between Rome and Carthage. This war was begun by Roman Emperor Augustus and saw the Romans regroup to attack and defeat Carthage in 146 BCE, conquering it. They exiled Hannibal and devastated Carthage. General Hannibal died at his own hand while the Romans colonized Carthage. Henceforth, Carthage began to serve as the capital of the Western Province of the Roman Empire in Africa. Subsequently, the Romans expanded their imperial empire to cover a greater part of North Africa—subjecting what later became present-day areas of Ghana, Mauretania, Morocco, Libya, Algeria, Western Sahara, and Egypt to Roman imperialism. These countries formed the Maghrib (also called Maghreb), and became one of the most fertile and richest parts of the Roman Empire.

The collapse of the Roman Empire in the West did not occur until the 5th century CE, when Odoacer defeated and deposed Emperor Romulus Augustulus. The empire's fall was the culmination of several hundred years of weakening of the empire by Germanic tribes whose warriors were called "barbarians" by the Romans. The Germanic tribes were peoples of northwestern Europe, and included the Huns, Norsemen, Goths, Jutes (Danes), Geats (Swedes, Anglos, and Saxons), etc. They migrated in late antiquity and the early Middle Ages, and produced great Germanic languages that became dominant along the Roman borders (Austria, Germany, the Netherlands, Belgium, and England). Their descendants include Germans,

English, Dutch, Norwegians, Icelanders, Luxembourgians, Swedish-Finns, Estonians, Swedes, Liechtensteiners, and Swiss Germans. These Roman enemies wore beards and, in Latin, "barba" means "beard." Hence, a barbarian was the bearded man, uncivil and uncouth in the eyes of the Romans. These Germanic tribesmen were fierce, rough, clothed in animal skins and course linen. The Romans viewed them as savage and primitive. They could not possibly be civil—they were hunters with spears, clubs, and shields that they used to destroy Roman civilization, civility, and trade.

By the time of the empire's collapse, the Roman Empire had left its mark on the lands it occupied. The landmass that was home to the Western Province of the Roman Empire was given a name by the Romans that most likely was the product of centuries of influence of many cultures and peoples, but the Romans gave it permanence. That name was "Africa."

WHY THE NAME "AFRICA"?

Diverse historical accounts differ on the real origins of the expression "Africa." According to some accounts, "Africa" is a term that originated from the Phoenician word "afar" meaning "dust," and the Romans twisted it to "afer" and called the inhabitants the "Afridi" (with "Afridi" being the Roman pluralization of "afer"). The Afridi were a tribe most probably of Berber extraction in Northern Africa around the area of Carthage.

The word "Africa" may also have been derived from the Greek word "phrike," meaning cold and connoting horror. Combined with a negative prefix, the expression becomes "a-phrike," meaning a land free of cold and horror. However, "aprica" also is a Latin adjective meaning "sunny." True, this continent does not only have lots of dust from the Sahara, it also has plenty of sunshine. So, it is not strange to learn that the Romans could apply the term "aprica" to Africa.

Nonetheless, whatever the origins of the name, "Africa" came into European use through the Romans who administered the Province of Africa—Carthage Territory—in modern Tunisia. Africa, as coined by the Romans in ancient times, originally referred to North Africa but with the passage of time, it was applied to the entire continent. Before the invasions of Africa by alien visitors, businessmen, and empire builders, very little was known of Africa. North Africa emerged as a cultural island between Europe and Africa, partly because of the birth of the Sahara Desert, and partly because of the cultural diffusion, as well as colonial, commercial, linguistic, religious, and other imperatives that were diverse but linked the northern part of the continent to cultural and commercial aspects that were alien to the southern part of continent. Consequently, the continent lacked a common bond that would have given it one homogeneous identity that required the continent to be known only by one name.

The globalization of trade, ideas, religion, and basic curiosity brought foreigners to the continent, among them Romans who built a great empire after the collapse of Alexander the Great's Greek Empire. With the various expressions used to describe different circumstances in Africa, and with the realization that the continent was, after all, larger than the then only known world stretching from the Mediterranean to Abyssinia, it became clear that a common name had to be applied to the entire continent. Islam made an important contribution to the search for a name for Africa.

Not only did the Arabs describe parts of Tunisia as "Ifrikia," especially during the Middle Ages they expanded their knowledge of Africa. For example, they engaged in legitimate and illegitimate (i.e., slave) trade throughout Africa in trans-Saharan caravans on camel and horseback that ventured to the west, north, and east of Africa, as well as to the interior of the African continent. In the Middle Ages, the Arabs named present-day Sudan "Bilad-al-Sudan", meaning the "land of black people." The Arabs named "Ghana" for a king of this rich territory where they bought gold and traded for other valuables in West Africa.

This expression, "Bilal-al-Sudan," like the one the Greeks invented for Abyssinia, was applied only to the country, but not to Africa as a whole. But whether you call it "the land of black people," or "the land of burned-faced peoples," or "the land of black men/people," "the land without cold and horror," "the hot land," "the sunny land," "the dusty and sunny land," etc., all of these expressions were applied to the continent that the Romans decided to describe as "Terra Africa," meaning the "Land of Africa."

It should also be noted that Africa was divided into five regions through a practice that probably emerged from the structure of the Western Province of the Roman Empire, which grouped together an entire region of North Africa—the territories of the Maghreb: Mauretania, Libya, Western Sahara, Morocco, Tunisia, Algeria, and Egypt. In these territories lived tribes including the Afridi—a Berber tribe. The Berbers, Bedouins, and other tribes of North Africa became absorbed into the cultures of Europe, the Mediterranean, and Arabia.

Thus, it was not until the arrival of the Romans in ancient time, their conquest of Carthage, and absorption of North Africa into the Roman Empire, that the continent received the name of "Africa." Today, Africa is more than the mere region. Africa is the people, the endowments, the geography, the topography, the cultures and civilizations, the geopolitics, the paradoxes, the natural beauty, the economy, the institutions, and the governments that govern the various nations that constitute Africa. Africa is everything that is Africa and that is African. For Africa to be successful today, Africa has to be African!

CONCEPTUAL UNDERSTANDING OF AFRICA, THE ENVIRONMENT

The environment is everything around us—land, air, water, as well as plants, animals, and the microorganisms that inhabit them. Man is the center of the environment. The challenge of the environment thus lies in man's ability to protect and prevent it from deterioration or degradation, so as to sustain its use and value to the present generation and preserve the environment for the use of future generations. In this sense, "environment" basically means the physical environment—a tangible concept, as opposed to intangible surroundings or circumstances, such as the political environment and the global climate.

Geography, however, is the study of man's habitat, its physical nature, topography, natural features, climate, resources, population, and related data that constitute a significant area of scientific study. All of these physical and related characteristics can be summed up in one concept: geography.

Physical Regions and Economic Zones of Africa

For a good understanding of Africa's physical environment, it is useful to divide the continent into physical and political/economic regions or zones. With this perspective, it is obvious that Africa's division into political/economic zones was created at the summit level of African leaders in the early years of Africa's political independence. Thus, for all practical reasons, five political regions of Africa were agreed upon: North, South, West, East, and Central Africa. To avoid the confusion of the South of Africa with South Africa the country, that part of the continent is better known as Southern Africa. In like manner, because of the various definitions of East Africa, it is often referred to as Eastern Africa, which comprises a larger area than the sensu stricto traditional definition of the subregion of East Africa. This originally comprised the countries of Kenya, Uganda, and Tanganyika (or Tanzania after Tanganyika and Zanzibar entered into a political union in 1964).

For practical reasons, the same five political regions are likewise referred to as the five economic zones of Africa. As follows, the five physical/geographical regions of Africa are:

1. The tropics, which are known for their savanna grasslands, grassy and flat plains that lie between the Tropics of Cancer and Capricorn, and occupy two-thirds of Africa with the largest population of the continent.

2. The arid and semi-arid lands (ASALs) that are Africa's dry grasslands.

3. The highlands (highland plateau), that give way to coastal plains and cover most of Sub-Saharan Africa, which has many non-navigable rivers. The

plateau partly explains why Africa remained an undiscovered Dark Continent for so long, with no beaches, but with steep rapids from the interior of Africa that flow through the coastal zones to reach the oceans. This topography, with the prohibitions of deserts (the First Belt of the Sahara, Kalahari, Namib Deserts, and others, as well as the Second Belt) tropical diseases, natural disasters, and the hostility of African warriors like Shaka Zulu, the legendary king of the powerful Zulu tribe in South Africa, reinforces the impenetrableness of the area.

4. The rainforest, which is the tropical jungle of Africa that covers the equatorial area from the Atlantic.

5. The deserts, especially the Great Sahara Desert, which is comparable in size to the United States, and is the largest desert on Earth, and the Kalahari Desert.

The Sahara Desert was formed about 7,000 years ago in 5000 BCE as a result of rapid climate changes. This desert marked the beginning of a new era in Africa because it divided the continent into North and Sub-Saharan Africa and, literally, ended the nomadic, traditional lifestyle of the Africans. These nomads were forced to start a new life in permanent settlements that necessitated the origins and development of civilization that fostered the growth of great cultural lifestyles and kingdoms that flourished for many centuries thereafter.

The Sahara covers one-third of Africa, with approximately 3,500,000 square miles (9,065,000 square kilometers). It has a topography of screw plains, rolling sand dunes, and sand seas. The Kalahari Desert is the second largest desert in Africa. It covers 100,000 square miles (259,000 square kilometers) and spreads through much of Botswana, southwestern South Africa, and western Namibia. There is also the Namib Desert in Namibia. The other regional deserts of Africa include the Libyan, Nubian, and Egypt's Western Desert.

The Sahel is a wide stretch of land running completely across north-central Africa on the southern edges of the ever-expanding Sahara Desert. The Sahel lies between the dry areas of the north and the tropical areas of the south. The Great Rift Valley is a series of geological faults caused by huge volcanic eruptions many centuries ago, culminating in the present-day Ethiopian Highlands.

Africa's major mountains include the following:

1. The Atlas Mountains, whose peak in the north is Mt. Toubkal at 13,671 feet. The Atlas run from southwestern Morocco along the Mediterranean coastline to the eastern edge of Tunisia. The Atlas mountain range consists of three sections: the High, Middle, and Maritime Atlas.

2. The Ruwenzori on the Uganda/Democratic Republic of the Congo border, is about 16,000 feet high.

3. Mt. Elgon in Western Kenya is about 14,178 feet high.

4. Mt. Kenya, the second highest mountain in Africa, is about 17,057 feet high.

5. Mt. Kilimanjaro in Tanzania, the highest mountain in Africa, is 19,340 feet high (official), or 19,332 feet high (accurate).

The Great Rift Valley to the east of Africa contains several huge lakes, including Lakes Nakuru, Naivasha, Elementeita, Baringo, and Turkana, which are situated in Kenya. Lake Albert is in Uganda, whereas Lake Victoria (called Lake Nyanza in British colonial times), is shared by Uganda, Tanzania, and Kenya. Lake Victoria is the largest lake on Earth. Lake Chad is another large lake in Central Africa.

Africa hosts many rivers, a good number of which are considerably large. They include the following:

1. The Nile River, which gets water from Lake Victoria, is the longest river in the world, at 4,160 miles (6,693 kilometers) long, and flows north from the highlands of southwestern Africa into the Mediterranean Sea.

2. Zaire's Congo River, at 2,900 miles (4,666 kilometers), is the second longest river in Africa and largest, covering 1,400,000 square miles (3,600,000 square kilometers). The River Basin covers the Democratic Republic of Congo, Angola, Cameroon, and the Central African Republic.

3. The Niger River is the third longest river in Africa at 2,600 miles (4,183 kilometers). It is West Africa's principal river and extends 2,600 miles (4,183 kilometers) from the Guinea Highlands in Southwestern Guinea through Mali, Niger, Benin (border), and Nigeria. The Niger Delta, with its oil rivers in Nigeria, flows into the Gulf of Guinea. The Niger River is exceeded in length only by the Nile and Congo. The Benue River is the Niger River's main tributary.

4. The Zambezi River at 1,700 miles (2,735 kilometers) is the fourth largest and fourth longest river in Africa. It flows through wilderness from Zambia near the Angolan and Congolese borders through Angola, Namibia, Botswana, and Zimbabwe, off the east coast of Mozambique and into the Indian Ocean. The Portuguese explorer Vasco da Gama was the first European to sight the Zambezi River when he anchored at the mouth of the river in 1498.

5. The Limpopo River, which flows through Central-Southern Africa and then eastward into the Indian Ocean, is 1,100 miles (1,770 kilometers) long. It is the fifth longest after the Zambezi River, but the second largest river in Africa, and drains into the Indian Ocean. The Limpopo separates South Africa to the southeast from Botswana to the northwest and Zimbabwe to the north. The Limpopo was immortalized in the short story, "The Elephant's Child," by the English author Rudyard Kipling in the *Just So Stories*, where Kipling described it as "the great grey-green greasy Limpopo River."[7]

6. The Nzoia River in Kenya, although relatively small at 160 miles (257 kilometers) long, nevertheless is an important river for Western Kenya, flowing through a region with an estimated population of more than 1.5 million people. The Nzoia rises from Mt. Elgon and flows south and then west, eventually

flowing into Lake Victoria near the town of Port Victoria. The waters of the Nzoia River provide irrigation all year round, and floods deposit sediments in Budalangi area that are good for agricultural production. The industrial region centered at Webuye and Mumias in Western Kenya gives the river a lot of effluent from the paper and sugar factories in the area, at Webuye and Mumias, respectively.

Political Regions/Economic Zones

As stated previously, there are five political regions/economic zones of Africa: North, Southern, West, Eastern, and Central. This section describes the nations that make up each region.

North Africa contains five countries (Tunisia, Algeria, Libya, Morocco, and Egypt) plus the disputed country of Western Sahara claimed by Morocco, which is also known as the independent Sahrawi Arab Democratic Republic (SADR).

Southern Africa is comprised of 10 countries (Angola, Botswana, Lesotho, Malawi, Mozambique, Namibia, Swaziland, South Africa, Zambia, Zimbabwe) and the island state of Madagascar in the Indian Ocean.

West Africa contains three island countries in the Atlantic (Cape Verde; São Tomé and Príncipe; and Guinea Bissau), Benin, Burkina Faso, Côte d'Ivoire, Gambia, Ghana, Guinea, Liberia, Mali, Mauritania, Niger, Nigeria, Senegal, Sierra Leone, and Togo.

Eastern Africa is comprised of 10 countries, including Burundi, Djibouti, Eritrea, Ethiopia, Kenya, Rwanda, Somalia, Sudan, Tanzania, Uganda, as well as three island states in the Indian Ocean (Mauritius, Seychelles, and Comoros).

Central Africa contains seven countries: Cameroon, Chad, Central African Republic, Democratic Republic of Congo, Congo, Equatorial Guinea, and Gabon.

Demography

The population of Africa, according to a December 2008 estimate, was 952,777,000. It is the second most populous continent after Asia, in which the estimated population of China is 1.4 billion and that of India is 1.1 billion.

NOTES

1. Gaius Plinius Secundus and Gabriel Brotier, *Naturalis Historiae* (Parisiis Barbou, 1779).

2. See Wikipedia Free Encyclopedia or World Factbook, 2010.

3. Genesis 1:26–28, *Holy Bible, New International Version* (Colorado Springs, CO: Biblica, 1984).

4. Georges Lamaitre, *L'Hypothese de l'Atome Primitif* [The primeval atom hypothesis] (Griffon, Neufschatel, 1946).

5. "Science Times," *New York Times*, Tuesday, January 9, 2007, pp. F1, F4.

6. Charles Darwin, *On the Origin of Species by Means of Natural Selection, or the Preservation of Favoured Races in the Struggle for Life* (London: John Murray, 1859).

7. See Rudyard Kipling, "The Elephant Child," *Short Stories.* (London: The Curtis Publishing Company, Frances Lincoln Children's Books, 1902) p. 10.

CHAPTER 2

Africa in Continental and Global Geopolitics

In terms of location on Planet Earth, and of human habitation, as well as isolation and marginalization in the world, Africa became known as the Dark Continent. The paradox of this African Condition has always been that the continent that served as the cradle of humankind and civilization was later described as the uncivilized Dark Continent. Africa was a vital part of the Old World, full of natural resources, and yet throughout history, Africa has been associated more with darkness, and ignorance than with enlightenment. Africa is unique in many respects. It has always been associated with disease and poverty, yet it is one of the richest continents on Earth. How did Africa evolve from her historical status as the Mother of Continents (Mater Continentium) to the Third World of which Africa is now a vital member?

CONCEPTUALIZATION OF AFRICA AS MATER CONTINENTIUM

Chapter 1 established that Africa emerged as the Mother of Continents after a long evolutionary process. The arguments supported the statement that Pangaeaism and Gondwanaism placed Africa at the center stage of the formation of continents, and now it is necessary to examine Africa's relationships with other continents, especially those normally referred to as Old World and Third World continents.

Four expressions have been coined to describe or refer to these geographical concepts. They are as follows:

- The Eastern Hemisphere is also known as the Old World. The geographical expression for this hemisphere is the half of the Earth that lies east of the Prime

Meridian (that crosses Greenwich, England) west of 180 degrees longitude. In a cultural or geopolitical sense, however, the Eastern Hemisphere is synonymous with the Old World, which comprises present-day Europe, Asia, and Africa, and is often referred to collectively as Afro-Eurasia, plus the surrounding islands. The term Old World is, however, usually used colloquially to refer to Europe. Today, the Old World houses about 85 percent of the global population, which is about 5.7 billion. The distinction of the Old World versus the New World, which refers to the Americas and Australasia.

- The Western Hemisphere is a geographical term for the half of the earth lying west of the Prime Meridian. This hemisphere is also known as the New World and includes North America, Latin America, the Caribbean, South America, and adjacent waters or islands. The New World was discovered only after voyages of exploration and discovery were undertaken by Europeans such as Vasco da Gama, Christopher Columbus, and others. The Western Hemisphere is home to about 15 percent of today's the global population.

- Afro-Eurasia is also known as Afrasia, and Eurasia is often used to refer to Asia and Europe only. Eurasia broadly includes North Asia, Central Asia, East Asia, South Asia and Southeast Asia.

- Eurafrasia is used to include Europe, Asia, and Africa as continents of the Old World. Europe can be divided into Northern, Southern, Western and Central Europe. Africa, since the appearance of the Sahara Desert, consists of North Africa and Sub-Saharan Africa, and all this divides Africa into five regions in political and economic terms: North, Southern (so as not to be confused with the country of South Africa), East, West, and Central Africa.

These geopolitical divisions of the world show that Africa is situated in a strategic location and affect how Africa will relate to the rest of the world politically, economically, etc. It should also be noted that following the colonization and decolonization of Africa, Asia, Latin America, and the Caribbean, a new world was born, which is better known as The Third World. This area is comprised of many of the countries in the southern portion of the globe and, in opposition to the rich and established nations of the north, they are considered the world's developing regions.

AFRICA: A CONTINENT OF PARADOXES

What is a paradox? A paradox is a contradiction.

Africa is not only the poorest continent on earth, it is the only continent to be poorer today than it was at independence almost half a century ago—that is a paradox. Africa is also the most ironical, and the most contradictory, of all the continents. Many of the prevailing conditions and situations in Africa should not be happening there today. The reasons that Africa is confronted with these numerous contradictory dictates need to be well understood because they affect the continent's international relations, foreign policy, and diplomacy. Many aspects of the African Condition form the foundations, determinants, and dictates from which African international relations (AIR), African foreign policy (AFP), and African diplomacy (AD) are based.

As a continent, if subdivided and clustered into historical analyses, Africa presents 12 paradoxes involving dwelling (habitation); humiliation; location/isolation/marginalization; fragmentation; acculturation; poverty-in-plenty (retardation); education deficiency; leadership deficiency; statehood; conflicts, coups, and corruption; categorization in global geopolitics; and natural beauty.

Dwelling or Habitation

The paradox of dwelling or habitation is seen in how although Africa was first the birth place for humanity and civilization In which humankind evolved through at least six stages, Africa was the last continent to be truly well inhabited. Africa is the second largest continent after Asia, currently housing almost a billion people!

Humiliation

The paradox of humiliation provides Africans with the distinction of having suffered the worst humiliation on Earth. Africa provided the cradle for humankind and civilization. The first human society was actually African society. Africa thus provided the human race to the world. Africans should hence have been given due respect, appreciation, and recognition, but instead, Africans were regarded as "primitive" and "savages," inhabiting a "dark continent." Africans were regarded as objects and sold as things without souls. There can be no greater paradox than the humiliation and dehumanization that Africans were subjected to. This is especially displayed over the centuries in slavery and the slave trade, in the use of slaves in the Americas and Asia; in Apartheid in South Africa. Even the Roman Catholic Church, which aims to be the champion of human rights and strives for the salvation of human souls, once believed that Africans had no souls, endorsed the by the slave traders' and slave-using countries' classification of Africans as "objects!" From the years of the slavery and slave trade in which captured Africans were sold to the Americas and the Orient, Africa has suffered from the scars of humiliation lasting through colonization. Africans were treated as objects, never as equals. There is an imperative need not only for extensive apologies to Africa for such humiliation but also for those nations and continents that sold Africans as slaves, treated them as objects, and sold these supposedly soulless objects to apologize and pay compensation to Africa. It is high time Africa demanded this.

Location, Isolation, and Marginalization

The paradox of location, isolation, and marginalization illustrates that despite Africa's central and strategic positioning on Earth, the continent has been marginalized, ignored, and isolated throughout history. Africa is the most politically peripheral and geopolitically neglected continent. The paradox of isolation exists and springs from the fact that as a continent, Africa was, for a long time, classified as the "Dark Continent." This is a paradox because North Africa serves as an island between Europe, the Mediterranean, and Sub-Saharan Africa. It is so near to Europe and the Near East. And yet the interior of Africa lay unknown to Europe for a long time because Europeans could not get into the African hinterland. The Dutch were the first Europeans to colonize the interior of Africa— from 1652 when a Dutch East Indies ship, *The Harlem,* anchored in Cape Cotonu in South Africa and started a settlement in the ensuing years. Thus, the lands of the Far East and Far West were visited and discovered by Europeans, but not neighboring Africa—until much later. That isolation of Africa by the external world had impacts on Africa that are still felt today in international discourse and conferences. Africa is still isolated and consulted only when, for example, her raw materials or votes at the United Nations are sought. Otherwise, Africa has constantly been isolated.

The fact, however, is that Africa does matter a lot and this fact has started to be considered seriously in international fora, and will continue to matter increasingly in the future. The same is true of the paradox of marginalization. Here is a continent strategically located in the world, with an Africa Diaspora present on every continent on Earth and with a growing influence in all spheres of international politics and economics. Yet Africa is still marginalized with all sorts of efforts to ignore Africa and consider her presence only when the rest of the world is interested in her resources or politico-economic support. This is a huge paradox. Nonetheless, it is increasingly becoming evident that marginalization of Africa is untenable. Other nations can isolate and exploit Africa, but to ignore the continent is becoming very hard to realize. This is because Africa matters.

Fragmentation

The paradox of fragmentation shows that Africa, the second largest continent on Earth (second only to Asia), is the most fragmented—a reality that was imposed on Africa during its colonization. Africa measures 11,725,385 square miles (30,368,609 square kilometers), including the adjacent islands in the Atlantic and Pacific. And yet Africa has 53 states, including Western Sahara as a dependence of Morocco, or 54 states with the Sahrawi Arab Democratic Republic (SADR) as recognized by the African Union in the early 1980s (however, Morocco has not recognized SADR but claims it as part of Morocco). The colonial "scramble" for Africa produced seven powers on the continent: Great Britain, France, Germany, Belgium, Portugal, Italy, and Spain. They introduced "divide et impera" policies and practices in Africa that Africans, so many years after gaining political independence, have not succeeded in overcoming. The location of Africa is central, strategic, and right at the center of the globe. Yet, the continent is bypassed too often. The division or fragmentation of Africa into so many political units is a residual effect of European colonization that continues to haunt Africa and to impact its foreign policy, diplomacy, and international relations.

Acculturation

The paradox of acculturation (i.e., the modification of the cultures of Africa by and through contact that African cultures had with Europe) reveals that although Africa has about 952,777,000 people that speak at least 2,000 different languages, Africans have to speak in a common foreign language in order to communicate and understand one another! Most of Africa's native languages should have become official languages of Africa. But they did not. Instead, a system was introduced whereby the ex-colonial languages became official: English, French, Portuguese, and Arabic (although Africa was not colonized by the Arabs but has a huge Arab heritage in Africa because of the Islamization of Africa) were introduced by colonizing foreigners and replaced the traditional indigenous languages and cultures because they were regarded as primitive by African newcomers. Although Western culture and civilization were imposed on Africans, it is astonishing that Westernization is preferred to Africanization culturally even by Africans themselves! It is very paradoxical that a country like Nigeria can have more than 250 languages and speak only English as its official language.

Poverty in Plenty

The paradox of poverty in plenty, retardation, or economic "backwardness" is perhaps the most paradoxical condition of Africa. A continent with vast natural resources, raw materials, and agriculture-based crops is still the poorest continent on Earth. Africa is one of the richest regions of the world with a huge human resource base and brainpower, vast natural resources and endowments (e.g., gold, copper, zinc, lead, energy including renewables, water resources, etc.). Yet Africa is the poorest continent—the only continent where people are poorer today than they were 40 and more years ago. Africa has many raw materials, manufactured products, minerals, oil, forest crops, grasslands, plants, agriculture, cattle, wildlife, fauna, rich soil, etc., yet Africa hosts the largest number of the world's poorest countries—34 of a total of 50. How can such a wealthy continent be so poor?

Education Deficiency

The paradox of education deficiency traces its roots to when the colonial system created in each African colony collided with the African value system and did not prepare Africans well for self-rule. Consequently, and since the African countries have retained the education systems of their ex-colonial masters, the education sector continues to suffer from deficiencies. Nonetheless, the blame for such educational deficiencies must be shared by the leadership of the African countries since, after independence, it has been the responsibility of the African governments to provide education. Generally speaking, the deficiencies in the education are worrisome because no nation can thrive in anything unless it has a sound education for its young men and women.

Leadership Deficiency

The paradox of leadership deficiency shows the cost of corruption, cultism, the God-like behavior of some African leaders, and the problems of elitism, incompetence, red tape, bad governance, no accountability, no transparency, and neglect of basic democratic principles and human rights. It has been argued for a long time that deficiencies in the leadership of Africa lead to this chain of problems.

Statehood

The paradox of statehood formed when colonial powers introduced subaltern statehood. The first system of statehood was created in Africa in 3100 BCE, when empirical statehood was used to create the united "Old Kingdom" of Egypt. Empirical statehood then consisted of the ability of a government to enforce laws and create institutions. Empirical statehood also gave a de facto ability to the government to use force to exercise authority within its territorial jurisdiction. Here, full control is exerted through a monopoly over the country's economy and assets from within the state. This subaltern statehood, based on the juridical statecraft created at the Berlin Conference of 1884–1885, still haunts African sovereignty today. Empirical statehood was ignored and replaced by juridical statehood. Statehood, as introduced in Africa, continues to pose many political problems among African countries. The European powers introduced a juridical kind of statehood—based on the signing of a treaty at

Berlin in 1885 among the Europeans after drawing geographical lines on the African map, which they called borders. Yet these were mere lines that either put together African nations into single territories the colonizers called nations, or separated the same people into separate territories called nations. Then they introduced colonial policies and practices of "divide et impera," which set the African peoples at daggers drawn. The end results were, and continue to be, conflicts and civil wars in Africa that have rocked the African states and retarded their economic development. If the Europeans had, instead of juridical statehood, introduced empirical statehood as they had done among themselves at Westphalia in 1648, the situation would be different in Africa today.

Conflicts, Coups, and Corruption

The paradox of conflicts, coups, and corruption is evident in that although Africa is a continent of African Socialism, of Ujamaa, Ubuntu, Harambee, Pan-Africanism, and African Nationalism, which should be promoting African identity, African unity, and cooperation, conflicts and civil wars have marked the entire independence period of Africa. Corruption and ill-advised development initiatives do impede the development efforts of the African countries. Thus, all the issues and challenges do not help in the promotion of good neighborliness and good inter-country/ group relations in Africa.

Categorization

The paradox of categorization of Africa in global geopolitics is that Africa was first almost in everything: in human society, in discovery and use of technology, in statehood, and in government. Yet Africa has been the least well-equipped and least prepared to lead in all these areas.

Natural Beauty

The paradox of natural beauty signifies the roles of innocence, burden bearing, abuse, and exploitation in any given society. Africa's extensive natural resources have been exploited and raped for so many years. In Africa, a terrible injustice was done to the African peoples and her traditional values. It was suffering and punishment without offence and victimization without crime. An innocent continent became the burden-bearer for another continent called Europe—Western Europe, in particular. Impoverishment of Africa and acculturization in Africa are two glaring examples of this injustice. All of these contradictions have had negative impacts on the development of Africa. Problems of ignorance, poverty, and disease haunt Africa on a daily basis. Epidemics such HIV/AIDS,

Ebola, Tuberculosis, Malaria, Dengue, Yellow Fever, Rift Valley Fever, and Highland Fever do not just haunt Africa, but retard her economic and sociopolitical development.

SUMMARY

Thus the implications for development and inter-state and group relations in Africa are negative because the paradoxes are friends of Africa's enemies. Lack of development, jobs, education, equality, and opportunity has a negative impact on Africa. Children, women, the youth, and the other marginalized strata of society cannot recover from their economic stress and mess unless the paradoxes are removed. Lack of population planning allows population explosions to happen and these retard economic development. Therefore, demography in Africa should be contained so as to control its growth. Whenever there are conflicts and disputes from within Africa or disputes with nations from outside Africa, this retards the development efforts of the African countries.

POLITICAL REGIONS/ECONOMIC ZONES IN AFRICA

In the first decades of political independence in Africa, the Organization of African Unity (OAU) decided to divide Africa into five regions for political and geographic reasons. The same regions were consequently designated as economic zones since it became necessary to establish regional economic integration arrangements for the respective regions of Africa. Since there are island states that are adjacent to Africa, they also form part of Africa. There are three island states in the Pacific that are former Portuguese colonies: Cape Verde, São Tomé and Príncipe, and Guinea-Bissau; and four island states in the Indian Ocean, all of which were French colonies: Mauritius, Madagascar, Comoros, and Seychelles.

In like manner, some territories and regions adjacent to Africa are still colonial possessions as explained in Table 2.1.

Africa is divided into five political, geographic, and economic regions. These groupings resulted in some of Africa's success stories, with their regional integration efforts to bring about economic and sociocultural development. They each have economic organizations dealing with economic development and cooperation issues and efforts: UMA in North Africa, SADC and others in Southern Africa, ECOWAS in West Africa, EAC in East Africa, and ECCAS in Central Africa.

• Southern Africa—COMESA (Common Market for East and Southern Africa); SADC (Southern African Development Cooperation); SA-BLS (the Customs Union of the Southern African States—Botswana, Lesotho, Swaziland).

• West Africa—ECOWAS, Lagos CFA (Monetary Union—Francophone), BCEAOC (Bank of West African States, Dakar, Senegal), UEMOA (Union Economique

Table 2.1
Territories and Regions Adjacent to Africa in the Pacific and Indian Oceans (2007)

Territory	Status	Location	Colonial Power	Population
Reunion	Colony	Indian Ocean	France	743,981
Western Sahara*	Colony Independent	North West Africa	Morocco Independent (AU)	393,831
Mayotte	Colony	Indian Ocean	France	170,879
Canary Islands	Colony	Atlantic Ocean	Spain	1,694,477
Ceuta	Colony	Strait of Gibraltar Off Morocco	Spain	245,000
Melilla	Colony	Mediterranean Off Morocco	Spain	66,411
St. Helena	Colony	South Atlantic Ocean	United Kingdom	4,000
Madeira	Colony	North Africa (Atlantic Ocean)	Portugal	

* Western Sahara is claimed by Morocco, but has been recognized by the Africas African Union as the independent nation of Sahrawi Arab Democratic Republic (SADR).
Source: Wikipedia Free Encyclopedia.

et Monetaire Ouest Africain/Economic and Monetary Union of West Africa), CEN-SAD (Community of the Sahel-Saharan States—Tripoli, Libya).

- East Africa—IGAD (Intergovernmental Authority on Development—Eritrea, Ethiopia, Kenya, Somalia, Sudan, and Uganda), EAU (East African Union), EAC (East African Community), EACU (East African Customs Union).

- Central Africa—BEAC (Bank of Central African States—Yaoundé, Cameroon), CCAS (Community of Central African States), UDEAC (Central African Customs and Economic Union), CEMAC (Communaute Economique et Monetaire del Afrique Centrale [Economic and Monetary Community of Central Africa]).

- North Africa—UMA (Union Maghreb Arabe—consists of the five countries of Maghreb (North) Africa (Algeria, Libya, Mauritania, Morocco, and Tunisia) plus the disputed SADR.

THE GREAT SAHARA AS A NEW ORDER IN AFRICAN RELATIONS: FROM STATELESS TO SOVEREIGNTY, INTER-CITY RELATIONSHIPS

As explained earlier, the appearance of the Sahara Desert 7,000 years ago marked the end of the beginning of more permanent relations, which replaced the pre-Saharan "stateless" and nomadic interactions of the African peoples as they moved from one corner of the continent to another, and even beyond Africa. Post-Sahara relations, though imposed on Africans by nature with the desert's division of Africa, became systematic and consistent among the political units that came into existence as dictated by circumstances requiring collective and more broadly based dealings between and among entities established within clearly defined borders.

While the African population was increasing, the land was shrinking, hence African societies were born into law-and-order settlements with governments and civil structures that were enforced by the tribal rulers, as well as the rulers of African empires and super empires. These African kingdoms, city-states, and empires started as tribes—combinations/amalgamations of African clans that, when several or many tribes merged, became a tribal kingdom with one tribal ruler or king. Several or many tribal kingdoms formed an empire headed by an emperor. In this case, an emperor had under him kings of kingdoms which the strongest ruler—the emperor—subdued and conquered. A super empire was an amalgamation of several or many empires. Thus, tribes grew into kingdoms and kingdoms into super kingdoms, and these into empires and super empires.

At this stage, inter-state relationships were driven mainly by the principles of sovereign equality and they assumed that nature of "across borders," and this raises the concept of statehood. Sovereignty, borders, delimiting a territory with a population that voluntarily agrees to live within those borders, and a small group of people appointed by democratic election, or consensus of the people (called a government), all lead to sovereign or inter-sovereign state relationships. This is why, after the appearance of the Sahara Desert and the forcing of the African peoples to live together north and south of the desert, the old traditions of nomads and stateless relations in Africa reached their end. A new form of relationships emerged that was based on inter-state and cross-border relations.

As regards city-states, the first city-state ever formed on Earth was in Egypt in 3,100 BCE. That city-state was formed when two kingdoms of Egypt, one in the north and the other in the south, merged or were united into one political unit, to form a city-state. Interestingly, that first ever city-state was born on the peripheries of Mesopotamia—the birthplace of civilization! Proximity to this novel way of living, born within the Great Valley between ("meso" in Greek) two rivers ("potamia"), the Tigris and the Euphrates (where modern-day Israel, Palestine, Jordan, Kuwait, Iran, Lebanon, and Iraq are located) had a tremendous impact on the neighboring regions of the world.

Egypt in Africa was thus one of the beneficiaries of that early invention of civilization. Subsequently, in Egypt new forms of civilization emerged with the invention of writing, hieroglyphics, etc. These novel forms of civilized living led to the birth of many other new ways of doing things. Egypt started to produce rulers called pharaohs whose ambitions, innovations, and visionary approaches to life led to the construction of some of the most durable and memorable wonders of the world—the pyramids.

These developments further led to the maturation and diversification in methods of governance and government in Egypt and elsewhere, including in other parts of Africa where city-states were born. In the idea of a city-state, one had to look for certain criteria or conditions for a political unit to qualify for that title of "city-state." There had to be a city or big town comprised of people who had voluntarily come to live together, both as relatives and co-workers, co-sharers of ideals, services, common aspirations and desires, living within borders or peripheries (no matter how small those boundaries or limits were), and agreeing to be subjected or governed (i.e., ruled, protected, defended, and provided for) by a smaller group of people who were charged with the important responsibility of governing. Thus, this small political unit had to enjoy a certain amount of cohesiveness, independence, and sovereignty within the borders of the territory they called a city—their city.

Certain criteria had to be met before a political unit could qualify for the status of a city-state. A clan was comprised of humans who were usually relatives, with "heads of families" starting from a father of a family unit who also was in charge of an extended family of relatives—parents, brothers and sisters, children, uncles and aunts, grandparents and all their siblings. All of these people and their friends and other "settlers" who voluntarily agreed to live in one place had to follow certain codes of behavior and use common services like wells, rivers, grazing fields, etc. They formed a village and decided through appointment/selection or election on their leader, better known as a village headman. This complex system led to the recognition of sub-clans in a clan, and several clans formed a tribe at the head of which was a tribal leader called a king. At that stage, a tribal kingdom was born.

At the stage of a tribal kingdom, many of the attributes of a city-state were still missing because in the relations between and among tribal kingdoms and even those between and among some of the super kingdoms, empires, and super empires, the element of sovereignty was missing in terms of inter-state relations. Thus a city-state of Egypt could, for example, enter into a binding treaty relationship with a foreign state of Europe. This was not possible with most of the tribal kingdoms and empires whose relations were still regarded as "stateless," because they lacked sovereignty under international law. They were not, however stateless in the sense of what the relations of nomadic African groups had been in ancient times.

One of the reasons for all this was that in a tribal kingdom, there were relatives of the king, and there were his subjects who were not his relatives. These could be, for example, captured prisoners of war, slaves, or volunteers who were all under the government and governance of the tribal king or emperor. Some of them had no choice but to be loyal to the king to avoid persecution and even execution. At the tribal kingship level, as at the clan level, it was not so much a question of sovereignty in governance and government as a matter of following the traditional ways of rule—by custom and tradition, by maintenance of relations between and among the subjects and relatives of the kingdom through marriages to maintain peace and security through diplomatic relations that often assured peaceful coexistence through intermarriages.

This practice also was found among the super kingdoms and even among the empires and super empires, which were much larger and more powerful than the tribal kingdoms. However, these forms of governance and government and leadership did not, sensu stricto resemble the kinds of government and governance that we know today. What is practiced in modern times is an improvement of the city-state system as established by the Treaty of Westphalia in 1648.

Nonetheless, it was Greece that produced the system of city-states par excellence that is best known and most quoted. The Greek city-state system emerged with clear "rules of the game" and practices that are compared here with similar systems that were adopted and adapted in ancient Rome and Africa. The emergent city-states, kingdoms, and empires in subsequent years in Africa demonstrate the sophistication of those practices of governance already in use in the early years of governance in Africa.

EARLY HISTORY AND CIVILIZATIONS OF AFRICA VIS-À-VIS OTHER CONTINENTS

The events and dictates determining Africa's early history can be highlighted as follows: Africa prides herself as being the only continent to have been inhabited by humankind for more than 5 million years of human life, and to have served as the cradle of humankind and of civilization. The first humans, at the hominid stage, date back to 10 million years ago. As the cradle of humankind and human civilization, Africa underwent a gradual but steady evolutionary process from the pre-history to early history and beyond.

Then, radical cultural and climatic conditions caused changes to the continent, especially between 12,000 and 5000 years BCE. These changes produced a new natural order in an area the size of United States where the Great Sahara Desert now dwells in Africa. Prior to those climatic changes, that vast area where the Sahara is today was once a great savanna territory (grasslands) with game and excellent climate, and inhabitants, even including those of Caucasian extraction. But when the Sahara Desert was formed, the face of Africa was altered forever.

In North Africa, invasions of alien cultures—but notably those of the Phoenicians, Greeks, Romans, Arabs—and of foreign religions over the centuries—introduced a new heritage in the first century CE for Christianity in Africa and Islam from the seventh century CE. These invasions by foreign cultures and civilizations were at first concentrated in North Africa following the migration of Saharan populations to two directions: to North Africa along the Mediterranean coastline, and south of the Sahara to settle along the banks of the Nile River. The Nile Valley became very fertile with the sediments of the soil gathered along the Nile banks in the valley. This attracted many settlements. First came agriculturalists or pastoralists who grew crops and domesticated wildlife. The Nile Valley became a haven for human habitation, development, and progressive prosperity. The land settlements were first forced on the migrant peoples, as migrations from the Saharan savanna went to the north or south of the desert. It was not just the Sahara, but the Kalahari Desert as well. Settlements grew along the Nile banks and in the Nile Valley because this was a very fertile agricultural land for human habitation where permanent settlements were able to provide agricultural, cultural, economic, and political benefits to the people.

Africa's early civilizations and kingdoms that had been homes for gatherers and hunters from remotest times when Africans developed survival skills and instincts, and invented tools from stone, metal, and other abundant natural resources, were of the kinship type. From those early kinships and ancient kingdoms and settlements emerged 3,000 years of empires and city-states found all over Africa—in Egypt, Nubia, Ethiopia; at Kush Axum, Meroe, and others in Northeast Africa dating back to before the common era. Then came the kingdoms and early states of West Africa, the Sudanic civilizations, and others from 10th century BCE to 16th century CE (but especially between 700 and 1500 CE) as well as many others in West Africa, such as the Savanna Kingdoms and Empires of Ghana, Kazem, Hausaland, Oyo, Benin, and others, which flourished especially between 300 and 1897 CE. Many of those such as the Hausa states (11th century CE), Kazem-Bornu (13th century CE), Igbo (16th century CE), and many others had existed for thousands of years, dating back to about 5000 BCE following the permanent settlements that the New Natural Order of the Great Sahara Desert created, forcing the African peoples to move north and south of the desert, and to form tribal kingdoms, empires, and city-states. That was long before the occurrence of the alien incursions into Africa. In East Africa, at least 40 kingdoms and city-states emerged. They included Mombasa Zanzibar, Lamu, Pemba, Malindi, Kilwa, and Mogadishu. In Central Africa, there were the Bakongo and other city-states and kingdoms in Angola, and other kingdoms in the Great Lakes Region. In like manner, Southern Africa produced some of the greatest kingdoms and city-states, such as the Zimbabwe and Zulu, as well as the Ndebele, Shona, Sotho, Xhosa, Tswana, Swazi, Khoikhoi, and San Kingdoms of the pygmies ("Bushmen" or so called "Hottentot") peoples. Then there were those formed in the Namib, Mozambique, and

Zambezi regions of Southern Africa. All in all, from antiquity to precolonial Africa, at least 10,000 states were created.[1]

All of this mushrooming of kingdoms and city-states in Africa was enriched by the Bantu migrations, which gave population pressures and foreign religions such as Islam and Christianity great influence in African societies. Bantu migrations, as well as Arab and Zulu migrations, compelled the globalizations of religion—especially Christianity and Islam. The migrations started from about 1500 to 1000 BCE (and probably earlier, between 3000 and 2500 BCE), but became great forces in Africa in the first century CE for Christianity, and from around 622 CE for Islam. This latter year marked the first arrival of Arabs in North Africa, and thereby started the great Islamization of northern Africa. These religions launched extensive conquests of the African populations. But the Bantus were themselves great conquerors who exerted a lot of influence. Wherever they went, they conquered and settled. In like manner, conversions of the Africans to Christianity and Islam introduced new orders in Africa, and the kinds of practices and inheritance in Africa that changed the behavior and attitudes of Africans who converted to these religions.

As centuries passed, prototypes of modern kingdom types emerged, especially from 1800 onward, which cemented the developments in kingdom rule as seen from the 17th century CE when absolutism and despotic authority started to grow in Europe especially as evidenced with the Treaty of Westphalia of 1648, and the Dutch settlement of South Africa of 1652, which marked the era of government in South Africa called Apartheid (separateness) that lasted until its collapse with the advent of majority rule in South Africa in 1994.

In later years of kingdom and city-state existence in Africa, other developments marked a new era in African history that would change and transform Africa perhaps forever. First, legitimate trade was developed between the Africans and their kingdoms and the first foreign traders to Africa—Phoenicians, Greeks, Romans, and Arabs in the early centuries, between 1200 and 814 BCE. Here, trade was in natural resources, mainly gold, salt, ivory, cowries, diamonds, and the like. Then came the era of illegitimate trade in Africa and the gold was now African slaves. This trading was between Africa and the rest of the outside world: Europe, the Arab world, and the New World across the Atlantic. Some Africans were willing to participate in the slave trade. Some chiefs and kings sold slaves to foreigners such as the Portuguese and Arab slave traders, using agents in the rural areas. These developments marked a new era in kingdom and city-state relationships between Africa and the rest of the world. The new order of relations thrived from the 15th through the 16th–19th centuries CE, even after the abolition of the slave trade at the beginning of the 19th century. Then followed the scramble and colonization of Africa by

Europe that marked a completely new order for Africa. Africa continues to experience the residual impact of colonization today in ways that are more negative than positive.

AFRICA: THE "DARK CONTINENT"

Africa was once called the "Dark Continent." Very little was known of the interior of Africa, which remained hidden and mysterious to the outside world. The seclusion of Africa was partly created by its topography, which included the world's largest deserts (the Great Sahara, Kalahari, and Namib), many non-navigable rivers and rapids, a hostile shoreline without harbors in which ships could anchor, and nearly impenetrable jungles. Those who made it past these physical barriers still had to survive the hostility of African tribes like the Zulus, who would defend their territories using spears, arrows, sabotage, etc., and the potential for contracting a potentially fatal tropical disease (tuberculosis, malaria, elephant disease, sleeping sickness, which is better known as trypanosomiasis, etc.).

Thus, much of Africa was cut off from the rest of the world until well into the 19th century. The following looks at the details of the African geography that enforced this isolation so well for so long:

1. The Great Sahara Desert very much discouraged communications across Sub-Saharan Africa. The trans-Saharan trade routes existing in ancient times did not extend too much to the south, but connected only the northern tip of Africa along the Mediterranean Region and the Middle East with the Sudan.

2. Almost all of Africa's great rivers descend to the sea via rapids and waterfalls, and hence fail to provide an easy means of transportation or communication from the coast to the interior, as is the case with other continents.

3. Much of Africa is covered with mangrove, swamp, and sand bar, with few natural harbors along its shores. The surf is very heavy on the Atlantic side.

4. Tropical diseases of the wide savanna areas affected both man and beast. The savanna is infested with tsetse flies, which carries sleeping sickness. In these areas, there could be no walking and carrying belongings on the head, and no draught animals could be relied upon as the main transport. Transportation was possible in these areas only much later (1–19th century CE), when mechanical transport arrived in modern times.

NOTE

1. Africa's history is full of such creations. For further information, consult, for example, Jared Diamond, *Guns, Germs, and Steel* (New York: Norton, 1999); G. Mokhtar, *General History of Africa*, Vol. 2 (University of California Press, 1990).

CHAPTER 3

Africa and the Cultural Order: The African Value System

CONCEPTUAL UNDERSTANDING OF AFRICAN CUSTOMS, TRADITIONS, CULTURE, AND CIVILIZATION

The term "culture" belongs to the group of expressions better known as pluralism. These expressions, although in singular form, actually have a plural meaning. Thus, for example, "African foreign policy" usually means a group of African foreign "policies." So, culture, civilization, and the like, although singular, actually mean many cultures and civilizations, and these terms should be conceptualized as being plural in meaning.

African culture and civilization can be best understood if analyzed in the global context. That is, one needs to know what culture generally means. Furthermore, it helps to know that civilization, custom, tradition, and culture are terms of Latin origin. In fact, most of the expressions that we read in terms of culture and civilization are derived either from Greek or Latin. This is partly because we are grandchildren of Roman civilization and great-grandchildren of Greek civilization. We are all byproducts of Greek and Roman civilization.

"Civilization" is derived from the Latin expressions "cultus," which in Latin means care or cultivation, and "civis," which in Latin means citizen or countryman or woman. In Latin, "civilis" means civic, civil, courteous, political, public, or polite. "Custom" arises when a group of people belonging to a given region, or sharing an ethnic background, follows a common practice. Custom is derived from the Latin "usus," meaning practice or practical experience. "Tradition" is from Latin traditio meaning handing down or handing over, instruction. Thus, it is the passing down of a culture from generation to generation, especially orally. In Africa, the value system has always been based upon custom and tradition. "Culture" comes from the Latin word "cultura," which stems from the Latin verb "colere," meaning to cultivate. Note the use of the term "agriculture" from two Latin expressions: "agri" (of land) and "cultura" (culture or cultivation, i.e., cultivation of land). This links culture to the soil. So the roots of culture are to be found in tilling the land. Culture generally refers to the patterns of human activity and the symbolic structures that give such activities significance. Generally, culture is manifested in all of the ways of life, beliefs, and customs (i.e., practices of people forming customary regulations and laws created over time by common practice) as shown in people's habits, behavior patterns, values, institutions, and all other material habits and products of human life that constitute the way in which a given people live. All characteristics of lifestyle, of a particular people's human work and thought, of the arts (music, dance, literature, painting and sculpture, film and theater, architecture, etc.) that they produce, are parts of their culture. All of these practices, habits, and lifestyle choices are cherished and passed down from generation to generation. Perhaps nowhere on Earth has culture played such a central role in society from remotest antiquity as in Africa.

African culture is thus a way of life followed by African peoples over the centuries and millennia, and this includes codes of manners and behavior, dress, arts (e.g., from wooden carvings and earthenware pots and figures to the pyramids in Egypt; from forms of music to types of storytelling), language, religion, rituals, norms of behavior and practices (i.e., customs and traditions), as well as morality, laws, systems of belief, and the like.

African cultures overlap because they have been influenced through centuries of interaction with foreign cultures, especially those of North Africa along the Mediterranean Sea. North Africa was the first to experience the invasion of foreign cultures, especially the first alien colonizers of Africa (the Phoenicians, Greeks, and Romans). The imposition of alien cultures, especially European cultures during the height of 19th and 20th century African colonization, not only had massive negative impacts on native African cultures, but indeed transformed Africa in a major historic way.

African culture has not only produced traditional lifestyles for Africans, but also has been influenced by European and other foreign cultures' religion—by Christianity and Islam, for example—which have prevailed through pastoral and agricultural lifestyles to modern, phonist lifestyles in post-colonial Africa. Thus, for all practical purposes, African culture is African civilization.

ORIGINS OF AFRICAN TRADITIONAL VALUES

African values are, in essence, African traditional values that provided the basis for African culture. These traditional values probably arose in ancient times around 5500 BCE, when early Africans created a tradition based on their values of truth, goodness, beauty, and other intangible and non-material things of worth. Africans also recognize the value of the challenges of modernization/westernization, restoration, reclamation, rehabilitation; the maintenance of customs and traditions; the need for education, the roles of women and girls, traditional leadership, and democracy in the African family; and the lasting influence of colonial heritage, urbanization, and civilization.

Interestingly, the expressions "traditional African value" and "civilization" arose more or less at the same time in antiquity that the city-state existed in Africa. Since a value is "a thing of worth," (like life which is worth living) African values are the things and practices worth having. They give cultural identity and personality to humankind, and an urge to make contributions to global knowledge, history, and civilization.

Thus, at the core of the African value system are customs, traditions, and culture. The African value system includes various kinds of values that have shaped the manners, behavior, and actions of Africans and commanded their respect and pursuit through custom and tradition observed over a long time.

ORIGINS OF AFRICAN CIVILIZATION

If civilization is (and should be) accepted to be an advanced and sophisticated form of culture—a complex human society characterized by the practice of agriculture and settlement in cities, with clear divisions of labor in that society and an intricate hierarchy of social order, organization and governance, then one can safely say that African civilization dates back millennia to remotest antiquity and started in Africa, when *Homo sapiens* migrated from Africa to inhabit all the continents of the world, except Antarctica. That was at least 200,000 years ago. As the years passed, throughout the Stone Age and earlier ages, African man developed the first human society. He developed the first technological know-how, domesticated animals and crops, and developed human knowledge and progress in the arts and sciences. He also made strides in refinement of thought and manners, of behavior and taste.

It has been estimated that civilization sensu stricto was born about 5,500 years ago, within the Nile Valley and the Great Valley between the Tigris and Euphrates Rivers (the area comprising modern day Jordan, Lebanon, Israel, Iraq, and Palestine). These locations are believed to be the sites of the first development of civilization. Nonetheless, as Africa was the cradle of humankind, the first human society was African society. Civilization must therefore have started in Africa, and Egypt was one such significant site for that development. Going back to the earlier definition of civilization provided in this chapter, it is easy to understand that civilization was born as a result of people living in settled sites and being required to share common services like water and land, communication services, and organized labor, and working in regulated places with government and standard forms of acceptable behavior and justice (note, the term "police" comes from "polis," which means city in Greek). Thus, as the cradle of humankind, Africa was first to experience civilization. With the rise of ancient Egyptian civilization, the valley between the Tigris and Euphrates Rivers advanced in "civilized" behavior and lifestyle. Later, in North Africa, the ancient Greeks and, later still, the Romans developed civilizations to which we can trace the origins of civilization as we know it today.

As years passed, civilized ways of living evolved. The concept of civilization as we know it today developed even further about 300 years ago when European intellectuals got inspired by the astonishing cultural changes that intellectuals had witnessed over the previous century (17th century). A superiority complex preoccupied Europe, and Europeans started to globalize and superimpose their civilization across the globe for many reasons.

It is noteworthy that Africa's culture and civilization play, and have played, significant roles in the formation and application of African foreign policies and diplomacy. Since foreign policy is the guide of a country's foreign relations and diplomacy—the major manager of such relations—it is obvious that a nation's traditions, values, customs, culture, civilizations, and related dictates—events, histories, decisions, etc.—form the major foundations and determinants of foreign policy and diplomacy.[1]

As ways of living and doing business on a daily basis, African civilizations are some of the oldest on Earth, partly because human society started in Africa and it was in Africa that human civilization actually arose. Developments in early African civilization can be summarized as first, African civilizations emerged (predominantly in Egypt) in remote antiquity. Unlike other parts of the world that developed much later (e.g., North America), Africa's ancient times date back to antiquity. *Homo sapiens*, having originated in the eastern and southeastern regions of Africa, went out of Africa through the northeastern part of the continent and must hence have passed through Egypt while spreading human life to the Middle East and beyond.

AFRICAN AND AMERICAN VALUES: A SHORT COMPARISON

African Values: Traditions and Cultures

Values give humankind a distinct sense of cultural identity and personality and enable humankind to make some contributions to society, global knowledge, history, and civilization.

African values are varied. In ancient times, around 5500 BCE, ancient Africans created a tradition based upon their values. Such values include non-material and intangible things of worth throughout all aspects of life, such as the following:

- African Socialism (especially in stateless societies), nationalism, Pan-Africanism, Negritude, majimboism, consensus in decision-making, leadership, governance, loyalty to ethnicity and parochialism, family codes, education of children, justice and equality, economic fairness;
- Land, life, inheritance, heritage, customs, culture, traditions, rituals; hunting, gathering, tool-making, fire-making, rain-making, farming, agriculture, barter; village, the home, and village parenthood, love for community, communalism, roots;
- The supernatural (as things such as stones or mountains found in nature, sun, moon, etc., or as gods, beings, ancestors), religion, nature, morality and moral values, worship of things that give food, luck, stability, health, peace, life sustenance; sacrifices to supernatural powers, gods, ancestors; celebrating to gods, ancestors;
- Human life, humanity; the family, children, love for/practice of the extended family, respect for old people (the aged and parents and grandparents), respect and honor (for seniors);
- Dance, music, songs, oral history, hospitality;
- African marriage, dowry, alliances in marriages and diplomacy, polygamy; dialogues and consensus; positive change of mental attitudes; division of labor among women (especially in rural areas) and women's role in family upkeep, as brides, as mothers bearing children, and other traditional family practices.

Another African paradox to be taken into account—many Africans believe in a supernatural being to which all creations are linked, even though Africans worshipped all sorts of gods, nature, events, stones, ancestors, etc. Africans believed in, and focused on, having relations with, and behaviors toward, fellow human beings and with nature. So no person had to be left behind. The object was to reach a heaven after life.

It is noteworthy that these roots of the African value system developed at the same time that an ancient and historically important civilization was emerging in the Middle East's Great Valley and in Northeastern Africa, in Egypt. At this same time, the Great Sahara, which appeared about 2,000 years earlier, had already caused Africans who had led nomadic lives for millennia to make their homes in permanent settlements north and south of the desert. This shift from nomadic life marked the start of the new natural order for the African population.

It should also be noted that ancient Africans developed their values following repeated practices—customs and beliefs over the millennia of hunting, gathering, fire making, tool making, rain making, farming, barter, communalism, etc., from which emerged African Socialism especially in stateless societies. Values are of two kinds: tangibles (i.e., material things) and intangibles (truth, democracy, etc.).

Things that gave or sustained life, like food, luck, stability, diplomacy, and the like, were also worshipped as they were important things of worth. Thus, worshipping appeared in various forms and for diverse reasons. The supernatural was worshipped for sustenance. Diplomacy, equity, and justice were valued for peace and stability. Sacrifices were offered to ancestors and gods for pleading, sparing help, and mercy. Women were honored for labor, especially in rural areas, and for family upkeep, childbearing, and the like.

Celebrations were commonly held for the glory, memory, and honor of past important events or ancestors, through traditions, songs, music, and other practices. Also celebrated were governance, Pan-Africanism, Negritude, etc.

From the foregoing analysis, one can safely state that with culture and traditional values arose brilliant civilizations. The habits and practices that emerged during this time still remain, even in relations between peoples and nations of diverse backgrounds. It is thus in these cultures and civilizations that lie the roots of AIR, AFP, and AD.

The clashes between African cultural values and alien values, especially those of the Western value system, were inevitable following the imposition of alien rule and foreign values on the African people. These new values came with the spread of urbanization. Thus, in urban areas, money, self-sufficiency, economic imperatives, and the like have introduced new determinants and dictates into the African value system. This change introduced a modernization in Africa that stressed the superiority of foreign (i.e., Western) cultures and values, and replaced African values, especially from the late 19th century to the 20th century, and up to the present. The advent of colonization, and later globalization of Africa, brought new values to Africa that constitute serious challenges to traditional African values. These include the use of money, which replaced barter, and other economic imperatives. Other latter-day values and challenges include the education of all children; roles of women and girls; traditional leadership and democracy in African society and family, modernization, westernization, and the loss of African identity; reclamation, restoration, redemption, and rehabilitation of African customs, traditions, and civilization, and the clash of colonial and African heritage.

Western Education

The replacement of the African value systems by the Western ways of living introduced in Africa foreign systems of education and living which wrongly regarded African values as "primitive" and "uncivilized", i.e., not conforming to Western values. It was, for example, believed that systems of Western education would help uproot the African values and transform the African continent into a European way of living. There could not have been worse intellectual arrogance, or a worse policy and practice in Africa, than imposing strange values on Africans and believing that the European values were superior to the African ones! Nonetheless, that calculated goal of "Europeanizing" Africans, though not completely successful, did succeed in transforming Africa and the Africans who consequently have been applying Western ways of doing things as a result of the colonial legacies of Europe in Africa.

The main promoter of Westernization/Europeanization of Africa was Western education. It did not only introduce new challenges to Africans, but also turned many of the obviously traditional African values and practices into big challenges to the African people themselves. These challenges include the following, among many others:

- Urbanization and urbanism with all its challenges and handicaps
- Multiple ethnic backgrounds
- Taxation
- Development of a new paradigm
- Employment and wage labor
- Knowledge and modern technology
- Education, both traditional and formal, which is a huge byproduct of colonization
- Goods and services in domestic and global economic relations—imports/ exports
- Other services such as mining, manufacturing
- Migrations of populations from rural to urban areas for settlement
- Village parenthood
- Self-determination, liberation, and African ownership requirements
- Self-sufficiency, self-realization, self-help, independence, and multidimensional development as inevitable goals in African development.

Summary

African values are founded in custom and tradition. They include the following: truth; goodness; beauty; morals; respect; other non-material and intangible things of worth; worship of the supernatural; worship of ancestors in African culture and religion: worship of nature, events, storytelling, etc.; hospitality; love for community; land; inheritance; alliances; diplomacy; urbanization; African Socialism; marriage; polygamy—an old practice whose significance has been diminishing owing to modernism and modernization; dowry/bride wealth; human life; love for/practice of the extended family; respect for the aged including parents and grandparents; music, dance, the arts, and artifacts.

Examples of the Patrilineal and Matrilineal Societies in Africa

Both patrilineal and matrilineal societies exist in Africa. The following are examples of patrilineal societies:

- The Tiv of Yoruba in Nigeria,
- The Kikuyu of Kenya,
- The Luhya of Kenya in East Africa,
- The Swazi of Swaziland,
- The Nuer of Sudan,
- The Zulu of South Africa, and
- The Gala of Ethiopia.

The matrilineal line of heritage is very rare in Africa but exists. Matrilineal societies of Africa include the Bemba of Zambia, the Wolof of Senegal, the Baule of Côte d'Ivoire, and the Yao of Tanzania, Malawi, and Mozambique.

The third category of heritage values of African customs and traditions consists of matrilineal and patrilineal values. Bilateral or cognation descent traces family members through both parents as in the United States and in other Western societies. This category also is very rare in Africa.

American Values

What are Western values? They are part of the modern system of new values for the African. American or Western values are predominant in urban areas and greatly promote urbanization. Thus, they are melting pot values of the multiplicity of ethnic backgrounds; they promote development; and stress love for other people instead of just "love of one's own ethnic group," which is still predominant in African social practices and promotes social and racial stratification as a value. Western values stress that knowledge is power; information is knowledge. Therefore, formal education, science, writing, arts, cities, technology, and development are inevitable, but formal education is meant to "civilize" Africans (i.e., bring Africans into the European value system). Formal education is hence a by-product of colonialism and colonization by Western countries. Individualism is a vital value in the American value system.

As a central object, American/Western values aimed at replacing African values, especially during the 20th century when Western colonization eroded African values and transformed Africa into a Western value system. American values should be considered as

- Constitutionalism—legal values (e.g., the American Declaration of Independence of 4 July 1776, the Constitution, the Bill of Rights), political institutions;
- Education;
- Equality of the sexes, rights and equal opportunities; and
- Prosperity, capitalism, and modernization.

Thus, significant Western values emphasize freedom, equality, liberty, opportunity, patriotism and the love of one's country. These are in opposition to most African values that stress ethnicity, land, tradition, family, customs, respect for moral values, age, and family codes. Other Western values include law and order and constitutional liberties, freedoms, democracy, individualism, health care, etc. Modernization, a Western value, was introduced to Africa through colonization and was enhanced by globalization of Africa through (1) inward economy (allocating a large role to endogenous influences on national economies), (2) tourism, and (3) international commerce.

Different political cultures have mushroomed in Africa, stressing equality of the sexes; protecting the community first; patriotism instead of regionalism (no majimboism); and superiority complex of race, power, and dominance. A fundamental question that can be asked is whether the differences in African and American values can be used to bridge the gaps between the two value systems for the common good of Africans and Americans.

In like manner, it would be instructive to find solutions to the challenges of values and culture clashes that confront Africans and Americans and the Western world in general. In this regard, it would be instructive to scrutinize the impacts of challenges to African–American relations, especially urbanization and modernization, as well as the restoration, reclamation, redemption, and rehabilitation of African values, customs, traditions, culture, and civilizations that were removed from Africa by the imposition of colonial rule.

Summary

American values are Western values, as set forth in the U.S. Constitution and its Bill of Rights. As follows:

- Inalienable rights of life, liberty, and the pursuit of happiness;
- Individualism;
- Freedom of expression;
- Democracy;
- Protection by government and government for, with, and by the people;
- Equal rights, equal opportunity, equality of the sexes;

- Education;
- Capitalism and the right of ownership;
- Different political ideologies;
- Protecting the country first, patriotism, not regionalism or parochialism;
- Superiority of race;
- Respecting and protecting laws—rule of law and basic freedoms;
- Education is believed to be the passport to success and to multidimensional development;
- Money speaks—the Western value system is almost predetermined by the availability of financial capacity—with money, everything is possible;
- Loyalty to the American flag, and aspiration for the American Dream.

DEVELOPMENT OF LANGUAGE AND CULTURE IN AFRICA

Premises and Origins of African Languages

Language is one of the most revealing discoveries in the evolutionary process of humankind. What is language? Who discovered it? When? Where and how? Accurate responses to these questions are not easy to establish. However, explanation of a few premises and conceptual definitions can help in the understanding of the origins and development of language as a tool for communication. Also important is the role that language has played over the millennia in facilitating understanding and cooperation among humankind and animals, as well as finding resolutions to problems and issues of peaceful coexistence that confront humankind and living creatures, most notably animals.

The term "language" is derived from the Latin "lingua," meaning tongue, speech, language, dialect. Although no definite indication exists as to the primordial author, location, timing, and mode of language, several premises can safely be advanced on the language issue. The first is that, if Africa was the cradle of humankind and civilization—and it was, given the existing substantial archeological and other evidence—then the first human society was actually African. The second premise is that, since the start of the evolutionary process dates back millions of years, starting with the hominids (or "near-men") more than 10 million years ago, as DNA, archeological, and other data also reveal, then the origins and development of language must have happened in Africa. Third, since there is evidence that humankind, originating in hominids, shared a common ancestor with the great apes and parted company or separated from the apes 6 million years ago, then it must be true that the roots of language preceded the emergence of humankind and hence the rationale for language which emerged from the need to communicate for survival, support, settlement, and steering of societies of living beings, especially animals and humans. The originators of language were the hominids, and the location was Africa. Furthermore, it was only in the human line that language emerged.

So, how did language arise? Language makes us human, and it emerged only in the human line along with all of the necessary brain structures for encoding thoughts into sounds, and transmitting them to other members of the species. About 2 million years ago, humans (*Homo genus*) spoke a precursor of language as we know it today, but the words had no grammar. Up to that time, these hominids had been living in forests, gathering and hunting wildlife for food, etc. Then about 120,000 years ago, these humans left the forest to live in savanna territory where they started to hunt systematically. They also domesticated wildlife and domesticated plants (crops) for food, etc. That was about 10,500 years ago.

At that stage, language started to develop among these earliest human beings in various stages. First humans developed "context free" vocal symbols such that the same word could be used in different contexts (e.g., The leopard is beautiful. The leopard is cunning. The leopard is stealthy. The leopard is unpredictable.). Then they developed signs and symbols as a means of communication. Later, whistling and writing were added to oral signs. These are the earliest known kinds of language.

Gradually, the population learned and developed the ability to communicate through language. Sounds were used to express emotions, feelings, wonder, and awe, summoning or calling (e.g., to express pain, laughter, crying, fear, or happiness; administration of warning; etc). Baby sounds (especially those of toddlers) resulted in expressions that became significant tools of communication, for example, a baby's communication with its mother, with lips biting, "mama," "papa," "tata," etc. Symbols (e.g., of objects such as drawings of giraffe, lion, leopard, etc.) were also an important stage in the development of language as shown in many early cave drawings including those discovered in ancient Egypt containing hieroglyphics, math, etc.

DEVELOPMENT OF LANGUAGE

Language thus occurred, gradually, with changing human behavior and experiences. As the human brain enlarged, thought and dialogue between and among humans had to be expressed in some form for emphatic and clear communication. This led to the birth of speech for communication with others.

The evolutionary process of language happening in various stages in the human mouth reached a kind of peak about 100,000 years ago when, with the use of his enlarged brainpower, humankind started to produce vocal outputs and engaged intellect and reasoning. Man developed further language from the symbols and signs of primates for alerting one another to the presence of enemies, predators, food, poison, etc.; advanced language use from imitations of sounds in the environment, and from cries and emotions of joy, pain, and other exclamations; used language signs for obtaining certain aims (e.g., privileges and advantages in society, such as a traditional rainmaker announcing that soon there will be rain so the villagers should get ready to plant their crops—such an act would earn the rainmaker privileges and advantages).

Language underwent considerable evolution in the era of *Homo erectus* (approximately 1.8 million years ago) and *Homo sapiens* (around 50,000 years ago). The *Homo erectus* stage marked the origins of sign language with considerable gestural communication. However, unlike primates, humans used language in order to obtain the power and ability of persuasion of other peoples, and to form alliances or accept the truth of something not happening before their eyes. In later years, humans, as political animals, used speech communication in spoken and written language forms that replaced sign language. At the *Homo sapiens* stage, humans invented vocal and spoken language.

NATIVE AND NON-NATIVE AFRICAN LANGUAGES

Africa has the greatest language diversity on Earth. However, at the creation of the world, mankind spoke and understood one uniform language. Genesis 11:1 reads, "Now the whole world had one language and a common speech." But after the great flood, sinful men defied God by uniting their skills and communications to create the Tower of Babel. So God said in Genesis 11:7, "Come, let us go down and confuse the people with different languages. Then they won't be able to understand each other." Since then, humans have been unable to communicate because of the diversity of their languages. Thus, after God scattered them throughout the world, descendants of the builders of the Tower of Babel began to change their natal speech and to develop symbols to communicate speech through writing.

There are at least 2,000 native languages spoken in Africa, all of which have countless dialects and language sub-groups. Africa has more spoken languages than any other continent. African languages can be described as native, i.e., indigenous to Africa, and non-native, i.e., not indigenous to Africa. The latter group comprises Arabic, which was introduced to Africa during the 7th to 11th centuries CE, and European languages, which were introduced to Africa starting from the 15th century CE, for example, English, Portuguese, and French. The Portuguese were the first Europeans to establish contacts with Africans in modern times: they invaded Morocco and occupied Ceuta in 1415 CE, which is an enclave in Gibraltar. Thereafter, more and more Europeans arrived in Africa in various roles. The Arabs, on the other hand, are believed to have arrived in

North Africa in 622 CE, and subsequently transformed North Africa through their culture and language.

The native African languages consist of four major groups. These are the Khoisan group, the Niger-Congo group, the Afro-Asiatic group, and the Nilo-Saharan group. Of the more than 2,000 languages spoken in Africa, about 50 have 500,000 or more speakers.

The Khoisan Language Group

The Khoisan language group is probably the oldest of the four African language families. But Khoisan is the smallest language group in Africa with about only 200,000 to 300,000 speakers. There are about 30 languages spoken in this group.

The Niger-Congo Language Group

The largest language family in Africa, with 300 million to 500 million speakers, is the Niger-Congo language group, which descends from a proto-language dating back 5,000 years. This group has very many languages, and has at least seven main sub-groups, six of which cover West, Central, Eastern, and Southern Africa. The seven sub-groups of the Niger-Congo language group are (1) Benue-Congo (including Bantus of the West Atlantic), (2) the Mande, (3) the Voltaic, (4) the Kwa, (5) the Adamawa East, (6) the Kordofanian, and (7) the West Atlantic. As one of the major sub-groups, the Bantu languages are spoken in most of the southern half of Africa. These languages expanded from Cameroon and eastern Nigeria in three major waves of migration 3,000 to 4,000 years ago. The Mande language sub-group is spoken in Senegal, Mali, Guinea, Liberia, and Sierra Leone. The Voltaic language sub-group spoken by the Gur is spoken in Mali, Côte d'Ivoire, Ghana, Togo, Benin, Nigeria, and Burkina Faso. The Kwa languages include Tuvi and Yoruba in Ghana, Liberia, Togo, Benin, Côte d'Ivoire, and Nigeria. (Yoruba is spoken by 22 million people.) Languages of the Adamawa East sub-group are spoken in Cameroon, Democratic Republic of Congo, and the Central African Republic. The Kordofanian sub-group is spoken in the Nubba Mountains of Sudan by fewer than 500,000 speakers.

The Bantu sub-group includes the Swahili language. Swahili comes from eastern Bantu and is the most widely spoken language in East and Central Africa, together with Hausa (in northern and western Nigeria). Swahili has nearly 50 million speakers. Intermarriages of Bantu and Arabs in Eastern Africa brought many Arabic words into Swahili. Swahili is thus both the language spoken on the coast of East Africa and the name of the people born from Bantu-Arab intermarriages who are known as the Swahili.

Other Bantu languages include some in Southern Africa, like Zulu Shona, Tswana, Khosa, and Ndebele, as well as others in Eastern Africa like Kiluhya, Kikuyu, Kisukuma, as well as Kikongo, Kinyarwanda, and Kirundi (Kirundi is spoken in Burundi and Rwanda, whereas Kinyarwanda is spoken in Rwanda).

Apart from the Hausa and Swahili language sub-groups in Africa, other native African languages include Hadza, spoken in Tanzania, and Ndorobo, spoken in Kenya. These two languages are spoken only by about 200 people—the smallest tribes in those nations.

There also are Igbo in Nigeria, Fulfulde in Senegal and Chad, and many other native African languages. Fulfulde is the dominant language in West Africa's Senegambia region, and is spoken by 13 million people in Cameroon, Senegal, and Chad. Wolof also is spoken in Senegal, whereas Temne is spoken in Guinea, and Bambara in Mali.

The Afro-Asiatic Language Group

The Afro-Asiatic Group is the second largest language group in Africa, with 200 to 300 million speakers, and is expanding in North Africa, the Horn of Africa, Southwest Asia, and parts of the Sahel. The stock is often described as the Hamito-Semitic group, as it embraces people from North Africa, such as the Berbers, Tamazight (Berbers), and Chadics; as well as the Middle East, such as Arabs and Egyptians; and Semitic peoples such as, Somalis, Cushites, Amharic, and Oromo.

The Nilo-Saharan Language Group

The Nilo-Saharan Group has about 30 million speakers. It is probably the most diverse language group, with about 100 languages spreading from northeastern to West Africa. It is spoken in Egypt, the Sudan, and even parts of East Africa such as the Maasai, as well as by Nubians and other Nilotic family populations. The Dinka and Songay and others also belong to this language group.

NON-NATIVE LANGUAGES IN AFRICA

The non-white languages in Africa are either Arabic or European. The globalization of Islam and Christianity, as well as the colonization of Africa, introduced foreign languages that greatly influenced African languages, especially English, French, Portuguese, and Dutch. The European colonial languages were imposed on Africa from 1500 CE onward. Arabic was introduced in Africa in the 7th and 11th centuries CE. Afrikaans is one of the official languages of South Africa. It was developed by the Dutch settlers who arrived in South Africa in 1652 CE.

The Malagasy language was/is spoken in Madagascar and belongs to the Austronesia group of languages with origins in Indonesia. Migration of people from Indonesia to Madagascar occurred when the Dutch visited the Far East via the Indian Ocean and colonized Indonesia and other Asian areas.

In North Africa, the dominant languages are Arabic and indigenous languages of the Berbers and other tribes of that African region, like the Bedouins.

SUMMARY

Language makes us human because it developed only in the human line after the separation of humankind from the great apes 6 million years ago. However, the origins of language can be traced to much earlier times in the hominid era. When the brain structures of humans became larger, man became capable of translating thoughts into sounds, and then, possibly 2 million years ago, transmitted these sounds to other members of *Homo genus*. At one time, humans spoke a precursor of language as we know it today (i.e., words without grammar).

Vocal language probably emerged when certain alterations happened in the human mouth about 100,000 years ago. Thenceforth, using their developing brain power, humans produced vocal outputs far beyond instinct and engaged reasoning and intellect. Then imitations of sounds, cries, and emotions (such as pain, joy, and other human experiences and exclamations), were used to send out messages to other humans in the environment. That kind of communication became extremely useful in environments and circumstances where and when humans had to alert one another using symbols, signs, and sounds to the presence of danger, enemies, food, poison, predators, etc. From about 1.8 million years ago, when the bipedal *Homo erectus* stood at 4'6" tall, gestural communication became the origin of sign language, which has developed especially for the hearing impaired in modern times.

In contemporary times, language, speech, signs, and gesticulation have become powerful tools used by politicians wishing to persuade and win to their side others in order to win elections, form alliances, ascend to power, or find solutions to problems through negotiation and by conveying their convictions of the most appropriate actions.

AFRICAN SOCIALISM AS A CONTINENTAL IDEAL?

Whatever interpretation may be given to African Socialism today, it was originally, and is still, a vital value within the African value system. African Socialism has really nothing to do with Western classical ideology, just like African democracy should never be interpreted as merely the Western concept meaning one man one vote.

African Socialism had its roots in the African value system, which is based on custom and tradition from the family unit to the extended family and clan stages to the tribe, and then extended to all of the African values of land, village parenthood, duty toward children, the elderly, the sick, etc. In short, African Socialism is a value that imposes on the society the duty to help without being requested, in order to settle problems by consensus. This motivates African society to do things without being rewarded and prompts Africans to take upon themselves the responsibility of helping, protecting, defending, and providing the necessities of life without seeking reward or gratitude.

In this sense, African Socialism is an excellent friend and companion of the African philosophy and concepts of Harambee (Swahili for "let us all pull together"), Ujamaa (Swahili for "extended family or family-hood"), Ubuntu (originating from the Bantu languages of Southern Africa where "-untu" or "-undu" has to do with a human being and "ubuntu" has to do with humanity. Ubuntu is a classic African concept or an ethic/humanist philosophy that focuses on people's allegiances to, and relations with, each other.

Jomo Kenyatta (c. 1894–1978) of Kenya was a staunch believer in Harambee. Julius Nyerere (1922–1999) of Tanzania made Ujamaa a national policy for socioeconomic development. Kwame Nkrumah (1909–1972) of Ghana is often referred to as the father of African Socialism as a political concept, and Nelson Mandela (1918–) of South Africa was a staunch advocate of Ubuntu.

In the African context, therefore, African Socialism was meant to be a key instrument through which peace and stability, collaboration, welfare, justice, equality of opportunity, assistance and self-sufficiency, sharing, and sustainable progress could be attained. African Socialism also found great promotion in Negritude, a concept that "blackness is beautiful and to be proud of if you are of African descent." This concept was promoted by Aimé Césaire (1913–2008) of Haiti, and found great favor in Sedar Senghor of Senegal.

AFRICA AND THE HUMAN ORDER: PEOPLING, DEMOGRAPHY, AND HUMAN EVOLUTION

Introduction: Creationism versus Darwinism

Discussions on the origins of humankind have been controversial. Was mankind created by divine command or natural evolution? As described in Chapter 1, the biblical story that appears in Genesis 1:2–2:2 states that God created man on the sixth day. However, some scientists and naturalists such as Charles Darwin have argued that natural evolution, not divine creation, presents the real story of the origins of creatures and the universe. Whereas there is disagreement in this regard, there is agreement that the evolutionary process has existed for millennia, and this is documented on the basis of DNA, scientific studies, archeological discoveries, and other evidence.

Thus, agreement exists on the following:

1. That Africa was the cradle of humankind and civilization. The first human society was thus African society.

2. That the great apes (gorillas, orangutan, chimpanzees) and humankind had a common ancestor, a species called hominids (hominidae), or "ape-like creatures" at least 10 million years ago and more. Originally, these hominids walked on four feet, like the great apes, hairy, just like gorillas and orangutans. They began to walk upright and became bipedal, stretching to about 4'6" foot tall, millions of years ago.

3. That the human species parted from the great ape species about 6 million years ago. Thus, the time range usually quoted when hominids lived, evolved, and developed separately from the great ape family as distinct hominids or "near-men" (i.e., ape-like creatures) is between 10 million and 2 million years ago. Humans evolved from these creatures of ancient mankind—the ancestors of man.

4. That in the hominid's family only did language evolve, most probably because the evolutionary process of at least 2 million years developed intellect and a larger brain in the hominids that were the predecessors of humans than in the ape family. As a result of this evolution, humankind developed a reasoning capacity that enabled him to have a sense of recognition, understanding, and communication between and among members of his own species. The first communication was through through the use of signs, emotionally based (warnings for danger, pain, pleasure, denial, approval, fear, etc.) and later through sounds, symbols, and writing.

5. That the origins of humankind are traced to eastern, northeastern, and southern Africa. This phase of *Homo* was also known as the *Australopithecus Africanus* (AA, or the southern ape of Africa). The scientific evidence of the existence of these "near-men" in Africa without interruption makes Africa not only the first habitat or humankind, but also the only continent to be continuously inhabited for at least 5 million years.

6. Even though some scientific studies have argued that the hominids as pre-human relatives of man actually lived in Africa at least 1 million years ago, the evidence that human life in Africa dates back to even more than 5 million years ago is overwhelming.

7. After *Australopithecus Africanus* started to walk upright at about 4'6" foot tall, he had human-like teeth, and began to use crude tools.

THE PEOPLING OF AFRICA: FROM *HOMO GENUS* TO *HOMO AFRICANUS AFRICANUS*

The process of human evolution has been traced in Latin terminology. In Latin, "homo" means human and "genus" means kind, So a juxtaposition of homo to genus produces "*Homo genus*," meaning humankind.

Thus, from *Homo genus* to *Homo Africanus Africanus* in the 21st century, there are six stages, as follows:

- Stage I: *Homo genus* (humankind) lived 2.5 million years ago.
- Stage II: *Homo habilis* (handy man or human being) lived between 1.9 and 1.6 million years ago and began the *Homo* line in Eastern Africa at Olduvai Gorge in Tanzania. Stone tools date back to this time and are evidence of Homo's further development of survival skills, especially in the Stone and Iron Ages when he roamed the African savannas, developed gatherer and hunter skills, learned how to make fire, and domesticated plants and animals for food. In this way, the hominid genus became skilled in making tools and using fire. By 1.7 million years ago, *Homo habilis* developed into the next stage.
- Stage III: *Homo erectus* (erect or upright man) lived at least 1.8 million years ago. He appeared in Eastern and Southern Africa, then spread to northern Africa and elsewhere including the Chad Basin, around Lake Nyanza (later Lake Victoria), and then into Eurasia. He coexisted with *Homo Neanderthalensis* and *Homo sapiens* from 1.6 million years ago. However, one did not evolve into the other. *Homo erectus* was the most adventurous stage, having coexisted also with *Homo habilis*. By the time *Homo erectus* wandered into Eurasia, he had developed considerable expertise in survival. In fact, the early genus of *Homo* moved out of Africa twice. He left Africa first about 1.5 million years ago and spread throughout Europe and Asia where the expression *Homo erectus* was coined to refer to the fossils of *Homo*. Thus, *Homo erectus* evolved outside Africa, but only in Africa did *Homo erectus* develop into *Homo sapiens*.
- Stage IV: *Homo sapiens* (wise man; knowing man) was very similar to modern man. He roamed Africa between 200,000 and 130,000 years ago. He gradually spread out in Africa and again migrated from Africa to inhabit all other continents except Antarctica some 200,000 to 100,000 years ago, and then he came back to Africa.
- Stage V: *Homo sapiens sapiens* (the real man, or true wise man). He was also known as Cro-Magnon—real man, our direct ancestor or the immediate ancestor of present-day humankind. He evolved from the archaic *Homo sapiens* 200,000–100,000 years ago in Africa, and appeared around 100,000 years ago (between 115,000 and 96,000 years ago).
- Stage VI: *Homo modernus* (modern human being or modern humankind) means that wherever he lives, he is modern. *Homo Africanus Africanus* in Africa; *Homo Asiaticus* in Asia; *Homo Americanus* in America; and *Homo Europaeus*, etc. We belong to this stage of humankind, and we are the proper modern human beings. Existing information on *Homo modernus* is rather confusing. In some cases, it is stated that *Homo modernus* is anatomically the same as *Homo sapiens sapiens* who lived 200,000 years ago in Africa, as evidenced by DNA in southern Africa.

Observations

Whatever the arguments, there is sufficient evidence to justify the conclusion that all people today are classified as *Homo sapiens sapiens* (i.e., the sapiens variety of *Homo sapiens*).

In like manner, creationism and Darwinism are not, and should not necessarily, be considered mutually exclusive of each other. In fact, creation by divine nature could have happened and been followed by evolution. It is this writer's informed conclusion that humankind was created by the supernatural, and that this creation was followed by the six stages through which humankind evolved.

SPREAD OF HUMANKIND ACROSS THE GLOBE

There is considerable evidence indicating that humankind's migrations out of Africa happened millions of years ago. By 600,000–200,000 years ago, there was a widespread migration of human species across Asia, Europe, and Africa.

By 500,000 CE, *Homo erectus* had been well established inside and outside of Africa (for example, in China and England), and excavations have found and describe the presence of African hominids. The survival instincts and skills of these near-men became further refined. Furthermore, within this same timeframe, between 600,000 to 200,000 years ago, other improvements enhanced the lives of our ancestors. For not only did man acquire mastery of making and using fire around 790,000–500,000 years ago, they also improved on their cultural and linguistic capacities and developed a keen sense of migration to distant lands (for example, from Africa to Eurasia). Excavations of the Acheulian culture in Africa about 1.6 million years ago show that people had not only mastered fire-making as long as 790,000 years ago, but that the prehistoric hominids from Africa settled outside of Africa in a significant way. Given this very early human migration from Africa, it is self-evident that the coloring of the human race, as translated in skin pigmentation, started in many millennia ago and resulted in the various colors of mankind that exist in the world today.

Archeological and anthropological evidence indicates that an African woman lived in southern England 200,000 years ago, and documentation of this is included in excavations of human origins dating back to 500,000 years ago. Three stages of *Homo habilis, Homo erectus*, and *Homo sapiens* converge in this period, with improvements in the cultural, tool-making, and linguistic dictates of their lives. The human brain grew larger, and this allowed mankind to develop better tool-making skills and better cooperation and communication among the members of the same species.

At least 11 different kinds of tools have been discovered in the Olduvai area of Tanzania where, for example, Richard Leakey was able to determine the existence of *Homo habilis* features, the culture of hunting, brainpower and intellect, as well as the ability to communicate using language tools for the education of the young, hunting for prey, sharing and preparing food, and using his large brain for survival.

Since *Homo sapiens sapiens* is the same as *Homo modernus,* this latter stage was already in evolution around 200,000 years ago when the first of the *Homo sapiens sapiens* species appeared. Between 89,000 and 35,000 years ago, a "systematic" migration of modern humans from Africa started to happen, and by 50,000 years ago, man had spread within, and out of, Africa. He established Stone Age cultures in Europe (he is estimated to have reached Europe around 40,000 years ago), Asia, and Australia.

By 60,000 years ago, *Homo modernus* (*Homo sapiens sapiens*) had developed and improved human behavior and forged the characteristics of modern political, economic, and social patterns by the time that the Sahara Desert appeared.

THE SAHARA AS GENESIS OF A NEW ORDER IN AFRICA

Defining the Sahara

Deserts in Africa form a separate geographical region, but the Sahara Desert constitutes an important sui generis case whose historical and other significance seems to be ignored. In most cases in which Africa is addressed as a vast region of diverse characteristics, a number of these features deserve a closer examination.The occurrence of the Sahara about 7,000 years ago marked the beginning of a new order, which not only changed the course of African history, but also provided to Africa a multidimensional approach to the African condition that went far beyond the description of the Sahara as a mere desert. For beyond the climatic, geographic, topographic, and natural disaster aspects that relate to deserts, the Sahara ushered in other historically significant considerations, and these included the shaping of Africa's cultures and civilizations; politics and economics; trade, including the slave trade and the African Diaspora; environment and ecosystem of Africa; as well as the peopling, history, and colonization of Africa on which the great Sahara Desert has had an impact in one way or another.

The word "sahara" is an Arabic expression meaning "desert." However, only a small part of the area is sand dunes. The rest is flat, gray wasteland of scattered rocks and pebbles, with occasional rock outcrops and ridges. The Sahara is the world's largest hot desert, about the size of the continental United States or the continent of Europe. The Sahara is approximately 9,100,000 square kilometers (3,500,000 square miles). It is about 1,610 kilometers (1,000 miles) wide, and 5,150 kilometers (3,200 miles) long (from east to west). Its topography comprises crew plains, sand seas, and rolling sand dunes.

Often, the western part of the Sahara is called "the Sahara proper." The desert has the following borders: to the west, it borders the Atlantic

Ocean; to the north, the Sahara borders the Atlas Mountains and the Mediterranean Sea; to the east are the Red Sea and Egypt; and to the south are the Sudan and the Niger River Valley Basin. The southern borders of the Sahara embrace semi-arid savanna called the Sahel, and south of the Sahel engulfs the Sudan and the Congo River Basin.

The story of the formation of the Sahara Desert is paradoxical and starts with the Ice Age. The Ice Age, also called the glacial age or glacial period, was a prehistoric geological period marked by cold temperatures and glacier advances. This period experienced long-term reductions in the temperature of the Earth's surface and atmosphere over a very long timeframe, resulting in an expansion of the continental sheets. The paradox with regard to the Sahara Desert lies in the fact that the roots and origins of this desert can be traced back to the Ice Age, which was distinguished by two divergent attributes: one was "glacial," meaning clearly marked by colder temperatures and the other was "interglacial" meaning it experienced, and was marked by, a retreat in the temperatures (i.e., it tended to possess warming features).

These two characteristics of the glacial era are actually quite proper to the features of all the four major documented Ice Ages, starting with the first one which was Huronian, dating back 2.7 to 2.3 billion years, and ending with the fourth Ice Age, which is actually the one that started 2.58 million years ago. The existing scientific determination of these phenomena reveals that the last glacial period ended about 10,000 to 15,000 years ago. It is noteworthy that that was the timeframe when the Sahara Desert started to form, in a focused and concentrated fashion, as a process of gradual but systematic changes and warming in the last Ice Age—about 12,000 years ago. The climatic changes between wet and dry were enormous, and became especially pronounced between 8000 BCE (about 10,000 years ago) and 6000 BCE (about 8,000 years ago).

Particularly noteworthy in this period were two phenomena. First, the Sahara region, a vast area, was subjected to considerable climatic alterations not just for hundreds of years but for a few thousand years. This region was once a fertile, great savanna grasslands area that enjoyed a moderate climate of the kind now prevailing in the Mediterranean and was inhabited by plenty of wild game and peoples of different walks of life from both African and even Caucasian extraction.

Second, and by the time the glacial era ended, the large Sahara area had been reduced in size. Changes in Earth's orbit caused the Sahara's abrupt desertification. A great increase in rain came to the Sahara between 10,000 and 8,000 years ago. Subsequently, low pressure areas arrived and lead to the collapse of the ice sheets to the north. Once the ice sheets were gone, the northern Sahara dried out. However, in southern Sahara, the monsoon winds brought rain further north than they appear today.

Monsoons happen because of the heating of our air over the land during the summer. When the hot air rises, it pulls in cool wet air from the ocean and causes rain. The Sahara was once wetter when it used to receive more solar insulation in the summer.

By 3400 BCE, the monsoons retreated south to approximately where they are today. This change lead to the gradual desertification of the Sahara. The Sahara is now as dry as it was about 13,000 years ago. Geographically, most of the Sahara had rocky "hamada" and large sand dunes called "ergs." Perhaps what is most noteworthy in the phenomenal story of the appearance of the Sahara Desert, is that it marked a new era of African history that would witness a lasting division of Africa into two sections: North Africa and Sub-Saharan Africa (SSA).

When Islam was globalized and introduced into African cultures from the 7th century CE, it spread to North Africa along the Mediterranean and converted the entire region of North Africa to Islam. Intermarriages also occurred and helped blend the cultures and traditions of North Africans and the people of the Mediterranean and the Arabs of the Middle East. The result was that the cultures and civilizations of North Africa were "crossed" and now the values and cultures of the African peoples of North Africa are closer to those of Arab cultures than African cultures.

Peopling of the Sahara

In analyzing the peopling of the Sahara, one needs to remember that prior to the appearance of the desert, the Sahara region had been inhabited for millennia by indigenous Africans long before the first foreigners—the Phoenicians who visited Africa between 1000 and 800 BCE for the first time—had contact with Africa. They came as merchants and businessmen from the Middle East (present-day Lebanon) and the surrounding regions inhabited by the Semitic peoples who were among the first to establish a civilization between the Tigris and Euphrates in the rich valley that lies between these rivers in what is now known as Mesopotamia (which, in Greek, means "between two rivers").

That the Sahara was inhabited for many centuries by African and other peoples and races has been established through archeological excavations, anthropology, fossils, rocks, artifacts, ancient skeletons, DNA, and remains found in various parts of Africa, including in the Rift Valley and in the Sahara Desert itself.

There is enough evidence to warrant the conclusion that humankind started in Africa, and that humans and the great apes had a common ancestry originating in Africa more than 5 million years ago. This makes Africa the only continent to have been inhabited by humankind for at least 5 million years.

Of the indigenous populations of the Sahara region, the Berbers, Tuaregs, and other African ethnic groups seem to have been the original inhabitants of the Sahara and spread all over from Carthage to Hippo to Tripolitania and Cyrenaica in present day Libya. These have always been nomadic peoples—desert-adjusting peoples—living along various oases in the desert. Alien arrivals in Africa were the Phoenicians, Greeks, and Romans, in that order, as described in Chapter 1.

Phoenicians in the Sahara

The Phoenicians were a people of Semitic extraction from the ancient maritime nation of Lebanon in southwest Asia, comprising city-states along the East Mediterranean. The Phoenicians were the first alien arrivals in North Africa. They settled in North Africa along the Mediterranean Coast and Egypt between 1200 and 800 BCE. They were the first alien colonizers of Africa: they colonized Carthage in 800 BCE just 14 years before the founding of the City of Carthage in present-day Tunisia. The original inhabitants of those places, the Berbers, were overwhelmed by the foreigners. Phoenicians then established confederates along the Mediterranean coast and flourished in kingdoms stretching across the entire Sahara, including Libya, which in ancient times produced great people who spoke Berber languages in North Africa and northern Sahara, where Berbers are still the dominant tribe. Another tribe, the Tuareg, is also an important inhabitant, especially in Central Sahara.

As the first foreign colonizers of Africa, the Phoenicians were followed almost 200 years later by the Greeks. These advanced their colonial ambitions in Africa between 633 and 530 BCE. Phoenician colonies were consolidated further between 633 and 530 BCE. During this period, Hanno the Navigator emerged and created Phoenician colonies in the western part of the Sahara.

Greeks in the Sahara

After the Phoenician colonization of North Africa came the Greeks, who exerted a new influence in the Sahara that resulted in the Greek colonization of North Africa. Greek colonial influence excelled between 631 and 332 BCE. They established important Greek settlements in Cyrenaica in 332 BCE and Tripolitania in present-day Libya. By 500 BCE, the Greeks had created a new, and considerable, influence on the Sahara. As traders along the eastern coast of the Sahara Desert, the Greeks established trading colonies along the Red Sea coast. Then in Carthage, business with the Carthagians flourished along the Atlantic coast of the Sahara.

As an island of sand, the Sahara divided Africa into that part which was to the north of the Sahara and the segment that was to the south of the Sahara. The Berber population was, and continues to be, nomadic, so the Greek colonizers established contacts with the nomadic populations both north and south of the Sahara. The Greeks colonized Cyrenaica and Tripolitania up to present-day Ethiopia which they believed to be the end of the known world and called "the land of sun-burnt-faced people" (in Greek, "ethio" means "burned," and "pia" means "face"). That description of Africa also was advanced later by the Arabs who described Africa as "al-Sudan," meaning "the land of the black people."

Alexander the Great of Macedonia expanded his empire to Egypt and founded Alexandria in 334 BCE, and that Greek city flourished for years as a hub for business in the region and became an important center for learning in the Greek African colony.

Romans in Ancient Africa

The third alien colonization of Africa, also confined to northern Africa, was by ancient Rome. The Roman conquest of Carthage in 146 BCE, followed the defeat of General Hannibal. That conquest marked the beginning of the long, imperialist rule of Rome over North Africa, which became a valuable part of the Western Province of the Roman Empire. It is noteworthy that the Romans previously had been humiliated in battle by the African General Hannibal, perhaps the greatest military tactician of all time, who led an army of Carthagians riding on elephants to present-day Italy for a successful attack.

By then, Carthage had become a renowned city-state with business and trade contacts all over the Mediterranean region, was well known for business in the Roman Empire, and was a great hub of the region for strategic, political, economic, business, and military business contacts in the Roman Empire. Trade continued to flourish in North Africa in subsequent centuries in that part of the Western Province of the Roman Empire, about which Pliny the Elder had talked in his competent Latin account of Africa, not only as a great continent possessing vast wildlife and other forms of nature, but also as a continent of great strategic location and various natural endowments with the wonderful, mild climate of the Mediterranean region, which would be great for international business.

NOTE

1. For an interesting account of African civilization before the arrival of the white man, see Richard W. Hull, *Munyakare African Civilization before the Batuure* (New York: John Wiley & Sons, Inc., 1972).

CHAPTER 4

Early Forms of Governance in Africa: From Remotest Antiquity to the State System

INTRODUCTION

African heritage and relations among various African societies and nations from colonial times show a steadily growing pattern of international relations development in, and for, Africa, which eventually led to the creation of diplomatic and other foreign policy initiatives and relationships that became important prototypes of African foreign policy and diplomacy. The problems of governance and government in Africa can best be clustered into three historical periods: pre-colonial, colonial, and post-colonial eras. These are broad eras with sub-periods in each era.

If governance is considered in pre-colonial times, then the period has to spread from the origins of governance in the period of time in African history, stretching from remotest antiquity until the European colonization of Africa in the late 19th century. That was the period of African heritage—consisting of African customs, traditions, cultures, civilizations, and ways of living best known and practiced by Africans.

The African pre-colonial period can be subdivided into smaller eras, as follows:

- From more than 5 to 7 million years ago to 700 CE, the period from remotest antiquity, which was marked by the peopling of Africa, from the hominids (near men) to *Homo genus* via *Homo sapiens* to *Homo Africanus*, steady births of African societies occurred following the evolutionary processes experienced by the hominids and ensuing humans over the millennia.
- From 700 to 1400 CE when African tribal kingdoms and empires flourished.

- From 1400 to 1883 CE, when the slave trade and slavery were a most lucrative business (this was also the age of European Renaissance, expansionism, exploration, globalism and globalization, commerce, discoveries, and occupations of foreign lands).

As millennia and centuries passed, African populations grew and various tribal stocks and groups also grew and evolved over the millennia from the expansions of family units to extended families, communities, villages, sub-clans, clans, chieftaincies, sub-tribes, tribes, and tribal kingdoms, to city-states, empires, super empires, and super city-states. They all matured after the birth of the city-state system in Egypt (3100 BCE), and subsequently following the birth of the great Saharan divide in Africa. That was long, long before the Greek concept of a city-state was born around 750 BCE from the political organization of the Greek Dark Ages, when the Greeks began to recover from the destructive wars that had been waged between 1100 and 759 BCE.

The African city-states witnessed great African civilizations, traditions, cultures, and kings and queens, like Queen Hatshepsut the "Beauty Queen" of Egypt, Queen Basheba of Ethiopia, and others. The city-states established relations between and among themselves and with the external world. Those relations promoted diplomacy, trade, protection of citizens and national interests, conquests, forging alliances with neighboring and other city-states and kingdoms, and settled disputes and conflicts via cooperation and diplomacy. The political units divided their countries into provinces and other smaller units for efficient administrative purposes. The European colonial masters adapted the African method of governance in colonial times.

That means that when the world's 14 powers assembled at the Berlin Conference of 1884–1885 to partition Africa into European colonial spheres of influence, they created juridical statehood for Africa, which would be imposed by 7 major colonial powers (France, Great Britain, Germany, Belgium, Portugal, Italy, and Spain). Political organization in Africa, up to colonization in the 19th century, appeared in various forms from family units headed normally by a man/husband/father to villages, each of which was headed by a headman or a kind of "askari" or "peacekeeper" for decent behavior and obedience to codes of life in the village. He represented the chief and the chief's assistants. Then came the sub-chief heading a sub-location. He served under a chief and was in charge of a location, as were several other sub-chiefs if the size of the location warranted such administration.

A senior chief was in charge of a large area consisting of chiefs. All these fell under a paramount chief. He was actually the tribal king before the Europeans overturned the traditional administrations in Africa and turned them into their administrative units. In essence, the colonial masters followed the traditional kingdom arrangements but abolished the kingdoms by making those institutions branches of the central government. Thus, the paramount chiefs who had been tribal kings became pensionable civil servants who were known as paramount chiefs or chiefs.

HISTORICAL ASPECTS

Throughout this study, the emergence of Africa as a continent and subsystem of the global system has been characterized by evolution and development—these being the two fundamental processes from and around which procedures have evolved in Africa. The dual and overarching goal is to promote, protect, improve, and defend the African human condition, and to develop and protect the African natural condition.

Thus the pillars upon which Africa must rest are her human and natural orders. Since Africa exists primarily for the benefit of the people who inhabit Africa, it is the human condition that must come first. This helps explain the reason why human governance and government must be well understood in any study of Africa. The roots of the success or failure of African leadership, African presence, and African international relations, foreign policy, and diplomacy must be traced in the early forms of governance in Africa. Later forms of governance and government will also succeed or fail depending on the kinds of foundation that were created in African society at or from the time when African human society became obligated to live on a given territory, within demarcated borders, and on a permanent basis.

Thus, to talk about early forms of governance in Africa is basically to talk about the African human condition, in historical perspective with government and governance being addressed and understood in historical context of the African evolutionary and development practicum.

To govern a people is to provide, protect, promote, and defend the people and provide their needs, promote their values, and defend their interests, image, integrity, and systems, among many other things. This is what any government has a duty to accomplish. Such a government, as a small group of people charged with these responsibilities on behalf of the governed, performs its duties well or badly, depending on what the government does, how it does it, and the result of its work. Here is where governance comes in.

The problems of governance in Africa thus prompt the government to exercise without power and control over the governed, as well as to make and administer public policy, under set rules and regulations, for the determination and implementation of these policies for the common good of the people.

A historical examination of the question of governance in Africa calls for tracing the art of government to the earliest years of human organization in prehistoric, as well as historic, periods of African evolution and development. As explained in Chapter 3, the prehistoric development of humankind dates back to the hominids (i.e., near men) who evolved over a period of more than 10 millions years and lived basically in nomadic and stateless communities moving in small groups, looking for green pastures, discovering things and places as they moved within and out of Africa. It can be stated with certainty that governance in those early years of humankind was not patterned on the dictates of large human communities, but rather on the needs of small human units starting with family units headed by the father of the family, then through the extended family, to the village, sub-clan, clan, sub-tribe, and tribe to the tribal kingdoms stage as years passed. But, for a long time, the management of affairs remained at the family or extended family and clan levels. Nomadism would not allow for long-term planning or settlement in areas. After all, the populations were quite small in Africa in those prehistoric and early ancient times.

When, however, populations started to grow large and spread elsewhere in Africa, life became more organized and eventful. Humankind started to invent and discover things, to domesticate crops and wildlife, to invent survival tools for hunting and gathering food as well as objects and commodities for barter. At that stage, unlike in prehistoric times where most aspects of culture were handed down from generation to generation, history became written, recorded, and documented.

In terms of governance, government, and their historical evolution in Africa, one needs to determine how such processes could have developed by looking from African historical perspectives. Prehistoric times in Africa, (i.e., more than 10 million years ago during the time of the evolution of hominids stretching from remotest antiquity up to 4000 BCE) was a period of undocumented, unrecorded, and unwritten history. With the invention of writing at approximately 4000 BCE, there is evidence of the beginning of written history. This marked the end of prehistory and the supplementation of oral history by written stories. When oral traditions and histories were documented, they helped save some of the rich oral traditions and the history that they recorded, that had been dying with the passing of the narrators/authors. The Middle Ages is recorded as stretching from 476 to 1453 CE. Although history of the Middle Ages is recorded, it mainly refers to European history.

ORAL TRADITIONS AND LEGENDS AS ROOTS OF GOVERNANCE AND GOVERNMENT IN AFRICA

Evidence from Stone Age and Iron Age legends and oral traditions suggests that the nomadic nature of humankind did not allow for fixed and systematic authority of individuals over other people. It was in the Iron Age that legends started to tell stories of some people trying to exercise power over others. The most convincing legend is the one that states that a locksmith started to force people to do his will in a gathering of individuals.

Nonetheless, many stories have been told orally that depict the origins of governance in Africa and indicate that the roots of governance and government from earliest antiquity in Africa were not limited to the well-known paternal authority that was then entrusted with more responsibilities to protect the people and guide them to conquer their problems and human enemies.

Then, as legend has it, in the Iron Age, a male founder emerged, who persuaded, or forced, people to accept his rule. This founder was a blacksmith who became a king, signaling the importance of iron in the evolution of the African kingdom. He invoked supernatural powers that signified the presence of supernatural sanctions behind the power of an African ruler. This complex beginning of the art and practice of governance in Africa is explained closely in the following analysis.

ORIGINS OF GOVERNANCE IN HISTORICAL PERSPECTIVE

The New International Dictionary defines history as "a narrative of events connected with a real or imaginary object, person or career . . . a systematic, written account of events, particularly those affecting a nation, institution, science, or art, and usually connected with a philosophical explanation of their cases. The branch of knowledge that records and explains past events as steps in human progress."[1]

Africa's prehistory and history can best be analyzed as recorders of issues, dictates, and determinants of governance and government when examined in the context of global history. In this sense, periods of African prehistory and history have to coincide with those of global prehistory and history. Thus, the prehistory of Africa is the period stretching from remotest antiquity to the beginning of recorded history around 4000 BCE. This is the period in Africa that began more than 10 million years ago with the birth and development of the hominids, our ancestors, and stretched to the beginning of the period of written or recorded history.

HISTORY OF AFRICA

In the African context, the period of African history is known by several descriptions and these range from early history, ancient history, ancient times, and antiquity in Africa. All these not only fit into the periods of global history, they especially signify specific eras that came into existence only after the initiation of recorded written history of both Africa and the world.

One needs to be careful here. For, although written or recorded history were possible only after the invention of writing in Egypt in the 4th millennium BCE, in the period better known as ancient history, it has to be stressed that the history of Africa in reality started in prehistory since it began with the first emergence of *Homo sapiens* about 100,000–30,000 years ago. Africa's ancient history can be defined as having started in antiquity (i.e., in ancient times that began with the rise of Egyptian civilization in the 4th millennium BCE), and advanced over the succeeding centuries during which diverse societies prospered throughout the Nile Valley until the extensive invasions of alien cultures and civilizations into Africa.

If African history started with the first emergence of modern human beings in Africa, continuing into its present situation, then one can safely delimit the eras of African and world history as follows:

- There is sufficient evidence to suggest that the period of ancient history, African history included, started in about 4000 BCE and ended with the fall of the Roman Empire in 476 CE. It is within this historical period from 4000 BCE to 500 CE that African ancient history or Africa's antiquity has been fixed.

- The period following this era of ancient world and African history was known as medieval time. Basically, this was a period in European history that stretched from the fall of the Roman Empire in 476 CE to the end of the early Middle Ages in 1453 CE.

- Modern European history began with the ending of medieval history and continues to the present. It also can be argued that the year 1453 marked the beginning of modern African history. But it was a period of dark African history, given the events that had been shaping Africa, especially following the invasion and conquest of Ceuta in Morocco by the Portuguese, who were the first Europeans to visit Africa in modern times and triggered the occupation of Africa by Europe. The slave trade in captured Africans that began at this time also marked a very dark period in African history.

- Modern African history, however, has different dates. For Africa, the three great ages of prehistory were the Stone Age, the Iron Age, and the Bronze Age. They mattered to Africa, since throughout the prehistoric times up to the 4th millennium BCE in Egypt, a long era of metallurgy had produced lots of lead and artifacts that flourished in the 4th millennium BCE. Copper artifacts have been dated back to pre-dynastic times in Egypt, when copper was in great use. By 5000 BCE, the Old Stone Age, the Middle Stone Age, the Late Stone Age, and the Age of Metals had each seen an increase in the demand and use of metals. Although the Iron Age is considered to be a part of the Late Stone Age, and the Bronze Age was an age of metals, they all date back to more than 10 million years ago as follows:

- The Old (Paleolithic) Stone Age
- The Middle (Mesolithic) Stone Age
- The Late Stone Age
- The Iron Age
- The Age of Metals
- The Age of Bronze

In the era of metallurgy there was a great deal of lead used, as shown in artifacts dating from Egypt in the 4th millennium BCE, and copper dating back to pre-dynastic times when copper was in great use. The use of bronze, which is an alloy of copper and tin, is found after 3000 BCE, especially in Nubia. Around 1750 BCE, gold and silver acquired increased use in Egypt during the pre-dynastic era.

MILESTONES IN THE PREHISTORY AND HISTORY OF AFRICA

In Africa's history, Egypt and the Neolithic North Africa saw the arrival of foreigners in North Africa who created colonies and empires there. The Phoenicians, Greeks, Romans, and Arabs were among these conquerors. Following the appearance of the Great Sahara, Africa was divided into two parts: North and Sub-Saharan Africa.

Religious Globalization

The spread of Christianity in North Africa to Egypt, Nubia/Sudan, and where present-day Ethiopia now rests caused the populations of these areas to convert to Christianity in 1 CE. By 33 CE, Christianity had been well established in Kush, Azum, and Meroe.

The spread of Islam after 632 CE to the 7th century CE first began in North Africa where Arab influence grew following the globalization of Islam. In subsequent years, Islam spread to East and West Africa.

These religions spread systematically in the Middle Ages, a time in which African kingdoms and empires had been flourishing in Eastern, West, Central, and Southern Africa. With the spread of these religions came a great deal of commercial and cultural influences in Africa.

As the empires and kingdoms mushroomed, they developed and refined issues of governance and government in Africa. Since the appearance of the Sahara, governance and government institutions and issues had been introduced and practiced everywhere in Africa—in Kush, Axum, Meroe, Nubia, and Egypt; in East Africa at least 35 city states emerged among the Swahili people of the Indian Coast; in Southern Africa, the Zulu and Zimbabwe kingdoms emerged; in Central Africa, the Bakongo and Angolan kingdoms; and in West Africa, the many kingdoms in Ghana, Dahomey/Benin, Oyo, Hausaland, Mali, Songhai, and territories where Christianity and Islam introduced new heritages in Africa. These religious influences, together with African heritage and subsequent European heritage, are still felt in Africa today.

ISSUES OF GOVERNANCE IN AFRICAN KINGDOMS, EMPIRES, AND CITY-STATES

Problems of government in Africa can be understood best when examined through the regional aspects of Africa (i.e., as they developed and were practiced in North, Eastern, West, Southern and Central Africa). In ancient times in Africa and North Africa (5000 BCE–500 CE), issues of governance arose in countries such as Egypt, and in city-states such as Carthage and Alexandria.

North Africa's Maghreb Region

The Maghreb Region of North Africa has a rich history, stretching from 3500 BCE to 1500 CE. As described in Chapter 1, the first foreigners to make contact with Africa were the Phoenicians in Utica in 1100 BCE and Carthage in 814 BCE. They were followed by the Greeks, most notably in the time of Alexander the Great who founded Alexandria in 332 BCE, and Romans who made what later became known as the Maghreb Region of Africa part of the Western Province of the Roman Empire in approximately 146 BCE. These conquerors all arrived before the common era. Ancient Egypt saw the formation of the world's first city-state in 300 BCE. All of Roman/Byzantine North Africa eventually fell to the Arabs in the 7th century CE.

In summary, Africa's prehistory was the recording of events that had been narrated in Africa by word of mouth. It was oral history as opposed to written history. Africa's prehistory can be said to have started in remotest antiquity, more than 10 million years ago when our ancestors the hominids, or near-men, became bipedal.

It should be noted that although prehistoric events in Africa form part of oral narrations, some of them have been recorded even though they happened when there were no written records. Such records reveal, for example, that one of the earliest dates of African prehistory, better known as the earliest southern rock art, dates back to 27,000 years BCE and included more that 4,000 paintings.

The features of prehistory included an evolutionary process of the spread of humankind after his origins in the eastern, southern, and northeastern parts of Africa where mankind roamed in small groups comprised mainly of extended family members looking for green pastures, exploring, and discovering, until the emergence of agriculture, domestication of crops and animals, and the development of survival skills.

By this time, mankind in Africa had entered into the Stone Age and subsequently went through the Iron Age. His gathering and hunting skills and inventions of tools and weapons for survival were improving, especially when metallurgy replaced the Stone Age skills with more sophisticated tools. Eventually, Africa underwent radical cultural and climatic changes leading to the birth of the Great Sahara Desert. This marked a new natural order for Africa. The hominids, who around 2.5 million years ago had discovered stone tools and materials in the Stone Age, were facing new life dictates with the new technology that they had invented. Thus, throughout Africa, from the Sahara to the Kalahari and Namibia Deserts, hunters and gatherers proliferated as they moved from one area to another. Then, agriculture spread on the continent and pastoralism emerged. By the 4th century BCE, conditions had been created for inventing writing and, with that invention, began a new era of history—no longer prehistory, but *African history* when events started to be written and recorded. Africa entered a second phase of history. This era coincided with population movements, especially expansions of Bantu stock in the southern and central regions of Africa.

In the south, there were the Khoisan in Kwazulu and Botswana. In Central Africa, the Bantus were spreading around 1000 BCE in the Congo and around the Great Lakes Region to Eastern Africa. Thus, although it is stated that African history as information about the past of the African people starts with the rise of Egyptian civilization in the 4th millennium BCE with the invention of writing and the use of language for recording history, African history actually started much earlier—in ancient times, with the first emergence of *Homo sapiens*. That was between 100,000 and 30,000 BCE. These are the dates of Africa's early history. It is believed that the oldest images and the oldest human skeletons have been found in Egypt. The *Homo sapiens* were hominids, modern human beings in Africa originating in East Africa, and continuing into its modern/present situation as an assembly of different and politically developing nation states. It is fascinating to note that the study of the documented past from the start of recorded history until the early Middle Ages in Europe is so closely associated with the history of Africa—a continent that has ironically been described as the Dark Continent.

In subsequent centuries, following the permanent settlements of Africans in Sub-Saharan Africa as forced by the rise of the Great Sahara, many African societies developed beyond the Nile Valley. Furthermore, the first alien arrivals in Africa—the Phoenicians—established commercial contacts between 1200 and 800 BCE along the Mediterranean. The Phoenicians were the first colonizers of Africa, although they were only in the north of the city of Carthage. The ancient Greeks arrived in 631 BCE in what is now Libya and was then the territories of Tripolitania and Cyrenaica, and by 322 BCE, imposed colonial rule in Egypt when Emperor

Alexander the Great ruled Macedonia. When the Romans arrived in 146 BCE, they eventually overthrew Hannibal to occupy, and ultimately conquer, Carthage.

ROOTS OF THE ARTS OF GOVERNANCE AND DIPLOMACY IN AFRICA

Like government and political science, governance is an art. In Africa, the skills, laws, and order for governance and government, stressing the administration of justice, African Socialism, and the protection and defense of the African society in which the governed lived, must have become essential following the permanent settlements of the African peoples north or south of the Sahara. To meet their needs and provisions, protect their interests, defend them from their natural and human enemies, and protect their assets, the leaders of the people had to develop leadership qualities gradually. This leadership was exercised by the rulers who relied heavily on the dictates of custom and tradition (inheritance). Governance and government in African tradition mostly started from patrilineal hereditary rule in which fathers or other male heads of families passed down rulership to their sons. In a few cases, where the power, authority, or governance was in the matrilineal code, the mother/queen became the ruler and handed her power down to her daughter, etc.

Thus, power and authority first belonged to the head of the family and then to the head of the clan, and, thereafter, it was exercised by the leader or ruler of the tribe. This head of a tribe was normally referred to as the king, and the tribe became the kingdom.

Where one ruler or king was in charge of several or many tribes, that ruler became an emperor since his rule was over the kingdoms of other tribes through expansionism and even by custom and tradition. Thus, several tribes formed a kingdom, several or many tribal kingdoms became super kingdoms or empires, and several or many empires formed a super empire. The leaders of these political units likewise assumed titles that were appropriate to their status as those who governed their tribes, kingdoms, empires, or super empires—chiefs, kings, emperors, and super emperors, respectively.

As observed earlier, empires and kingdoms flourished in the years 800–1500 CE in Africa. It was also within this timeframe that many city-states were born in Africa. The most important feature of the city-state was its possession of territorial sovereignty.

The earliest states of ancient Africa, whether called city-states or kingdoms, arose and developed with little or no direct contact with the outside world. Those early states arose along two main axes: one axis ran east and west across the broad belt of the Sudan. The other axis ran north and south along the highland spine stretching from Nubia in present-day Sudan and Ethiopia, to Kipling's "great grey, green greasy" Limpopo River at the other end.

Each king had a council of advisors—or elders—applying mostly custom and tradition as the guiding principles of governance. Africans existed in loosely organized groups of tribes and peoples, not as the subjects of feudal monarchs held together by bureaucrats whose loyalty was to the king alone. A state's fate was determined by diplomacy and long-distance commerce.

One of the most remarkable methods of dealing with matters of state was the application both of advisory mechanisms for solving differences and disputes, and of diplomacy as the art of negotiation and management of disputes—and even wars—which aimed at avoiding war and clashes between and among sovereign or non-sovereign political entities. In early African diplomatic practice, intermarriage played a major role. When for example, the Arabs arrived in East Africa from Oman and Arabia, one way of cementing trust and relationships with the Bantu-speaking people of East Africa was through intermarriages between Arabs and Bantus. A new culture emerged from these practices, which became the Swahili culture of the Swahili people. "Swahili" is an expression derived from the Arabic term "sahel," meaning "coast." So, the Swahili are people of the coast who, until nowadays, were found in the coastal areas of Kenya and Tanzania, along the coast of the Indian Ocean. They were and are still farming, fishing, and trading people. The Sudanic Belt, running from the Ethiopian Plateau to the Atlantic Ocean, had a large population settled there since 3000 BCE. These have always been people of mixed racial composition, but those who generally were Negroes. They were mostly food collectors who struggled against nature, as well as other Africans to the south. In Sub-Saharan Africa, the Stone Age was replaced by the Iron Age, which created advancements in hunting, fishing, farming, and warfare. Iron technology developed in ancient Africa led to better agricultural methods.

Since ancient times, Africa—meaning the physical land—has maintained a special place in African society, in which agriculture has retained the roots of African civilization. In the African tribal kingdoms and empires, before attaining those positions and eventually graduating to city-states, pre-colonial rulers were constantly reminded by their council of elders that African societies traced their roots and civilizations to agriculture, family ties, religious worship, dance, the arts and music, matrilineal and patrilineal systems, etc. These reminders were crucial to the kings and emperors of the African societies who later developed and established inter-kingdom and inter-empire diplomatic relations, which became cross-border relations in cases where sovereign political entities were concerned. By the time kingdoms, super kingdoms, empires, and super empires attained the status of sovereign entities, they had actually become city-states, or simply

African states, that had the authority to deal with other sovereign entities. Good cases in point were the Barbary State and Egypt in North Africa, which maintained sovereign state relations among themselves and with other non-African sovereign states.

With the emergence of the city-state system, African political establishments have discovered ways of creating and maintaining diplomatic contacts as a means of promoting good political, economic, and business relations. These were essential for promoting non-violent ways of solving differences (e.g., through intermarriages or by cementing cooperation with other entities to defend themselves and their dependencies against human and natural enemies). Any steps taken to resolve disputes through negotiation and compromise, land, slaves, prisoners, and other possessions—but not by war—could be described as diplomatic.

Then there was a steady growth of business and trade relations that thrived during the kingdom and empire centuries (5000 BCE–1697 CE) in various countries of Africa: Carthage, Alexandria, Egypt, Kush, Nubia, Axum, Ghana, Meroe, Mali, Songhai, Zimbabwe, Buganda, Timbuktu, and Mombasa, Angola, Congo, and other commercial hubs and nations of Africa. These were savanna, forest, coastal, and mountain empires and kingdoms that thrived by trading in gold, ivory, salt, diamonds, and slaves. Diplomatic relations also were facilitated through rapid and durable common commissions and courses around Africa: from the Niger River in Mali to the Nile in Egypt to the Limpopo and Zambezi in Southern Africa, and other waterways, like Lakes Victoria, Albert, Tanganyika, Rudolf, Elementaita, Nakuru, Naivasha, and rivers in the Rift Valley and the Great Lakes regions of Africa. This not only established and facilitated commerce between and among the African kingdoms and empires, but helped to develop vital diplomatic tools during the advent of the city-state era.

By that time, the origins of foreign policy, diplomacy, and international relations—as supported by city-state services across borders and strongly backed by the royal advisory council of elders—had taken strong root. By the 6th and 7th centuries CE, African civilizations of this period in late antiquity were thriving close to the Roman Empire and near the Red Sea. Men and women had been assigned clear roles in society where diplomacy and foreign policy started to play increased roles of mediation and negotiation, and these, in turn, enhanced the roles of peaceful coexistence, inter-city-state networking, and the establishment of consultative mechanisms for dispute settlement, cooperative promotions, friendship promotions, and the like.

Africa and the Origins of the City-State System

From the existing data, taking into account Africa as the cradle of humanity where the first human society originated, one is bound to conclude that the concept of the city-state system must have originated in Africa and became real and applicable after the formation of cities (i.e., places where people voluntarily assembled to dwell within definite borders of a demarcated land, with law and order codes or legal powers bestowed upon a few people in the same place). Usually, these codes were enacted through selection or sanctioning by all of the inhabitants of the place, and those legal powers or stipulations were enacted or put in a document called by different names such as charter, constitution, declaration, etc., but with a binding force in which the governed people had to obey and follow the government.

This kind of societal order did exist in Africa but also arose later in Greek societies. Thus, it is evident that around 5,500 years ago, when the city-state process started to exist, it must have been in Africa, since around that time, the evolutionary process of radical climatic and cultural changes was overwhelming Africa and leading to the birth of the Sahara Desert. The process leading to the appearance of the Sahara started around 12,000 BCE, and by 5000 BCE, the desert had taken root in that part of Africa known today as the Sahara. This is a huge area in Africa, the size of United States, where there had been excellent moderate climate, plenty of wild game, and great grasslands—ideal for human and animal habitation. There also is evidence that people of Caucasian extraction likewise lived in that region.

When the Sahara divided Africa into north and south of the Sahara, amid the new natural environment, new human, sociopolitical, and cultural orders ensued. Among many requirements, the people were forced to give up nomadic life and live in permanent settlement so that they could share common assets and services, share leadership and governance, and be protected by their leaders against common enemies like famine, hunger, insecurity, politically driven human invasions, and natural enemies such as animals.

Thus, 5,500 years ago, African peoples already had been living in such permanent settlements north and south of the Sahara for 2,500 years—since the Sahara Desert appeared in 5000 BCE—about 7,000 years ago. This fact leads to further pertinent observations. Long before the colonization of Africa there were no states, but many small, loosely associated families and tribal kingdoms. Tribal kingdoms especially emerged after 5000 BCE, with the migrations of African populations in the Sahara area into North Africa and the Nile Valley where settlements flourished, mainly due to fertile lands and acceptable living conditions. Thus, nomadic and expansionist ways of life had been brought to an end, and Africans had to live not in cities but in settlements. Then discussion of the city-state system starting as a process and existing in Africa through state-building around 5,500 years ago with the advent of civilization in Egypt should be interpreted to mean that the appearance of civilization was a slow but steady development. It started in Mesopotamia between 3500 and 300 BCE. With this development, living conditions of peoples before then, especially in Africa around 5500 BCE—had to change to give way to civilized behavior and living in common demarcated places, with sophisticated ways of living, acting, and governing. It was thus from civilization that the true city-state system had to emerge. In Africa, that code of behavior and living came through Egypt mainly because of Egypt's proximity to Mesopotamia and also due to Egypt's strategic location between Africa and the Near East—what was then the seat of civilization.

Advent of Civilization in Mesopotamia

Mesopotamia is the region in the great and rich valley between the Tigris and Euphrates Rivers. In Mesopotamia ("meso," meaning "between" and "potamia" meaning "rivers" in Greek), civilization started in this part of the world for a number of reasons, which included the following:

The availability of the Great Valley for agriculture, civilization, and other facilities—river waterways, common services, and advanced societal refinements—were useful for advanced living through the domestication of food crops and animals, organized work in urbanized areas, the growth of industries, refined living as evidenced by flourishing arts (music, dance, painting, etc.), advanced law, and systems of governance and government.

As stated, Egypt became an early beneficiary of the Mesopotamian civilization because of Egypt's location but Egypt had to import civilization from Mesopotamia. Egypt became the first country on Earth to experience city-state governance and government when the northern and southern kingdoms of Egypt decided to merge into one state under one king, Menes, who was called a pharaoh, in 3100 BCE. But it was in Greece that the city-state system emerged par excellence, and it is that ancient Greek form of city-state, later imported into ancient Rome, that has become the best known. The best known does not, however, mean that the city-state system was born in Greece, as wrongly argued in some literature.

The Greek city-state started as a city ("polis" in Greek) or town. The concept of city administration grew out of the political organization of the Greek Dark Ages (1100–750 BCE). In Greece, the city-state originated from the city or capital of a nation state. The city-state was a political unit and form of government, expressing military and political strengths and might, political values, and local patriotism. The city-state system continued to grow steadily from 500 BCE to 700 CE, by which time the system had been clearly solidified.

During the Iron Age, the concept of rule for, and in, organized society began to take shape. Governance started to be talked about, and many legends arose that describe how governance and government started, as well as their importance to law, order, and justice. So, as the legend goes, a blacksmith in the Iron Age started to call people around him and became their leader. He started to give them directives of work and behavior. He became their ruler/king by requiring them to obey his authority, which was given to them through his instructions, and to be governed by a certain way of behavior toward him as their leader/king/instructor, and toward one another as a group or people who voluntarily decided to be his subjects. Here, the test of governance and governments lay in knowing how to relate to subordinates, maintain their loyalty, require them to work as a team and collaborate for their common good, as well as the good of their dependants. Then there was the need for peaceful coexistence, for sharing of values, assets, and services that were essential for the common good of all and of their society. The leader/king then had to select—usually on the advice of the people—his subjects. A small group of advisers, usually wise men (elders) of their own families, were familiar with their customs, traditions, values, and ways of living, coexisting, collaborating, and solving problems collectively from family to relative and societal circles for law and order, justice, education, and acceptable decent behavior that ensured coexistence. It was in those very early years of organized human society that governance and government arose as essential arts for law, order, prosperity, and the development of communities in nation states.

After originating in Greece, the city-state system found application later in ancient Rome, where it was increasingly refined for purposes of rule, law, order, and civilization. Between the 8th and the 19th century, great city-states flourished in Africa and spread throughout the continent. As in Greece, the city-state in Africa started as a small town, then spread into a city-state administration engulfing the neighboring lands and populations who were subjected to the rule of the king or emperor and owed allegiance to him. Normally in Africa, the kingdoms were tribal structures ruled by a tribal king. An empire was a collection of several tribal kingdoms, and a city-state combined all these under one ruler. The element of sovereignty and statehood, as well as territorial integrity and endogeneity, went beyond the tribal kingdom structures and fell under the city-state organization. A city-state was thus a nation state and maintained inter-city-state relations that, for all practical purposes, were international relations under public international law.

Africa and the City-State Systems of Greece and Rome

By the time the Greeks colonized North Africa around 631 BCE, their city-state system had been operational for centuries. The Greek city-state system evolved from the tribal kingdom system in the 8th century BCE. A small but sovereign unit emerged in which all important activity was concentrated at one spot, and in which communal bonds—expressed in terms of law—were more basic than personal ties. It is, however, noteworthy, that a system of city-states had existed long before it emerged in Greece. The city-state system existed in Egypt in 3100 BCE. The Greek polis, meaning city, became a city-state unit and grew out of the political organization of the Greek Dark Ages from 1100 to 750 BCE, when the city began to include the surrounding countryside. From the same concept of a polis came the expressions policy, politics, police, and politician. Apart from the big island of Sparta, which controlled 400 square miles, most Greek city-states controlled around 50 square miles. The city-state was thus a small but sovereign political unit, in which all important activity was conducted at one spot, and in which communal bonds that were expressed in terms of law were more basic than personal ties with natural borders (mountains, rivers, lakes, seas hills, etc.). Its citizens—meaning men only, since women, children, and foreigners were not Greek city-state citizens—assembled periodically to vote on major issues and to elect officials. Councils were formed as early as about 600 BCE at Sparta and Athens. The councils represented the aristocracy and ran the government. Government members of the polis were chosen in one way or another virtually for life. Kings were in charge. Political values, strong military and political strengths, and patriotism were highly respected.

City-states, in their original form, differed in size, wealth, location, population, power, and importance. However, a city-state's size generally was similar to that of a county in America. Whether in Greece, Rome, or Africa, it had natural borders, (sea, mountains, etc.) and its citizens assembled periodically to vote on major issues or to elect officials.

Councils were formed as far back as about 600 BCE at Sparta and Athens. The council represented the aristocracy and ran the government. The government members of the polis were chosen in one way or another virtually for life. They were not always elected though. In some cases, they could be appointed or endorsed by acclamation. Kings were in charge, military and political features of the city-state were strong, as was local patriotism. Aristotle once said, "man is by nature an animal intended to live in a polis."[2]

Africa, Greece, and Rome: Common and Divergent Features of City-State Systems

The first and earliest city-state was created in Egypt in 3100 BCE when the northern and southern kingdoms of Egypt merged and started a system of governance and government similar to what is seen in government today. In other words, a system of sovereign dealings was commenced whereby relations with an Egyptian official was regarded as being form within sovereign borders such that any relations between that city-state and any other would have to be regarded as across-the-border dealings. This is the beginning of inter-city-state or international relations. That system of governance and government in Egypt/Africa would be experienced elsewhere in the world—especially in Greece, and also in Rome. In Greece and Rome, only men could be citizens of city-states, not women, children, aliens/subjects, or slaves. Only citizens in the city-states had the power and authority to act or inherit.

In like manner, in Greece and Rome, governance, government, or rule started in the city, then it expanded to cover and include neighboring territories/kingdoms, empires and super empires, which could comprise kingdoms, small empires, and city-states. In some cases, city-states were bigger than kingdoms, but generally kingdoms and empires were larger than city-states. Initially in Africa there were no cities, as was the case in ancient Greece and Rome. In Africa, government was hereditary, as dictated by custom and tradition. The city-state system in Africa evolved from the tribal kingdom system. In this latter system, traditional forms of law and order, justice, defense against natural and human enemies, and a clear division of labor among men and women had been developed and practiced for many centuries in Africa.

In tribal forms of governance in the kingdoms of Africa, African Socialism, rule by consensus and democracy, had evolved, and payments of periodic tributes to paramount rulers (kings, chiefs, etc.) for protection and use of certain assets (such as lands, rivers, grazing fields), among many other practices, occurred even before the city-state system appeared.

Other kinds of African heritage in pre-colonial times included democratic governance according to custom and tradition; intermarriage for the purpose of forming alliances and coalitions; the use of diplomacy when making contact with external groups; and many forms of trade, including long-distance trade in gold, cowries, copper, ivory, ornaments, barter for cloth, animals, weapons, monkey nuts, kola nuts, groundnuts, etc., that were exchanged for natural resources (horses, foodstuffs, salt, etc.). Additionally, tariffs, customs, fees, and taxes were levied on behalf of emperors, kings, and other tribal leaders, as well as hostages taken to be used as slaves for administrative offices.

Thus, prosperity and trade flourished in the ancient kingdoms, empires, and city-states of Africa in pre-colonial times. These political units learned how to use and share the environment, knowledge, and global public goods—the life-support systems of our ecosystem.

As previously described, kingdoms and city-states arose and flourished all over Africa, dating back to ancient times in West and North

Africa, in East and Central Africa, and in Southern Africa. The requirements for a city-state included the following:

- Democracy, governance and government, practiced collective responsibility, the absence of a monarch, single ruler, or king and central authority by individuals, as well as natural borders.
- Decision making through discussion not dictatorship was provided to the governed. Government decisions were to benefit the people.
- A population voluntarily assembled in one place to settle and live there.
- Acceptance of authority over the people usually after selecting the few to rule them by voting acclamation or in consensus. That was central authority, individuals in power held collective responsibility.

In Greece the city was known as polis, literally meaning "public affairs." The use of polis arose between 750 to 650 BCE. A city-state was the area surrounding the city, plus the city itself.

In Rome, a city-state was called "urbs" (Latin for town or city). The Roman city-state emerged between 800 to 575 BCE.

In Africa, no cities were created that did not progress from a tribal kingdom system to an empire, an empire to a super empire, and a super empire to city-state. Sometimes, city-states were smaller than empires. In other cases, city-states were larger than empires, but normally a super empire was larger than a city-state. Most of the city-states in Africa arose and flourished between 500 BCE and 700 CE. This was the period in Africa when kingdoms, city-states, and super kingdoms flourished.

The system of city-states continued to grow and flourish even beyond 1648, the date that is historically believed to have been the start of the modern city-state system when European powers, desirous of attaining European peace for Europe after many years of war for conquest, power, and territorial aggrandizement, signed the Treaty of Westphalia in Germany. This treaty introduced a system of empirical statehood. The city-state system was in place and practiced in Africa by Africans until the European colonization of Africa was imposed on Africans by the European colonial powers following the partition of Africa by the Berlin Accord of February 26, 1885.

Further Characteristics of African Governance and Government Procedures

Apart from repeatedly stressing the roles of custom and tradition in the governance procedures from the earliest systems of tribal kingdoms and city-state entities, the legends of oral traditions dominated the beliefs and practices of governance in Africa.

Origins of governance practices in oral traditions in African kingdoms stated that the Iron Age produced the need for tools and weapons for gathering and hunting to provide for the people and defend them from their individual or common enemies. There arose a heightened demand for a figure who, although playing the role of a family leader like a father and head of a family unit, had to be accepted in African society as a leader of the people upon whom the society could depend for protection, provision, and defense of interests and just governance.

EARLY KINGDOMS AND CITY-STATES OF AFRICA

Ancient Egypt[3]

Ancient Egyptian civilization developed in eastern North Africa, concentrated along the lower reaches of the Nile River in what is present-day Egypt. This civilization began around 3150 BCE with the political unification of Upper and Lower Egypt under the first pharaoh. Egyptian civilization continued over the next three millennia. Egypt grew into kingdoms separated by stable periods called Intermediate Periods. After the end of last kingdom, known as the New Kingdom, the civilization entered a period of slow, steady decline. The rule of the pharaohs officially ended in 31 BC when the early Roman Empire conquered Egypt and made it a province.

Ancient Egyptian civilization thrived within the Nile River Valley in part because of controlled irrigation of fertile agricultural land that produced surplus crops, which led prosperity, social development, and cultural advancement. Ancient Egypt also is known for mineral exploration of the valley and surrounding desert region, early development of an independent writing system, collective construction of agricultural prospects, trade with surrounding regions, military might, a strategic location, mathematics, elite scribes, pyramids, temples, religion, art and architecture, a system of medicine, and scientific investigation. Prior to this civilization, nomadic hunter-gatherers started living in the region 1.8 million years ago in the Pleistocene. The fertile flood plain of the Nile River gave humans the opportunity to develop, settle agriculturally and economically, and become sophisticated and centralized.

Nubia

Nubia is a region in southern Egypt along the Nile, most of which is now what is considered northern Sudan. In ancient times, Nubia was composed of kingdoms as a super independent kingdom. Situated adjacent to

Egypt, Nubia witnessed the first clearly Africa civilization and had numerous rich cultures and languages that stemmed from various populations of Kordofan extraction. These peoples later became known as "Nubia." By the 100th millennium BCE, peoples of Nubia had fully participated in the Neolithic revolution of the prehistory of the area. Around 3800 BCE, the first Nubian culture emerged, and is termed the "A-Group." Their policies were similar to those of Upper Egypt.

Around 3300 BCE, there was a united Nubian kingdom that maintained substantial cultural and genetic interactions with the culture of the pre-dynastic Nuqadan of Upper Egypt. These people contributed to the unification of the Nile Valley and the birth of the pharaohnic dynasty.

In early history, Nubia became the homeland of one of Africa's earliest black civilizations—their monuments, artifacts, and written records eventually reached Egypt and Rome. In antiquity, Nubia was a land of great natural wealth that included gold mines, ebony, ivory, and incense. In 2300 BCE, trade missions between Egypt, Nubia, and Aswan were recorded. From ca. 2240 to 2150 BCE, there was an evolution from the B-Group, or invaders during the 6th dynasty of Egypt. A C-Group also emerged and continued its interaction with Egypt's Middle Kingdom. Different cultures emerged among these groups, and Egyptian expansion into Nubia left its influence.

By 350 CE, Nubia was invaded by the Eritrean and Ethiopian kingdom of Aksum. The Nubian kingdom collapsed and smaller kingdoms emerged. By the 4th century CE, Christianity had penetrated the region. The king and nobles of Nubia's Nobatia converted to Christianity around 545 CE. In 569 CE, the Kingdom of Acodia converted to Christianity. Christianity spread through the 7th century CE and later. By this time, the Arabs and Islam had taken Egypt.

Kush (Cush) Kingdom and City-State

Kush (Cush) was originally a town/city in Nubia (present-day Sudan) in the 4th millennium BCE (i.e., more than 3,000 years ago). Kush lay in the fertile Nile Valley. It later became the first major kingdom of Sub-Saharan Africa, but was under Egyptian domination for 1,000 years (2000–1000 BCE).

As a kingdom, Kush developed a great culture and civilization with enormous influences from the Egyptian, Nubian, and Assyrian cultures and civilizations that had been prospering because of their sophisticated irrigation schemes, agriculture, domestication of plants and wildlife, etc. Kush in Nubia also owed its prosperity to trade in ivory, ebony, gum, hides, ostrich plumes, and slaves along the Nile to Egypt and across the Red Sea to Arabia and Mesopotamia.

By 1070 BCE, Egypt's grasp over Nubia ended and Kush arose as an influential kingdom and city-state in the region.

In 751 BCE, the Kushite King Piankhi led an army down the Nile and conquered Egypt. In the same century, Kush, under the leadership of King Piye, invaded and controlled Egypt during Kush's Ethiopian dynasty. In fact, the rulers of Kush had started to exert independence around 1000 BCE, when they broke away from their dependency on Egyptian pharaohs and developed their own distinctively Kushite African civilization and culture around 540 BCE. By around 690 BCE, a descendant of King Piye, King Taharqa, was crowned and ruled over Nubia and Egypt.

Kush flourished for a long time, and became an empire until King Taharqa left his city of Memphis under Assyrian assault. But Taharqa reconquered Lower Egypt and ruled there for years until his death in 664 BCE. Another Kushite, King Aspelta (593–568 BCE), reorganized the empire, and decided to learn more about Egyptian civilization that was so advanced in writing and kingdom rule. He transferred the capital of Kush from Kerma to Meroe.

Thus, as an ancient nation in northeastern Africa comprising large areas within present-day Egypt and Sudan, Kush flourished as a city-state partly because of its strategic location in the Ethiopian highlands with Kerma as the center of its kingdom. For all practical purposes, Kush was an ancient African city that lay in confluences of the Blue Nile, White Nile, and the River Atbara in present-day Sudan. The influences upon it from its location made Kush one of the earliest civilizations to develop in the Nile River Valley. This is one reason why Kush civilization has been referred to as Nubia and also as Ethiopia in ancient Greek and Roman records.

As a state, Kush was established before the period of Egyptian incursion into the area. Josephus and other classical writers have stated that the Kush Empire covered all of Africa and some part of Asia and Europe at one time or another. However, the Egyptians eventually conquered Kush in about 1500 BCE.

Influence of the Early Kingdoms of Africa and the Middle East

It is noteworthy that these early kingdoms and city-states—Egypt, Kush, Nubia—in Africa and the Middle East in the great and fertile valleys of Mesopotamia and the Nile Valley, led to the domestication of wildlife and plants. In East Africa for example, coffee was domesticated in Ethiopia, whereas in North Africa, rice, wheat, barley, and donkeys, camels, and horses were domesticated more than 4,000 years ago. By 3000 BCE, agriculture in Ethiopia produced coffee, tuft, barley, millet, sorghum, pearl, cowpea, groundnut, monkey-nut, cotton, watermelon, bottle gourds, and other domesticated items. In like manner with Sahel, peas, finger millet, lentil, and flax were also domesticated. In West Africa, African yams, oil, palms, millet, and cowpeas were domesticated.

As civilizations developed, the indigenous populations grew in sophistication. By 1000 BCE, the Bantu peoples along the Great Lakes of East Africa and Central Africa (the Congos, Chad, Kanein Empire and others), as well as the indigenous Southern Africans like the Hottentots, pygmies, and others had advanced the domestication of animals and crops for their survival.

Between 200 BCE and 700 CE, the Bantu-speaking families and populations in Sub-Saharan Africa, especially along the Nigeria-Cameroon border and elsewhere, emerged and developed Iron Age tools for hunting and spears. They cultivated food crops like cassava, yams, and bananas. They learned the skills of being great mediators in local disputes. With the expansion and consolidation of Islam in Africa after the 7th century CE, several kinds of civilization were born in Africa. Thus, Islam and the Bantu-migrations greatly influenced the way of living and governing in Africa.

EARLY KINGDOMS AND CITY-STATES IN EASTERN AFRICA

Aksum (Axum) Kingdom emerged in northeastern Ethiopia in the 4th century CE. In 6th to 7th century CE, Axum was the capital of a kingdom called Ethiopia. However, this mountainous city had become a naval and trading power much earlier, way before the Roman era that ruled the region from ca. 400 BCE into the 19th century CE. By then, Axum had become a kingdom that was occasionally referred to in medieval writings as Ethiopia. The kingdom became a Christian city-state in 324 CE. Before this date, the kingdom of Axum had Meroe as its capital at Merve. By 300 CE, Axum had become very rich and powerful through trade between the Red Sea and the African interior.

Axum conquered Egypt and ruled over the Nile for 70 years. Axum traded with Greece, Rome, and Egypt. Axum's farmers grew spices and Arabic gum, and exchanged these for tortoise shells collected along the Red Sea. Ivory and gold were exchanged for Egyptian cloth, linen, articles of flint, brass, glass, sheets of soft copper, iron ingots, wine, olive oil, gold, silver, and the like.

Axum became an ally of the Byzantine Empire in its struggle against the Persian Empire. The Kingdom of Axum had a great and skilled army that conquered Yemen and other Arabian kingdoms. This explains how the fruits of ancient civilization in the Nile, the Near East, and the Mediterranean grew further to embrace the southern tip of Arabia, which was very rich in minerals and incense in what is now Yemen. In those days, around the 10th century BCE, and even earlier, camels had been used widely to carry spices, gold, and precious stones. Dating back to ca. 1000 BCE, the Queen of Sheba, ruler of Ethiopia though a descendant from Yemen, travelled to visit King Solomon of Israel on his invitation and brought him gifts of gold and incense. She had an affair with the king, and their son became the first emperor of Ethiopia as Menelik I, around 982 BCE. This is the date selected as the start of Ethiopian independence.

Axum was much influenced by missionaries from Syria and Axum rulers who adopted Christianity—the Menophysite Christian faith. In 350 CE, Axum's King Exana unified his African holdings and converted himself and his kingdom to Christianity. The Axumite kingdom developed into modern Ethiopia, but started to decline in the 7th century CE when Islam and Islamic groups occupied trade routes. Those heading for Alexandria, Byzantium, and Southern Europe were captured by Arab traders.

Christian Axum quarreled with Islamic groups over religion. Aksum's last known king was crowned ca. the 10th century CE. His influence and power declined and Axum was replaced by Ethiopia. Meanwhile, Islam began to penetrate into Sub-Saharan Africa, soon after the Arab conquest of Egypt in 641 CE, after which the kingdom of Ethiopia emerged.

Meroe City Turned into a Kingdom

Meroe was Saba in what is modern Yemen. In 2500 BCE, Meroe contributed to the rise of the Kingdom of Kush (Cush). Meroe thus also started as a city situated near the Nile, and became a home to a Kushite royal family in 550 BCE. Later, Meroe became a very important city-state on the east bank of the Nile about 4 miles northeast of Kabushiya Station near Shendi, in Sudan, approximately 125 miles northeast of Khartoum. Meroe gained prominence between 800 BCE and ca. 350 CE. It adopted many ancient Egyptian customs, but with a unique culture. It developed its own form of writing, first by using Egyptian hieroglyphs, and later creating an alphabetic script with 23 signs. Meroe also had many pyramids. The kingdom maintained an impressive military force. In 332 BCE, Alexander the Great invaded the region with a great force, but was met by a brilliant military formation of Meroe's warrior, Queen Condace of Meroe, who led the army from atop an elephant. (This event was repeated around 146 BCE when General Hannibal led an army of 38 elephants against the Roman Army's invasion of Carthage.)

Alexander the Great was forced to withdraw his forces in 332 BCE, and turned his attention to the invasion of Egypt, which he conquered and occupied the same year.

Another Queen of Meroe, Queen Candace, was blind in one eye but, using a Nubian archer, she led the Meroe Army against the Romans and did very well, until her defeat after attacking Roman territory. She surrendered but negotiated a peace treaty with the Romans on favorable terms. In the 1st–2nd century CE, the kingdom of Meroe began to fade, sapped by war with the Roman province of Egypt and the decline of Meroe's traditional industries. Meroe was defeated anew by a rising kingdom to their south: Axum under King Exana of Axum.[4-5]

EARLY STATES AND KINGDOMS OF EAST AFRICA:
1100–1500 CE

In view of the development of civilizations in the Nile Valley and its proximity to Mesopotamia, it is understandable that the earliest civilizations, kingdoms, and city-states in Africa emerged in the northeastern part of the continent. Eastern Africa was particularly important historically in view of the human evolutionary process that began in the eastern and southern parts of Africa. Human societies emerged in full force in East Africa where at least 40 city-states were established. Geography also played a major role in shaping African history. The Nile River strongly influenced life not only in ancient Egypt, but also in the countries that emerged along the Nile. Historically, these kingdoms and city-states flourished both in precolonial times and up until the 19th century European colonization of Africa that eventually suffocated the glory and historical significance of African societies and their achievements as sociopolitical entities that were the precursors of the modern sociopolitical systems of African nations.

Early immigration to Eastern Africa happened when immigrants to the region during the 700s CE came from inland to the coastal areas of East Africa. Most of the immigrants to East Africa were Bantu-speaking people who settled on the east coast of Africa and intermarried with the Arabs who had settled in East Africa from Arabia, especially from Oman. The Sultan of Oman and other Omani frequenters to East Africa came in dhows, boats steered to Africa by the monsoon winds. The merging of Arab and Bantu-speaking populations produced a new people known as the Swahili. Many Arab Muslims fled from their homelands to Africa in order to escape political enemies and persecution.

In North Africa, Islam was imported through the arrivals and settlements of Arab immigrants into Egypt and the other countries of North Africa. Ancient Egypt was indeed an integral part of the Mediterranean world. The term "Sahara" is an Arabic word, "sahra," meaning "desert." The birth of the Sahara was an event that marked a big divide that had cultural, religious, and geographic implications and forced the African peoples to cluster themselves into two parts of the continent—north and south of the great desert—thereby placing Egypt in the cultural groupings of North Africa and the Middle East.

The Sahara Desert also deprived many people living in that area of Africa, which is equivalent in size to the entire United States, of that formerly fertile and traditional home as hunters, gatherers, domesticators of animals, etc. When the people lost that vast area of grasslands, also called savannas, that were filled with a lot of game, they were forced to move south or north of the great divide and many centuries later more than 40 city-states and kingdoms were established in what are now Uganda, Tanzania, Kenya, and the other nations of the East African region along a 1,000-mile strip of the East African coast.

The kingdoms and city-states included the kingdoms of Buganda (who had Kabaka as their king), Toro, Ankole, and Busoga, of Uganda, as well as the kingdoms of the Baluhya and Kikuyu tribes of Kenya and the city-states of Mombasa, Malindi, Lamu, Zanzibar, Pemba, Kilwa, Mogadishu, Lamu, and Sofala, some of which are on the East African mainland but most of which are islands in the Indian Ocean. These kingdoms and city-states were homes to flourishing traditions, civilizations, and cultures that celebrated their ancestors and customs and enjoyed enormous wealth.

EARLY KINGDOMS AND CITY-STATES
OF WEST AFRICA: 300–1600 CE

Like East Africa, West Africa witnessed the emergence of many prosperous kingdoms, city-states, empires, and super empires. These included many in Dahomey, Benin, Kazem, the Mossi (and its great constitution), the Sok, Yoruba, Hausa, Igbo, and many others.

Nigeria and the Mali Empire

In what is present-day Nigeria, there arose city-states and empires at Sok in central Nigeria where the people were skilled in farming and iron work. These included Yorubaland, Hausaland, Igboland, and the Nok Kingdom, which was the oldest recognizable pre-colonial society in Sub-Saharan Africa and a great cultural center and city-state. In Mali, there was the Mali Empire of Songhai (Songhay), which was a city-state that was a great cultural center, and Timbuktu, which was another great center of culture and learning.

The Mali Empire was established around 1230 CE as a kingdom. It was a big center for commerce and culture. Commerce included gold and ivory, as well as a big slave trade system where influential Arab traders made fortunes by buying and selling slaves within Africa and to customers out of Africa—notably Arabia, the Middle East, and the Far East. The kings and rulers of the Mali Empire were converted to Islam in the 14th century CE.

Songhai Empire: 1255–15th Century CE

The Songhai Kingdom, like Timbuktu and its university, flourished over many years and centuries but, especially, between 1464–1500 CE. Unlike many who have argued that Africa was home to savages and uncivilized people, it is clear that great centers of learning like Songhai and Timbuktu; Cayor in Ghana; Alexandria in Egypt; Carthage in Tunisia; Kampala in Uganda; Calabar, Kano, and Ife in Nigeria; and many others existed in Africa long before European educational systems were introduced in Africa in colonial times.

Songhay was a significant pre-colonial African state in West Africa, which flourished especially from the early 15th to 16th century CE. One of the largest African empires was born in Songhai. The huge city of Timbuktu became a thriving cultural and commercial center for many years and was visited by Arab, Italian, and Jewish merchants who gathered in Songhai for trade. By 1500 CE the Songhai Empire had more than 1.4 million inhabitants.

Ghana Empire: 750–1076 CE

Ghana got its name from King Ghana of Awkar Kingdom, which was the territory in Ashanti Kingdom that had plenty of gold. In 1874 when Ghana fell to the United Kingdom as a colony, it was called the Gold Coast. The country received many alien traders, including Arabs, and because of the greatness of the king of the "Land of Gold" (the Kayamaga territory also called the "Land of the God") the Arabs gave his name to the country and called it Ghana. He was the richest and most powerful monarch of the Biladal Sudan, which was known as the "Land of the Blacks."

As an empire, Ghana flourished between 750 and 1076 CE. It was also known as Wagadou Empire between 790 and 1076 CE and was located in present-day southeastern Mauritania, western Mali, and eastern Senegal. The first of many medieval trading empires in West Africa, the Ghana Empire became very wealthy between the 7th and 13th centuries CE. Gold and agricultural crops became the empire's main cash crops (kola nuts in West Africa were exchanged for natural resources). But salt trade, horses, foodstuffs, ivory and other minerals, and slaves also became important exchange commodities especially when trading with Arabs as Islam moved to West Africa and converted many indigenous populations.

As ruler, Ghana, the king of the Soninke tribes people, probably was visited by Arab traders for the first time in the 4th century CE. Ghana's city-state of Cayor had a great constitution already in place between the 3rd and 10th centuries CE.

Other Empires and Kingdoms in West Africa: 7th–16th Centuries CE

By the time Islam was introduced to Africa in a big way, it was also received in Spain, which, like Africa, was subjected to Islamic culture. When Christianity also spread everywhere in Africa, these two alien religions were globalized, and they also spread a new heritage in Africa. This is especially true of Islam in Egypt, North Africa, Songhai, Mali, Hausa, and in other northern parts of Africa that were frequented by Arabs traders.

Benin Empire: 1440–1897 CE

The Benin Empire, also known as the Dahomey Empire, flourished between the 11th and 13th centuries CE. When Arab immigration into Africa grew from Arabia, the caliphs of Baghdad and the sultans of Oman increased their immigration into Africa. The other dynasties that flourished between the 7th and 16th centuries CE included the mid-dynasty in Egypt/Cairo in 968 CE; the Turks who seized Egypt in 1517 CE and established regencies of Algeria, Tunisia, and Tripoli between 1519 and 1551. From the 11th century CE, Arab invasions of North Africa left their cultural influence on the African Berber tribes. Then came the Persians and Indians who immigrated to East Africa, Mombasa, Malindi, and Sofala. Arab Moors in North Africa were affected.

Moreover, the Islamization of West Africa included Senegambia and the Niger regions.

Birth of Dynastic States in West Africa: 9th–17th centuries CE

The period from the 9th to 17th centuries CE saw the rise of many dynastic states in West Africa (e.g., Hausa states arose across sub-Saharan savanna territory from the western coast to central Sudan). The affected areas included Ghana, Gao, the Mali Empire (1235–1400 CE), and the Kanem-Bornu Empire.

The Arab travelers (explorers) to West Africa included Ibn Battuta, who arrived in Timbuktu in 1352 CE, then went to Kilwa (Quiloa). Swahili Muslim cities flourished in subsequent centuries. Another traveler to this area was Sonni Ali (1464–1492 CE). He founded the Songhai Empire in Niger and western Sudan, and controlled the trans-Atlantic slave trade. He seized Timbuktu in 1468, and Jenne in 1473. He also established flourishing commerce in West Africa, along the West African coast, the coast of Guinea, and in Nigeria's north, Yoruba city-states (such as Ife and Oyo), and the Benin Empire from the 17th century CE onward.

Mali Empire: 13th Century CE

In ancient Mali, a great empire developed during the 13th century CE in the upper Niger area of the western Sudan region. "Mali" is derived from a local word meaning, "a place of the king." Several smaller kingdoms and states had prospered previously in this area. In ca. 1235 CE, the remaining part of the ancient Ghana Empire, led by King Sumaoro Kante, was conquered by King Sundiata Keita (1217–1255), founder of the Mali Empire, and his army of Mandinka (southern Mande-speaking people). Sundiata continued to develop the Great Empire of Mali.

CENTRAL AFRICA'S KINGDOMS AND CITY-STATES

Central Africa was home to the Kongo Empire and its Bakongo tribe in the present-day Democratic Republic of the Congo and the People's Republic of the Congo, as well as the city-states that appeared in the Central African Republic, Angola, Chad, Gabon, Malawi, and the Kalonga Kingdom, all of which possessed great civilizations and wealth. Other kingdoms emerged along the great rivers and lakes of Central and Eastern Africa, including the Zambezi River, Lake Tanganyika.

SOUTHERN AFRICA: KINGDOMS AND CITY-STATES

The African kingdoms and city-states that flourished in Southern Africa include Zimbabwe Kingdom in the 1400s CE. "Zimbabwe" means "stone enclosure" or "dwelling of the chief." It was called the Great Zimbabwe. Other kingdoms and city-states were the Zulu (kwa Zulu) Kingdom, the San Khoikhoi, the Pygmy and Hottentot populations, the Xhosa, Shona, Ndbele-Matebeleland, and many others in Namibia, Zimbabwe, and the Tswana, Sotho, and Swazi Kingdoms.

Monomotapa Kingdom was a kingdom that existed from 1250 to 1629 CE, and ran between the Zambezi and Limpopo Rivers, which flow through Zimbabwe and Mozambique.

NORTH AFRICAN ISLAMIC STATES AND THE ISLAMIZATION OF AFRICA

As previously described, North Africa developed a sui generis kind of status in Africa mainly because of its proximity to the Middle East and Europe. As an African Mediterranean region, North Africa experienced considerable pressures from the Islamic and European worlds, but it was the Arab-Islamic influence that became dominant. North Africa had a long and fascinating history of colonization by the Phoenicians, Greeks, and Romans. Then there followed the invasion of Islam in North Africa.

The Arab conquest of Africa was a piecemeal process that was triggered by the spread or globalization of Islam from around 632 CE. The founder of Islam, Mohammed, born in Saudi Arabia in 570 CE, became a prophet and presided over the globalization of this religion that reached North Africa quickly and easily because of the proximity of North Africa to the Middle East. This new religion introduced an Arab culture in North Africa whose strength among the northern Africans succeeded in reducing and even replacing Christianity, which had reached North Africa as early as the 1st century CE.

However, the situation in northwestern Africa was different. The Greeks and the Romans had colonized it in the classical period as explained earlier in Chapter 1. It was only after the Banu Hilal and Banu Swaim Bedouin invaded and settled in northwestern North Africa in the 11th century CE that the area was Islamized. Arab nomads ensured that Islam crossed the Sahara to West Africa. This was facilitated by trade contacts that had been established between West Africa and the Arab world even before the slave trade was conducted in subsequent centuries. Camels became the ships of the Sahara, and Islam spread even further to Sudan, Chad, and even East Africa. The settlement of Arabs in East Africa was prompted both by the slave trade and by the arrivals at the East African coastal areas by the Oman Arabs who also conducted commerce with East Africa and used to frequent the East African Indian Islands. Even the Omani sultan himself used to spend vacation time in Zanzibar and adjacent islands. The means of transportation was the dhow—a small boat that was propelled by the monsoon winds. It is noteworthy that there was considerable resistance to Muslim settlers in those parts of Africa like in the Sudan and Abyssinia where the conversion of the inhabitants to Christianity had created Christian kingdoms, which were subsequently conquered by the Arabs.

As explained earlier in this chapter, Islam and Christianity introduced new kinds of heritage, which, together with European heritage, collided fundamentally with African heritage.

Christianity's globalization reached Africa in the 1st century CE, much earlier than that of Islam. Thus, by the time Islamic states were established in North Africa, Christianity had reached Europe, including Spain, where Islam had penetrated by the 11th and 12th centuries. By then, the Nasirid and Marinid were the two Berber dynasties that had conquered Spain and Islamized the country. However, fierce Christian attacks on the Islam dynasties during the Spanish Inquisition led to the latter's defeat by early 13th century in most of Spain, except in the south of the country, in the Iberian Peninsula (Granada and Andalusia), which remained under Islam and underwent deep Islamic culturization.

In the entire northern part of Arica, two great Berber dynasties emerged between the 11th and 13th centuries. These were the Almoravids, or Al-Mumbits (1056–1147 CE) and the Almohads, or Al-Muwahhids (1130–1269 CE).

The Empire of the Almoravids (1056–1147 CE)

The Empire of the Almoravids, a desert people, began in about 1050 CE and lasted until 1147 CE. In 973 CE, the Fatimid Arabs moved from Ifriqiya to Egypt and settled in Egypt. With their seat of power in Egypt, the Fatimids gave Ifriqiya over to the governorship of the Zirids, who subsequently lost control of their homeland to their Hammudid kinsmen. This shift in the power structure of North Africa led to the domination of

Western Maghrib by the Zenata pastoral nomads. Subsequently, however, the Zenata nomads were defeated by the Almoravids. These were a puritan Muslim population of Saharan Berber tribes and Sudanese who had moved north across the desert in order to attain the power, plunder, and opportunities that were offered by the Muslim occupation and civilization of Morocco and Spain.

As plunderers, the Almorvids destroyed the rich agricultural civilization of Ifriqiya, as the Zirids reclaimed their orthodox Abbasid allegiance and rejected that of the Fatimid caliphs. Disputes and grave quarrels arose among these ruling Arab groupings.

The Fatimids (909–1171 CE)

"Ifriqiya" means "Arab Africa," and is the area where present-day Tunisia is situated. Just as the Romans began their African influence in Carthage, which later spread to include the entire Western Province of the Roman Empire, the Arabs started at Ifriqiya in Africa. The Fatimids, Shiites led by the Kutama Berbers from Little Kabylia, conquered Ifriqiya during 902–909 CE and created an independent caliphate. The presence of the Fatimids continued to be felt throughout 900 CE. The Fatimid caliphs sought to challenge the Abbasids in Egypt and to assert authority over the rest of the Maghrib. The Abbasids were orthodox Arabs in Egypt who lived in an Abbasid caliphate. In 969 CE, the Fatimids established themselves in Egypt. In subsequent years, they conquered Syria, taking it from Abbasid control.

This type of power struggle indicates the growing Muslim influence on North Africa, which continued until Islam absorbed the African region into the Arab world—not only religiously, but also culturally, politically, and economically. This influence continues today. In subsequent years, Arab settlements in Africa spread across the entire continent, ranging from the settlement of Yemeni Arabs in Ethiopia that produced Queen Sheba to the modern day Arab presence in the Barbary states.

The Fatimid caliphs attacked the Zirids by sending the Banu Hilal and Bau Sulaim Bedouin Arabs to fight the Zirids. Then the Normans attacked the empire of the Almoravids from Sicily, and all of these wars and conflicts weakened the Almoravids. The relationships among these Arab dynasties became complicated, but they included international relations conducted among sovereign entities.

When the Amoravids started to advance northward across the Sahara from the Sudan, they encountered stiff opposition, especially from rulers such as Ibn Tashfin, who between 1061 and 1066 CE staged strong campaigns against the Almoravids, but the Almoravids captured him in 106 CE. The Almoravids captured the town of Fez in 1069 CE. With the Norman attacks from Sicily came Christian attacks, and the combination of these attacks overwhelmed the Almoravids. Their choice was to compete with their attackers (but they were too weak) or to reckon with another Arab dynasty in North Africa—the Almohads.

The Empire of the Almohads (1130–1269 CE)

The Empire of the Almohads came into prominence in the year that the power of the Almoravids declined. The Almohad Empire began in around 1130 CE and lasted until 1269 CE. The origins of this empire can be traced to the Moroccan mountains where the Berber tribes rose against the control and extortion of the tribal population of the Almoravids. The Almohad Empire had its roots in a religious and political movement that aimed at silencing the Almoravids. The strain of repelling Norman and Christian attacks weakened the Almoravids' base of power and made them quite vulnerable to further external attacks, especially by the Almohads. The Christian attacks came mainly from Spain, and so the first demand of the Almohads to the Almoravids was for the Almoravids to free the Spanish Muslims. Soon thereafter, the Hammudid power of the Almoravids in central Maghreb was destroyed by the Almohads, who also defeated the Hilalian group in Ifriqiya and advanced to Egypt. The struggle for supremacy among the Arab dynasties continued throughout the 13th century. Though the Almohads seemed to succeed in their conquests, they did not last long before they themselves were silenced by Christain princes of Castile, Aragon, Navarre, and Portugal at the Battle of Las Navas de Tolosa, in which the Almohad Ruler, al Nasir (1199–1214 CE) was defeated.

Maghrib Nations: 13th–14th Centuries CE

The fierce rivalries and wars between and among the Arab powers in North Africa forced the birth of a new order in which the North African Almohad Empire split into three rival Berber dynasties or dominions. The first was headed by the governor of Ifriqiya in the 13th century CE. He proclaimed independence of the Almohads and thereby created a new dynasty of the Hafsids.

The second and third regions were controlled by the two Zenata Berber tribes of the Abd-al-Wahid dynasty and the Banu Merid dynasty, respectively. The former controlled the central part or dominion of the empire whereas the latter controlled Morocco, which was the third dominion or region. This became the Marinid dynasty, and was the most powerful of the dynasties. In 1212, the Muslims were expelled from the Iberian Peninsula in Spain by the Christians at the Las Navas de Tolosa.

RELATIONS AMONG OTHER ISLAMIC STATES OF NORTH AFRICA, INCLUDING THE SUDAN

As stressed before, what bonded the Muslim nations in Africa was the Arab culture, religion, and trade—both in legitimate commodities such as gold, salt, and diamonds and the illegitimate trade of slaves. These types of commerce were exchanged between and among Arab states as well as between Arab and African states. In those early years, the trade, religion, and culture of Islam spread across the Sahara to the west and northwest of Africa, as well as to East Africa where the Sudan, the largest country in Africa, lay both in the eastern and northern parts of Africa.

Thus, Ghana, Niger, Mali, Mauritania, Gao, Nigeria, and other West African states established contacts with the Arab dynasties mentioned previously in this chapter that had empires in Morocco, Algeria, Tunisia, Egypt, and other parts of the Maghreb. These states discussed diplomatic and inter-state relations, including border disputes. The Sudanese states became strongly Islamic and created many fruitful relations with the Maghreb and West African city-states.

Barbary States[6]

The Barbary states were the North African states of Algeria, Tunisia, Tripoli, and Morocco that flourished between the 16th and 19th centuries CE. From the 16th century, these states were autonomous provinces of the Turkish Empire. Morocco pursued her own independent development.

The expression "Barbary" or "Barbary Coast," was used by Europeans from the 16th century until the 19th century to refer to the above-mentioned states. Corsair Barbarossa and his brothers led the Turkish conquest to prevent the region from falling to Spain. In 1541 CE, the last attempt by the Holy Roman Emperor Charles V to drive out the Turks failed. Piracy was a weapon that the Muslims of North Africa used as a component of their wars against Spain. Piracy became quite a lucrative business, and as the young United States, under presidents John Adams, Thomas Jefferson, and James Madison, failed to resolve the piracy problems in the 17th and 18th centuries, the Turkish hold on North Africa weakened, and the local Muslim rulers enriched themselves with bloody ransom and slaves in North Africa and the Mediterranean coastal lands.

Toward the end of the 18th century CE, the United States and the Europeans took advantage of the decline of Turkish power and launched more attacks against piracy. At that time, Europe was rocked by the Tripolitan War and the Napoleonic Wars. In 1827, Tunisian and Ottoman troops fought in Greece, but the Europeans overpowered the Muslims. In 1830, France began conquest of Algeria after the French blockade of Algeria for three years, which ended in 1830.

NOTES

1. *Webster's Third New International Dictionary of the English Language* (Springfield, MA: G. & C. Merriam, 1965) p. 1073.

2. Aristotle, *Politics* 1.1252a2.

3. *Nagel's Encyclopedia Guide on Egypt,* (Geneva and Paris: Nagel Publishers, 1978).

4. David W. Philipson, *Ancient Ethiopia: Aksum: Its Antecedents and Successes,* (London: British Museum, 1998), 53–54.

5. Basil Davidson, *The Lost Cities of Africa* (Boston/Toronto: Little, Brown and Company, 1959).

6. Cheikh Anta Diop, *Precolonial Black Africa* (Westport, CT, Lawrence Hill & Company, 1987).

CHAPTER 5

African Foreign Policy and Diplomacy in the Ancient and Medieval Periods

INTRODUCTION

As stated earlier, the division of history into periods of time can be tricky. Readings on African foreign policy, diplomacy, and international relations are many and varied, but research into this topic is time well spent.[1-5] In terms of historical periods of Africa's foreign policy, diplomacy, and international relations, it would be difficult to determine the ancient and medieval periods. Nonetheless, it is safe to state that whereas Africa's prehistory ranges from more than 10 million to 5 million years ago to the end of statelessness in recent centuries and is heavily influenced by the advent of the Sahara Desert, the start of ancient African history can be identified by the invention of writing in Egypt in the 4th millennium BCE. This development in human communication coincided with the appearance of the Sahara Desert and the origins of permanent settlements in Africa as explained earlier.

In this regard, African ancient history ran from 4000 BCE to the end, or fall, of the Roman Empire which was in 476 CE. Medieval times in African history started in 476 CE and lasted until the fall of Constantinople in 1453 CE. This kind of divisor fits well into the accepted clustering of the periods of world history. Therefore, modern times in Africa started from the fall of Constantinople to the present (i.e., from 1453 to today).

In this writer's view, however, it would be wise to state that to draw a line of demarcation between ancient history or antiquity and modern African history, one needs to consider a number of other dates that could mark the beginning of modern history. These include 1415 CE, when the Portuguese attacked Morocco's enclave at Ceuta and occupied it. That was the first contact that Africans had with Europeans in "modern times."

Another important date is 1648 CE, when the European powers met at Westphalia, Germany, and negotiated a peace treaty for Europe that ended many years of European conflicts and wars. That date could be considered as marking the origins of modern Africa because the treaty, in effect, did begin the state system as we know it today. Since Africa later became a by-product of Western civilization through European colonization and the imposition of western values on Africa, the modern history of Africa could as well be regarded as having started in 1648 CE.

However, 1652 CE is also an important date in African history. This is the year that marked the beginning of European colonization of the interior of Africa—when the Dutch started to colonize the cape region of South Africa.

Likewise, 1800 CE is important as the date that marked the beginning of Pan-Africanism. Americans, with the Back to Africa Movement, witnessed the abolition of the slave trade in 1807 and the developments that culminated in the return to Liberia of freed African slaves. Forty years later, in 1847, the world witnessed the birth of Liberia's political independence.

The year 1909 CE, in which World War I ended, arbitrarily also has been suggested as marking the beginning of the modern world.

For this writer, however, it is the year 1800 that seems to be the most appropriate date for the beginning of modern Africa. The year 1800 marked the beginning of serious talks of Africa being united and freed of such injustices as slavery and the slave trade through concerted actions by all Africans to prevent future exploitation and to encourage the return of Africans Americans to Africa. This is the date that will be referred to in this book as marking the beginning of modern history in Africa.

In discussing the problems of African diplomacy and foreign policy in ancient and medieval times, however, a number of conceptual understandings and clarifications need to be made. First and since the main object of this study is to determine the origins and foundations of Africa's foreign policy, its development, and the implementation of Africa's foreign policy, diplomacy, and international relations, it is necessary to examine the dictates and determinants of these disciplines in historical and global perspectives.

Additionally, an analysis of these dictates and determinants needs to be performed as they appeared and were shaped in the vapors of the historical periods in which Africa has lived. In this chapter, while examining African foreign policy and diplomacy as shaped and practiced in ancient and medieval times, it is necessary to establish what happened in the prehistoric period, what happened in the pre-colonial period, and how these disciplines have faired in the post-colonial period—which is considered as having started in 1960—the year better known here as the "Annus Mirabilis," or miracle year, of Africa's surge toward independence.

On the basis of the definition of African international relations as the totality of the actions that internationalize the domestic policies and practices of the African countries, it has to be remembered that foreign policy is a pluralitantum expression—while appearing in the singular, the expression has a plural meaning. Thus, African foreign policy is, in essence, Africa's "foreign policies."

It also should be remembered that African international relations appear at two levels: at the intra-African level (i.e., when African countries engage in activities, relationships, actions, and interactions between and among themselves), which is bilateral or multilateral and confined to the African continent, and at the international or external level, when all of these actions, inaction, and dealings of African states are conducted with the external world.

It is important to note that African foreign policy simply means the elevation of domestic African policies of the individual and collective countries of Africa to the international or global level. Like international relations, African foreign policy can, and does, also appear at bilateral and multilateral levels. The dictates of foreign policy are many and varied and include protection, defense, and promotion of national interests; attainment of international peace and security; promotion and attainment of trade and development, peace, and security; peaceful coexistence and the promotion of socioeconomic justice in international relations of all kinds; provision of the basic needs of the nation; and protection and promotion of good governance, democracy, cooperation, and understanding among nations.

Diplomacy, which is also a pluralitantum term, basically means the art of negotiation and the management of international affairs in such a way as to seek to resolve differences through peaceful means and to promote, defend, protect, and maintain the national interest and good use of the country that sends its diplomats forth. By promoting peaceful coexistence and facilitating friendly relations and cooperation among nations of various cultural, political, economic, and social orientation, diplomacy is an inevitable tool for the promotion of the civility of nations. Among nations, diplomacy endeavors to ensure the observance of the standards of "civilized states" and "civilized behavior" as dictated by the principles of public internationalized law, international business codes, and many other requirements. Then, there is the role of foreign service, which, together with foreign policy and diplomacy, helps manage a country's relations with other political entities, including international legal personalities.

Put in the context of this section's explanation, issues of foreign policy and international relations could be considered in prehistorical times, since these were periods of human evolution that were occupied with adventures, nomadism, expansionism, the search for green pastures through which life could be sustained, and the inevitable interactions of small groups of people as they moved throughout the land to better their own lot in life. The land was plentiful, and power and governance were neither international nor inter-state at this time.

GOVERNMENT IN ANCIENT AFRICA

In ancient times in Africa, for example, a man (and only men, not women) assumed power through hereditary methods. Whether called a chief, paramount chief, monarch, or king of a people and territory, normally the leader was an administrative ruler who managed other people in supervisory roles. Even in territories that differed in size, significance, wealth, etc., this leadership system was common. The social and political organization of power and administration was as described in this section, but required no foreign policy or diplomatic arrangements.

A family unit was headed usually by a man—a father who could have several or many wives. An extended family unit existed under the control of the head of the family. Several or many extended family units formed a village and were headed by an appointed headman, who worked under a sub-chief.

Several or many villages formed sub-locations headed by a sub-chief (a sub-clan). A location was a small administrative unit consisting of several or many sub-locations, headed by a chief or a chieftaincy or clan. Several or many locations formed a division, administered by a divisional ruler who was in charge of chiefs and their locations or sub-tribes. Several or many divisions formed a district that was headed by a district officer or ruler who was in charge of divisions and divisional rulers (sub-tribes). Many districts formed a province that was headed by a provisional chief who was in charge of district officers and their districts. These titles and divisions existed in pre-colonial Africa since there were decentralized forms of governance, but were changed by colonial practices.

The patterns of expansion comprised the following, especially after the long years of colonial rule and the voluntary mergers of villages and families either through war or peaceful union. Villages were merged into chieftaincies, chieftaincies into communities, communities into divisions and districts, and districts into provinces.

The administration/government and governance of these units was executed as follows. At the village level, leadership remained hereditary; control was exerted by local partrilineage. At the sub-location and location levels, rule was by appointed chiefs and chieftaincies. At the divisional and district levels, governance was by officers who were the appointees of the king. At the provincial level, rule was by the paramount chiefs who were tribal kings. Empires were ruled by monarchs, kings, emperors, and other rulers of comparable status.

GOVERNMENT IN MEDIEVAL AFRICA

At the city-state level, government was organized differently than that of ancient Africa. The city-state was actually a sovereign political entity. Some city-states were smaller that empires. The city-state of Egypt, created in 3100 BCE by the merger of the northern and southern kingdoms under one king, was the first on Earth. The features of a city-state included sovereignty, borders, territorial integrity, a population, and a government for the people. The above features confirm that diplomacy was possible to be applied even at the not-state entity level when requirements arose for the settlement of disputes and differences through peaceful means. Thus, whereas foreign policy was not applicable until the elements of statehood, sovereignty and issues associated with sovereignty (e.g., borders) arose, among African societies in ancient times and necessitated the use of foreign relations and diplomacy long before medieval times.

Furthermore, the dictates for diplomacy, foreign policy, and international relations could be the same for sovereign and non-sovereign entities in Africa. Thus, the issues of territory/land and inheritance, borders and natural resources (i.e., water, geography, topography, mountains, grazing lands, herds of cattle, hunting grounds), customs, traditions and the value system in Africa, trade, settlement of differences, alliances for common strategies for collaboration or against common human and natural enemies, as well as issues of statehood, sovereignty, territorial integrity and many others, were all common determinants of diplomacy, foreign policy, and international relations. And these were applicable at all times, throughout all periods of history in Africa.

In Africa's antiquity, the issues were mainly of cultural civilization and "common survival." From around 5000 BCE when the Sahara Desert emerged, big changes occurred in the likes of African societies. Permanent settlement had to happen, which, in turn, required organized authority through the use of government and governance skills. The reasons for this change included the birth of the desert, which followed climatic and cultural changes in Africa. The same series of changes was necessary in the Kalahari and Namib Deserts in Southern Africa. Another factor that promoted change was the shrinking of available land with the growth of the African population and the demand for human settlements, organization, and protection from natural and human enemies.

Further, there was the need to exercise power and control over the ruled population and territory. The increased population gathered in given settlements called for law and order to attain prosperity, provide defense, protect the people, and provide them their basic needs. In short, there was the need for government and governance. The division of Africa into North and Sub-Saharan "Africans" produced new challenges of different cultures, religions, civilizations, etc., that posed increased challenges to the rulers and leaders of African societies.

Problems of leadership thus arose long before African societies gained permanent statehood and sovereignty for inter-state relations.

Responsibilities of governance and leadership confronted all rulers and heads of families from the father of a family unit and lineage as husband and head of the extended family. Usually, a man became the head of a clan by inheritance, or by designation because of a dying/outgoing ruler, or even by unanimous "corona turn" of family elders. In most cases, inheritance in Africa and leadership of families were through patrilineal descent, and passed down through the male line of a family for many generations. However, some tribes did have government and governance exercised in the matrilineal heritage.

A senior chief was a tribal ruler under whom fell several tribes, but a paramount chief ranked higher in governance. Often, he was a tribal king over a large area of tribes. The position of chief was by appointment, as were the positions his deputies held. In most cases, the position of king and monarch was used interchangeably with the title of tribal ruler or king. Some tribes were huge; others were small. In like manner, an emperor was a monarch and ruler of tribes who presided over a larger area than that of a tribal king or super king. The emperor was a "big paramount chief," and a super emperor was even larger in power and authority because he ruled over the empires that fell under his rule. Among these kings and emperors arose autocratic rulers or kings and even chiefs.

SELECTED ISSUES OF GOVERNANCE, GOVERNMENT FOREIGN POLICY, AND DIPLOMACY IN ANCIENT AND MEDIEVAL AFRICA

In general, as explained in this chapter, the determinants and dictates of issues relating to foreign policy and diplomacy in ancient and medieval Africa were similar. The main difference lay on the status of the Africa community at the time in question. In ancient times, settlements and formation and consolidation of power and relationships between and among African societies involved diplomacy and inter-tribal relations more than inter-state relations.

In medieval times, however, after the birth of the city-state system in Africa and especially after 700 CE, the policies of foreign relations and diplomacy predominantly involved the cross-border relations of sovereign entities.

DICTATES AND DETERMINANTS OF INTER-TRIBAL RELATIONS AND WARS IN ANCIENT AND PRE-COLONIAL AFRICA

In pre-colonial times, dating back to remotest antiquity, the causes and consequences of peace and/or war were many and varied. They included the following, among many others: land and other natural resources such as geography and topography (lakes and rivers, mountains and forests, borders); slavery and slave trade; common hunting and grazing grounds for herds of domesticated animals and wildlife; territorial aggrandizement, expansionism, and legitimate trade; inheritance; peaceful settlements or disputes for peaceful coexistence and collaboration; problems of statehood, territorial integrity, and sovereignty; defense against common enemies, both human and natural; disasters, etc.

INTER-TRIBAL RELATIONSHIPS AT HOME AND ABROAD

Inter-tribal relationships were shaped by many factors, including those mentioned in the previous section. These customs and traditions dealing with tribal lands, regulating territorial issues, and other matters in cases where cultural and linguistic clashes happened (e.g., slaves and slave trade posed problems; invasions of small tribes by larger tribes, prisoners of war and the like), often meant resolution through village and tribal tribunals that were set up to resolve those differences. This process generally relied on the doctrine of African Socialism—the rule of consensus.

Peaceful coexistence codes of behavior for enforcing African values were cited, and oral traditions were cited. In cases where diplomacy failed to resolve differences, special negotiators were appointed who were mutually acceptable to the warring sides, and their verdicts were implemented. The traditions of following the modes of tribal groupings from clan to tribe to tribal kingdom to empire, to super empire, and to city-state were respected. Envoys were selected from one tribe to travel to another on various errands.

When the peace process failed, traditional indigenous warfare involved testing warrior skills, intelligence, and courage. Tutsis and Hutus in Rwanda and Burundi were elevated to false positions of power by the colonial policies and practices of the Dutch. The assumption was that Tutsis had more Caucasian-looking features than the Hutus. Such colonial myths allowed the West to exploit Africans and encourage inter-tribal warfare. The non-indigenous people of Africa have, over millennia, been responsible for such unnatural causes of inter-tribal conflicts, including cultural politics and social stratification or injustice; stereotypes of racial, ethnic, and class prejudices; exploitation, slavery, and dominance; religious beliefs, discrimination; and color bar.

Trade Relations in Pre-Colonial Africa

The trade and business history of Africa can best be analyzed if clustered into three eras: the pre-colonial, colonial, and post-colonial periods.

In pre-colonial times, the causes of nomadism and expansionism among the African population groups were associated with gathering and hunting, as well as the domestication of plants and animals. Those early business relations gradually were replaced by more permanent farming and agriculture. Land was the root of the African value system, even though barter continued to be the means of exchange in the commercial areas. Barter exchanges were common long before the Europeans arrived in Africa. Arab Africans had conducted business among themselves for millennia. When Arabs arrived in North Africa, trade was carried out between African kings and Arab traders across the Sahara for many centuries before Europeans glimpsed African shores.

As the trading skills improved among the African populations over the millennia, it became clear that business relations in Africa would be based on two forms of trade. Trade in agriculture-based goods and services, and trade in natural resources-based business. Under agriculture, the crops would consist of what became known as subsistence crops (cassava, millet, sorghum, maize or corn, wimbi, kolanuts, groundnuts or peanuts, sweet potatoes, beans, bananas, pineapples, passion fruit, guavas, and various kinds of vegetables) that took a relatively short time to mature and were hence ideal for African families. There also were those crops that required long periods of time before they could mature. These long-maturing crops were the "cash crops" (cocoa, coffee, tea, pyrethrum, rice, wheat, barley, sugarcane, sisal, rubber, mangoes, palm oil trees) as described in colonial times and grown primarily for export.

Then came the so-called natural resources that comprised water, energy, and mineral resources. Among these should be included cowries (seashells) and salt, as well as diamonds, gold, platinum, zinc, copper, manganese, asbestos, tin, silver, uranium, phosphates, and other minerals as well as oil and coal.

Africa has always been enormously rich in all these natural and agricultural resources and commodities. However, it is ironic that Africa is a continent of such vast natural resources and yet hosts some of the world's poorest countries. Africa is poor in plenty, and this is Africa's huge paradox, as discussed in Chapters 2 and 7 of Volume I and in Volume II.

Prior to European colonization of Africa, economic and trade relations had been established among the African peoples and had, in fact, flourished. When European currencies were introduced in African colonies, the barter system of business was replaced by the cash crop system. Some crops were grown to be sold for money instead of consumption, and the main market was European nations. The Africans were left with what were described as subsistence crops such as cassava, monkey-nuts, millet, and wimbi. The outcome of this transformation was the serious, systematic, and steady European impoverishment of Africa, because Africa has not been fairly compensated for these goods. The cash crop system shall be explained in great details in this study.

The economy and business could not thrive in colonial Africa since the colonial masters and administrations only allowed trade with the motherland of each colony. African entrepreneurs could not sell anything to anyone outside of the colony, and there was no free-market system or competitive price structure for goods, no matter how high the demand for them reached. This type of monopoly seriously affected the ability of Africa to trade globally and to develop trading partnerships like those that existed elsewhere throughout the world.

Moreover, the legitimate trade in goods and services was almost replaced by the illegitimate trade in African slaves. "Gold" now became the African slave and hence the talk from the 15th century for almost the following 400 years would be about human and natural resources even though the African slave was treated and regarded as an object.

Thus, there were various forms of trade after the introduction of the trade in captured Africans—slaves. Legitimate trade in goods and services from land, agriculture, and natural resources, and illegitimate trade in slaves, which was quite common. Both forms of trade—legitimate and illegitimate—existed side by side. In fact, it should be noted that slavery predates the colonial period in Africa. The Arab slave trade in Africa lasted for 10 centuries from the 9th to 19th centuries CE. In pre-colonial times, trade was an important occupation among the African tribes. Trade between Africans and the alien arrivals (the Phoenicians, then the Greeks and Romans) of classical times was common and an important element in the pre-colonial African economy. Starting in medieval times, Africans traded with both Arabs and Europeans. The Islamic and Barbary states established in North Africa and the African city-states that arose and flourished all across the continent of Africa, as kingdoms, empires, and city-states were all involved in trade, which was guided by the complexities of inter-kingdom, inter-empire, and inter-state/inter-city relations that relied on diplomacy, foreign policy, and external relations.

War in Traditional Africa

Wars among the African peoples, as with other human societies, have been fought from time immemorial and for various reasons as explained above. This does not, however, mean that traditional African societies were simple and savage as is often supported by Western stereotypes. The time between some wars was generations, whereas other conflicts recurred after relatively short periods of time.

Among the major causes of war in Africa should be counted the greed for power and glory; territorial aggrandizement, natural resources (geography and topography included), and the desire for political dominance; alien invasions and the fights to repel them; commerce; Christianity, and civilization. The three Gs (glory, gold, and gospel) led to many European invasions of Africa and prompted much of the colonization of Africa by European countries. Conflicts arose over grazing and hunting fields. Natural phenomena like drought and desertification caused movements and migrations from one area to another that imposed a new presence in places where such a presence was/is not welcome. Trade and empire-building as pursued by the stranger against weaker indigenous peoples and conquest, exploitation, slavery, supremacy, grasping for authority and political power also were all causes of conflict. The imposition of religious beliefs on other peoples left its mark on Africa as well. However, traditional religion played a valuable role in promoting peaceful community relations in African traditional societies. The slave trade as the most luxurious form of acquiring "human gold" was a contributor to wars, as have been human rights violations and inequality in society (e.g., against the weaker gender). Solutions to the battle for gender equality have included the empowerment of women and clear divisions of roles and labor between men and women in traditional Africa. Women have played important roles in African development, food production, agriculture, and the promotion of people in African societies. The place of womanhood in traditional Africa was vital both in inter-tribal relations as well as in promoting collaboration and understanding in African societies and in stressing the need to resolve differences through negotiations and other ways that avoided armed force and violence.

It is, nonetheless, clear that traditional Africans enjoyed military strategies that prevented the vestiges and devastation of war. Good examples of excellent African military strategies included the defeat of the Romans by the African (Carthaginian) general Hannibal around 146 BCE and the military mastery of the Zulu king Shaka Zulu (c. 1787–1825) in Southern Africa. Other examples also include the military leadership of African women such as Queen Hatshepsut of Egypt (1503–1482 BCE), Queen Makeda of Basheba (c. 960 BCE), and Queen Asentewa of Ejisu (1863–1923 CE), who led their armies against invaders of their countries and kingdoms. Besides diplomatic negotiations and consensus resolution of differences through concerted searches for solutions to the problems that cause war, as elsewhere in the world, solutions to differences and wars in Africa have included war itself.

Intermarriages and Alliances

As diplomatic tools, intermarriages and political alliances have been sought in Africa in order to resolve disputes and/or wars. Two kings who decide to cement friendship and cooperation through alliances both human and natural are able to protect each other whenever necessary to live peacefully or through peaceful coexistence and set up consultative mechanisms for collaboration and co-ordination of efforts and the like.

Intermarriages in like manner helped cement cooperation between and among rulers and leaders of the African kingdoms. Cases in point included kings agreeing to marry off their children as signs of permanent friendship and co-operation in times of need. These practices greatly promoted diplomatic and foreign policy relations among the African political units and kingdoms of ancient and medieval times. The practices continued even during the colonial times of Africa.

Peaceful Coexistence as a Fruitful Tool for Exogeneity

As stated above, peaceful coexistence among the African tribes, kingdoms, empires, and city-states naturally promoted peace and welfare; it also helped develop inter-state and inter-tribal relations which later proved to be inevitable for foreign policy and diplomatic relations of Africa from pre-independence to post-independence eras of Africa. The phonist system introduced in Africa by the alien colonization of Africa, as we shall see, became a big divider, only made worse by the Cold War. Thus, peaceful coexistence in Africa is still a big tool for Africa's multi-dimension.

METHODS OF GOVERNANCE, DEMOCRACY, AND DIPLOMACY IN PRE-COLONIAL AFRICA

Closely linked to the management of affairs between and among different political units and entities in Africa were the methods of governance that the African leaders of ancient, medieval, and even earlier and later periods employed in domestic circles as determinants of external links and relations.

In pre-colonial times, governance and government were political arts exercised in various forms. For example, despotism, absolutism, kleptocracy, as well as democracy and diplomacy; centralization and decentralization; formation of alliances for peaceful coexistence and control; protection and perpetuation of power and governance; confederation and federation with the application of custom, tradition, and inheritance.

DEMOCRACY AND DIPLOMACY AS PROMOTERS OF INTER-TRIBAL AND INTER-STATE RELATIONS IN AFRICA

In ancient and medieval Africa, as in earlier and later eras, democracy and diplomacy were vital tools for advancing peaceful collaboration of concerted efforts among different political entities in Africa. These tools were acknowledged as being valuable for the attainment of cooperation, even among close relatives and within families. However, the African sense of universality, requiring loyalty, harmony, and reverence to the royalty of the king/ruler was not to be broken. Thus, a universal harmony existed in which each being had to recognize their place and role in society. In this society the king was supreme and represented the greatest vital force in the whole kingdom. The king was sacrosanct, an all-powerful mediator, and a superior in the universe. He was irreplaceable and no external influence was allowed into the kingdom. He had to lead a life strictly regulated by custom—in some kingdoms the king had to ride around his capital on horseback or by other appropriate means, meeting and hearing or investigating the complaints/grievances/presentations of his subjects.

Role of the Councilor

In most cases, the king was appointed by a council of advisors according to tradition after a thorough examination of each case. The king then became the guarantor of the terrestrial and social order. Each king had a council of advisors applying mostly custom and tradition as the guiding principles of governance. The councilors in African states/kingdoms/empires held great power since they often commanded military units and possessed vast tracts of land that affected many villagers. In ancient rituals, officials acted as protectors of the forest kingdoms, and advisors of forest kings. Councilors often participated in selecting, installing, and disposing of successive monarchs. For example, impotent kings were ceremoniously killed or replaced with healthy monarchs.

Councilors also collected tributes and taxes in their own provinces. Apart from taxes, the other sources of their revenue were customs, gold from mines, booty, royal treasures, fees for administrative offices, and ransom for hostages. A complex system of checks and balances curbed monarchical authority. Divine kings ruled the states whose prosperity depended on their ruler's well-being.

African kingdoms were loosely organized groupings of tribes and peoples (not feudal monarchs) held together by bureaucrats whose loyalty was to the king alone. Local chiefs governed their own domains and owed to their paramount ruler not so much detailed obedience as periodic tribute and as the availability of their men and supplies in time of war.

Thus, the kings ruled via councils or societies of leading elders or titled hereditary aristocrats, and dynasties governed the super states (e.g., in Yorubaland, Ghana, Dahomey, Benin, Congo, the Sudanic states, and Zulu empires). The savanna empires of Ghana, Mali, and Songhai flourished between 300 and 1600 CE. The East African city-states prospered between 1100 and 1500 CE. The inhabitants of the East African coast came as migrants from inland Africa during the 700s CE. They mainly spoke Bantu languages. Other settlers there were Arabs—Muslims who had fled their homeland to escape political enemies.

Despotism and African Monarchs

In early African states, despotism was strong a form of government. Monarchs tended to be despotic and introduced new forms of taxation and assigned their own approaches to collecting taxes. This practice enhanced their economic power.

Monarchs also controlled the governed by imposing their own (monarchical) royal nominees in new provinces. They often worked for a reduction of powers of the hereditary chiefs by transferring their fiscal functions to a new class of personally appointed officials whose tenure the monarchs controlled directly.

Assertion of Authority in African Pre-Colonial Times

Authority was asserted by African leaders in various ways (e.g., via gift-giving, a system and practice widely applied in pre-colonial Africa) between the rulers and the ruled, governed, or conquered chiefs and their subjects. Gifts could be slaves, cloth, beads, or other cherished items.

Tribal intermarriages between families and between kings and chiefs (subordinates) were also used to assert or maintain authority. Among the Bunyoro of Uganda, the king/monarch/chief would assert his authority by sharing milk from sacred royal herds with others whose favor he wished to reward or retain.

Many objects symbolized the bond of loyalty and subordination: royal drums, turbans, trousers, sacred tools, spears, daggers at ceremonies, etc. Items such as these symbolized power and authority, and their use was common among the royal families, especially those of the Baganda in Uganda, the Wanga in Wanga-Nabongo, etc.

Centralization, Decentralization, and Confederation of Government

The confederations of Shona and other states emerged in Eastern, Central, and Southern Africa (e.g., in Congo-Katanga, Malawi, the Sotho-Tswana, Zulu and other African groupings of empires in Southern Africa), as well as the Zulu and Zimbabwe empires and autonomous city-states such as the Maritime city-states in East Africa where intermarriages between the coastal Bantu tribes and the settlers from Shiraz in Arabia, Oman, and the Persian Gulf produced a new ethnic group called the Swahili.

Muslim city-states in pre-colonial Africa included the war-time groupings of the Kilwa, Malindi, and Mombasa. Even in West Africa, in Hausa-land, there were war-time groupings of the Kano in the African grasslands.

Ancient traditional Africa also produced rulers whose sources of authority and power came from the ritual needs of the tribe or clan, lineage, and extensive support of clan elders. The royal councilors also gained their status in society by exhibiting themselves as deserving of councilor positions by election or appointment. These wise men—arbitrators in conflict—were Omwami Omukhongo in the Kiluhya language, meaning Great Ruler.

NOTES

1. Sir Arthur Harold Nicolson, *Portrait of a Diplomatist: A Study in the Old Diplomacy* (New York: Harcourt, Brace and Company, 1930).

2. Douglas Busk, *The Craft of Diplomacy: Mechanisms & Development of National Representation Overseas* (London: Pall Mall Press, 1967).

3. Garrett Mattingly, *Renaissance Diplomacy* (Boston: Houghton Mifflin Company, 1971).

4. Konrad Repgen, "Negotiating the Peace Treaty of Westphalia: A Survey with an Examination of the Major Problems," in *1648: War and Peace in Europe*, 3 vols., ed. Klaus Bussman and Heinz Schilling (Catalogue of the 26th Exhibition of the Council of Europe on the Peace of Westphalia, 1998).

5. C.W. Wedgwood, *The Thirty Years War* (New York: New York Review of Books, 1938).

CHAPTER 6

Major Extra-African Actors before the 19th Century

ANTIQUITY IN NORTH AFRICA: 500 BCE–1500 CE

An important part of ancient African history began with the origins of recorded history (i.e., when history or events began to be discriminated from around 500 BCE to the end of the early Middle Ages). Thus, the period from around 500 BCE to 1453 CE marked a new but important period in African history that concentrated on the northern part of Africa.

The first foreigners to visit North Africa along the Mediterranean coast were the Phoenicians who created flourishing trade links with the indigenous populations of North Africa, including the Berbers. The Phoenicians were followed by the Greeks and, subsequently, by the Romans.

Although Ghana was the first Roman colony in Africa, the Romans concentrated their colonization of Africa in the north, in what was later called the Maghreb by the Arabs who arrived there for commerce. North Africa became very valuable as the Western Province of the Roman Empire. The Maghreb included Mauretania, Tripolitania (where present-day Tripoli stands in Libya), and Cyrenaica, which was founded by the Greeks in 631 BCE in ancient Libya.

The Phoenicians arrived in Carthage for the first time in 814 BCE but they had been roaming about along the Mediterranean Sea from 1200 to 1000 BCE. In 332 BCE, Alexander the Great, who colonized Egypt, founded an important business hub in Egypt and named it Alexandria.

The Greek empire and colonization in Africa thus was extended to Egypt, and the whole northern part of Africa was brought under Mediterranean control with significant trade links/routes across the Sahara Desert involving traders of Berber, Bedouin, Phoenician, Greek, Roman, and later Arab extractions.

The Arabs came to North Africa in the 7th century CE and imposed their culture and the religion of Islam on the people of North Africa. When intermarriages occurred, a new light-colored race arose in North Africa whose base was tri-fold: Arab, African, and European.

Of particular interest and vast cultural influence in North Africa were the Muslim Arabs whose Islamic religion was brought to Africa starting around 622 CE. When religion combined with commerce and culture, the Arab presence became overwhelming. The result was that many African countries assumed Arabic ways as a mode of life that was even more important to the inhabitants of North Africa than the traditional African lifestyle.

EUROPEAN COLONIZATION IN AFRICA: 1400–1800 CE

The scramble to colonize Africa was born much earlier than 1885, the date by which it was officially cemented by the accords in Berlin. There seemed to be no difference then between politics, economics, trade, and conversion. The European powers whose agents had been working at grabbing big parts of Africa emerged as the British, Dutch, Germans, Portuguese, Spaniards, Italians, Belgians, and French.

The Spaniards did not grab too much of Africa's cake because they went to the Americas instead.

In northwest Africa, it was the French and the British who took the largest pieces of Africa. The Germans tried in the west but did not get much of it. However, the French were prominent in Morocco, Tunisia, and other parts of North Africa.

In West Africa, the British and French dominated. In the Central Africa, the French were everywhere. In East Africa, it was predominantly the British, although the Germans occupied Tanganyika. A protectorate for the Sultan of Oman was granted by the British on a 10-mile strip of land form the coast of Kenya along the Indian Ocean. In Southern Africa, there were several European influences. First, the Dutch colonized the Cape region of South Africa and became the first Europeans to colonize the interior of Africa. The British then came and struggled with the French and the Dutch for Southern Africa. The British emerged as the imperial power in Southern Africa, although the Dutch continued to colonize South Africa with a dehumanizing policy called Apartheid. Apartheid, colonization, and slavery can be compared, but Apartheid was a sui generis kind of brutal discrimination against Africans based solely on the color of their skin, which forced South Africans to be subjected to separate development.

The Portuguese occupied Angola and Mozambique as well the three adjacent islands in the Atlantic Ocean called Cape Verde, Guinea-Bissau, and São Tomé and Príncipe in the Indian Ocean, the four islands of

Madagascar, Mauritius, Seychelles, and Comoros, which gained independence, as well as the other island territories of Reunion and Mayotte, which became French and are still French dependencies. These territories and countries of Africa will be analyzed in later sections dealing with the questions of colonization and decolonization of Africa.

The only Spanish territory in Africa that was reported is Western Sahara. This nation still faces controversies because it is claimed by Morocco even though it was recognized by the African Political Unity Organization as far back as 1980. The countries of North Africa, including Egypt, Libya, Tunisia, Morocco, and Algeria, were brought under European imperialism—Egypt under the control of the British, Algeria under the rule of Morocco, and Tunisia under the control of the French and Libyans.

But the winds of change blew against imperialism and colonialism. Especially after the First and Second World Wars, pressures and struggles against imperialism increased and these countries eventually emerged as sovereign members of the Organization of African Unity.

The Ottoman Empire, or Turkey, or the Ottoman State was an empire that lasted from 1299 to 1922 CE as an imperial monarchy. The zenith of Ottoman Empire power was in the 16th to 17th centuries. It spanned three continents and controlled much of Southeastern Europe, the Middle East, and North Africa, including the Sudan. The Ottoman Empire was the center of interaction between the Eastern and Western worlds for six long centuries (13th–18th centuries).

EGYPTIAN INVASION OF SUDAN: 1820–1838 CE

In July 1820, Mohammed Ali, viceroy of Egypt under the Ottoman Turks, sent an army under the command of his son Ismail to conquer the Sudan. Ali was quite interested in the gold and slaves that the Sudan could provide and wished to control the vast hinterland south of Egypt.

By 1821, the Funj and the Sultan of Darfur surrendered to Ali's forces and the Nilotic Sudan from Nubia to the Ethiopian foothills and from the Atbarah River to Darfur became part of his expanding empire. Ali then started to impose very objectionable practices on the Sudan, including the collection of taxes, and the confiscation of gold, livestock, slaves, and the like.

Opposition became strong in the Sudan, leading to rebellion and murder of Ismail and his bodyguard. The rebellion was brutally suppressed. Turmoil and unrest continued until 1826 when Ali Khurshid Agha was appointed governor general of Sudan.

This new ruler improved the Egyptian/Ottoman–Sudanese relations when he reduced taxes, consulted the Sudanese on various affairs of state, and respected the Sudanese leader Abda–Qadir wad az-Zayn. After consultation with the Sudanese authorities, the governor general also engaged in diplomatic activities including granting letters of amnesty to fugitives and introducing a system of taxation. He further supported self-rule among the Sudanese tribes, which were led by their powerful class of holy men and Sheikhs or tribal chiefs—administrators of their areas—whom he exempted from taxation.

Furthermore the governor general opened trade routes and promoted and protected them in the Sudan. He developed Khartoum as the administrative capital and launched agricultural and technical improvements in the country. By the time of this return to Cairo in 1838, Ali Khurshid Agha had restored the Sudan to its former condition, and left it in a prosperous and contented mood.

Egypt and Sudan remained Ottoman provinces until 1914. Thus these two African states fell under the imperial rule of the Turkish Empire, which was, in effect, a vast sultanate of Turkey comprising the southwest part Asia, the southeast portion of Europe, and northeastern Africa.[1]

OTTOMAN EMPIRE[2-4]

The Ottoman Empire was founded in the 13th century by Osman I and ruled by his descendants until its dissolution after World War I. The empire started as a small state controlled in Ottoman by the Osmanli Turks. It then spread rapidly, superseding the Byzantine Empire in the east.

In 1922, following post–World War I treaties that dissolved the empire, the sultanate was formally abolished by Mustapha Kemal Ataturk, who proclaimed the creation of the Republic of Turkey in 1923.

The Turks under the Ottoman Empire came to rule over the Sudan via Egypt with which Sudan had established long relations in neighboring African states—not that those relations were all good, but rulers of both states controlled them "back and forth" through wars, mergers, diplomatic, and other arrangements until the British colonization of these Africans in 1922.

It is noteworthy that a part of present-day Sudan was nominally an Egyptian dependency. The Egyptian occupation of Sudan set up a new government there in 1821, known as the Turkiyah or Turkish regime, where soldiers lived off the land and exacted exorbitant taxes from the populations as explained above. The Turkish soldiers also destroyed many valuable ancient meroitic pyramids while searching for hidden gold. Furthermore, trade in slaves increased causing many of the inhabitants of the fertile Al Jazirah, the heartland of Funj, to flee while trying to escape the slave traders. Within a year of appointed Governor of Egypt Muhammad Ali Pasha's 1805 victory, some 30,000 Sudanese slaves went to Egypt for training and induction into the army, but very many perished due to disease and unfavorable climatic conditions in the Egyptian desert.

Other causes of the strained relations between Sudan and Turkish/Ottoman-led Egypt included Egypt's parasitic bureaucracy, recruitment of Turkish mercenaries and their use in Sudan in garrisons of Khartoum, Kassaha, Ul Uhayyid, and other places in Sudan. The original occupation was brutal and much resented by the Sudanese people.

To subdue rebellion, the Egyptian rulers of Sudan divided the country into smaller administrative tribal units in 1850, and Khartoum became the seat of the governor-general called the Hakimadar. The legal and trade system that the rulers of Sudan introduced from Egypt under Ottoman rule, favored the foreigners, not the Sudanese populations. Thus, Sudan became Turkiyah and was completely under the Ottomans between 1821 and 1885. Many that tried to resist Ottoman rule left Sudan. Others, such as those in Darfur, were suppressed, brutalized, and conquered by the Ottomans from Egypt. Slavery continued in Sudan as before and flourished until the abolition of the slave trade in the 19th century by the British and Americans.

OMANI ARABS OF EAST AFRICA

The whole area of the East African Coast, called Uswahili, was ruled by an Omani sultan for centuries. Zanzibar rebelled at times, as did Lamu. But, predominantly, their ruler was always an Omani Arab. Then, around 1886, the sultan of Zanzibar created his own sultanate and broke away from the Uswahili region. He and his subjects in Zanzibar rebelled against their home rulers, just like 13 American colonies in the New World had rebelled against Great Britain in 1776.

In East Africa to this day, Omani Arabic is still the primary linguistic influence. Swahili is the language that emerged from the blending of Bantu and Arabic people inhabiting the East African coast. Swahili is thus both the language and the people that speak Swahili.

East Africa

The earlier Arab traders who settled on the East African Coast had come from Oman, learned the Bantu language, married local women, introduced Islam, and brought to this part of Africa much of the Arabic culture and vocabulary that is used today. The Arabs maintained their Arabic language but also spoke Swahili, the form of Bantu language common on the East African Coast. Arabic was a minority language.

Trade between the Kenyan coast and Arabia was brisk by 100 CE. Arabs settled on the coast during medieval times and soon established several autonomous city-states including Mombasa, Malindi, and Zanzibar. Farmers and herders traveled south from Ethiopia and settled in Kenya in 2000 BCE. Between 500 BCE and 500 CE, some Bantu and Nilotic peoples from South Sudan also settled in Kenya.

In 1729, the Portuguese who had visited and settled in Kenya starting in 1498 were permanently expelled from Mombasa and were replaced by the Arab dynasties on the East African Coast. The Busaidi from Masqat in Oman and from Zanzibar came around 1832, and the Mazrui dynasty was based at Mombasa. The Busaidi and Mazrui quarreled and fought in 1837.[5, 6]

East African Arabs, especially those from Zanzibar and Tanganyika, should be classified as speaking a dialect of Omani Arabic, but not many speak it nowadays. The Arabian Arabs, as opposed to the Kenyan or East African Arabs, are Yemeni. The coastal Kenyan Arabs are basically business people who speak Swahili, not Arabic. Even if they can speak Arabic they do not use it, as they prefer to use Swahili.

On the East African Coast, especially in Kenya today, the majority of the Arabs are of Yemeni and not Omani extraction. This is only in recent decades, however as they were originally of Omani extraction—especially those in Zanzibar. It was in the early days of Arabs in East Africa that the Omani sultan used to come to Zanzibar on vacation, using the dhow as a means of travel. As the Arab presence grew, their culture followed and the Arabs were granted a protectorate status when the British colonized Kenya as Bantus East Africa. A treaty signed between the British and the sultan granted 10 acres of land from the Indian Ocean into the Kenyan interior to the Omani Arabs to inhabit and use. In 1895, Kenya became part of the British East Africa Protectorate, and would later become the Kenya Colony in 1922.[7] The colony and protectorate of Kenya were administered as a single unit with a single flag under international law, a protectorate in an autonomous territory, protected diplomatically or militarily against third parties by a stronger state or entity.

EUROPEANS IN AFRICA BEFORE THE 19TH CENTURY

Before the advent of European colonization in the late 19th century, two events of historical significance occurred in Africa. As described in Chapter 5, the first was the slave trade between Africa, Europe, and the Americas, which dealt in captured Africans and was very lucrative for many years. The second was the Arab slave trade in captured Africans who for 10 centuries (from the 9th to 19th centuries) were shipped to the Middle East and the Far East by Arab slave traders. The slave trade, in effect, replaced legitimate trade in goods and services that had been conducted between Africa, Europe, and the Arabs for centuries. The slave trade as an institution was abolished at the beginning of the 19th century both in Europe and in the United States (President Thomas Jefferson signed the Abolition Act in 1807, but it became effective on January 1, 1808). Thereafter, the European traders and adventurers turned to Africa again, but this time in order to be engaged in the study of nature and other interests that became famous as the following three Gs and Cs:

- Glory/civilization (Western),
- Gold/commerce (natural resources), and
- Gospel/Christianity (conversion of Africans).

Before the 19th century however, the most notable colonizing force had been the Phoenicians—who invaded and colonized Carthage in 814 BCE. As described in Chapter 1, the Phoenicians were followed by the Greeks, who colonized parts of North Africa between 631 BCE and 332 BCE, and later by the Romans in 146 BCE when they made North Africa part of the Western Province of the Roman Empire.

NOTES

1. *Britannica Concise Columbia Encyclopedia of the Middle East and North Africa: History 1450–1789.*

2. Timothy Childs, *Italo-Turkish Diplomacy and the War Over Libya: 1911–1912* (New York: Brill, 1990).

3. P. Wittek, *The Rise of the Ottoman Empire* (London: Royal Asiatic Society, 1938).

4. "Ottoman Empire" in *Macmillan Encyclopedia 2001* (Aylesbury, UK: Market House Books, 2000).

5. R.A. Oliver, et al., *History of East Africa*, 3 vols (Oxford: Oxford University Press, 1963–1976).

6. Byron E. Farwell, *The Man Who Presumed: A Biography of Henry M. Stanley* (London: Longmans, 1958); *Burton: A Biography of Sir Richard Francis Burton* (London: Longmans, 1963); *Queen Victoria's Little Wars* (New York: Harper & Row, 1972); *The Great War in Africa: 1914–1919* (New York: W.W. Norton, 1986); *The Great Anglo-Boer War* (New York: W.W. Norton, 1990); and *Over There: The United States in the Great War, 1917–1918* (New York: W.W. Norton, 1999).

7. *Britannica Concise Encyclopedia* (2009).

CHAPTER 7

What If the Foundations of African Foreign Policy and Diplomacy Had Been Solidified in the Middle Ages?

The overview of African history provided in this chapter leads one to wonder what condition Africa would be in today if her foreign policy and diplomacy foundations had been solidified in the Middle Ages. Would Africa have developed differently? Would many of Africa's present burdens have been prevented? For example, would slavery and the slave trade in captured Africans that was conducted by Europeans and Arabs have occurred? Would Africa have been vulnerable to the exploitation and impoverishment forced on her by the European powers? Would European colonization and transformation of Africa into a by-product of Western civilization have been possible? Would Africa have suffered the heavy losses of African cultures and civilizations that were regarded as primitive by the European invaders? Would the excessive fragmentation of Africa through the European conspiracy permitted under the Berlin Accord of 1885 have occurred? Would Africa still experience the excessive and perpetual poverty syndrome she struggles with in the midst of her vast human and natural resources? Would Africa still experience the unending conflicts, coups, corruption, and ethnocentrism that have rocked the continent and dominated life in Africa throughout Africa's post-colonial era? Would Africa still be home to the paradoxes of acculturation, isolation, marginalization, education and leadership deficiencies, humiliation, and the like?

To pose the above questions in a different way: if Africa had been left to develop according to her own value systems, without external,

European influences, what would be Africa's Condition today? How would she be conducting her foreign policies and diplomacy today? Can and will Africa reclaim her lost civilizations and redeem them in the 21st century?

The answers to these questions are hard to give, and no one can really tell what would have happened if Africa had been left to develop according to her own identity and destiny. The viewpoint of this writer, however, is that things in Africa would be quite different today if no foreign invasions of the continent had taken place. This is especially the case if the African path to the future would have been shaped by Africa and Africans in the Middle Ages—that is, if Africa's foreign policy and diplomacy would have been solidified in medieval times.

WHY THE MIDDLE AGES?

Various reasons prompt the conclusion that Africa lost a golden opportunity and "missed the boat" in the Middle Ages—a unique era in world and African history that offered unique opportunities for learning from past mistakes as medieval times demonstrated. Africa, with all her flourishing kingdoms, empires, super empires, and city-states already in medieval times, was ripe for cementing foundations for her future internal and external relations with other political entities. These could, and should, have allowed for an independent African forging of Africa's future visionary strategies and approaches for multidimensional development of Africa. Strategies that would have produced diplomacy, foreign policy, and international relations disciplines in medieval times could have prevented many of the ills, injustices, deprivations, burdens, exploitations, corrupt practices, lootings, and impoverishment that Africa has been subjected to for millennia, and that continue to haunt the African continent today.

In the Stone and Iron Ages

Already in the Stone and Iron Ages events had happened in Africa that had not yet happened anywhere else on Earth. The Stone Age was a prehistoric period during which humans widely used stone for making tools that improved their chances for survival and quality of life. It was the earliest known period of human culture, characterized by the use of stone tools. The Stone Age began probably around 2.5 million years ago, with hominid (near-men) toolmakers in Africa.

There were other ages, notably the Iron Age, Bronze Age, and the Age of Gold, these being the best documented of the prehistoric ages. During those ages, there was a lot of gathering, collecting, and hunting, and it was in those times that humankind advanced his survival instincts. Those were the Ages when animals and crops were domesticated progressively. That led to increased inventions in the thoughts of those early Africans. After all, when the first humans roamed the planet they were on the African continent and it was Africans who were the first technologists and inventers of tools, weapons, and fire.

The Iron Age began in the 12th century BCE in the Near East in the vicinity of ancient Iran, India, and Greece. Archeological evidence suggests that the Iron Age was a stage in the development of any people in which tools and weapons whose main ingredient was iron were prominent. Ancient Greece split into two eras during the Iron Age, one of which was the "Greek Dark Ages." There was Iron Age I, stretching from 1200 to 1000 BCE, and Iron Age II, which stretched from around 1000 BCE to the early Middle Ages in 476–1453 CE. The Iron Age coincided with other social changes, including changes in agricultural practices. That age was preceded by the Bronze Age. Known as the ages of man, and the ages of human existence, the three ages marked significant and historically memorable developments in human evolution, through which the African man went systematically unto today.

Thus, without Africa, those events and discoveries of significant, historic proportions would probably not have been possible. These events started to shape Africa long before medieval times. They also included the development of language as a means of communication. The movement from nomadism to permanent settlements and civilized styles of living were known in Africa long before they happened elsewhere on Earth; as was the development of governance and government in permanently settled areas where living conditions had to be improved and protected, with provisions of common services for the people, law and justice/order, codes of living, etc.—all that following the appearance of the Great Sahara with the development of skills in agriculture, animal husbandry, and peaceful coexistence as well as skills in barter trade, food and clothing discoveries, divisions of labor in society; inter-human, inter-tribal and inter-state contacts thereby replacing stateless relations with cross-border contacts and relations. This brought diplomatic ways of settling differences among groups of peoples via alliances, compensatory means of dialogue, cooperation, consensus compromise and coordination of efforts for development and peaceful coexistence. Thus, already long before the Middle Ages, Africans learned how to use diplomacy to manage their relations and use tools for what became known as peaceful relations—the prototype of international relations—through African diplomacy and leadership based on custom and tradition.

With these facts in mind, the present writer believes that the Middle Ages were a reservoir and an acme of opportunities and lessons for visionary use. The period in world history in which a great divide existed between antiquity and modernity, and hence the Renaissance, should have marked a new and significant era for, and in, Africa for political evolution as well. Antiquity had been the period of ancient times of prehistory, long before written history, and before the fall of the Roman Empire in 476 CE. The skills and development that Africa witnessed and experienced from remotest antiquity (i.e., from more than 10 million to more than 5 million years ago) when hominids began to walk upright at 4'6", to the 4th millennium BCE when written history began, and right to the Middle Ages, were unique and may not have happened in quite the same way if they had not occurred in Africa.

What Lessons do the Middle Ages in Europe have for Africa?

It is useful to note here how things were in Europe before the Middle Ages, and how Europeans overcame their problems. Can Africa not do the same? One could safely conclude that the future of Europe as the colonial power over Africa was probably cemented between the time of feudalism and the Renaissance in Europe. European expansionism started after the Renaissance, which was a time of rapid cultural, scientific, technological, and economic advancement in Europe. This created an excessive curiosity that fueled exploration, colonialism, imperialism, conquest, etc. Before Medieval Times, all of Europe and North Africa had been parts of the Roman Empire, which fell in the 5th century CE. By the 9th century CE, landlords in Europe had taken control of ruling and governing large European manor estates and farms.

THE MIDDLE AGES AS THE WATERSHED BETWEEN ANTIQUITY AND THE RENAISSANCE

Background

If the Middle Ages fell between antiquity and the Renaissance, then we can safely conclude that medieval times started at the fall of the Roman Empire (in the West) in 476 CE, and lasted until the fall of Constantinople (in the East) in 1453 CE. The Renaissance was greatly influenced by the Middle Ages. In turn, some historic developments, like those of medieval times, could have influenced Africa quite differently than as a by-product of Western civilization that Africa became in subsequent centuries.

The Middle Ages were a very long but uncertain period of time characterized by plagues and progress; commercial revolution; great expansionism that brought with it global governance, globalization of commerce, and the spread of religion (especially Christianity in the Catholic tradition); the Crusades; the creation and destruction of empires and city-states; the growth of universities as centers of learning; and the rise of mercantilism.

Europe experienced many changes in the Middle Ages. It saw the first sustained urbanization of North and West Europe; the fixing of the current borders in Europe; as well as a substantial deterioration in the art of diplomacy, owing mainly to the disintegration of the Roman Empire in the 5th century CE. It would take extraordinary efforts on the part of European leaders, including in particular the popes in Rome, to revive diplomacy as a tool for settling differences among nations, without resorting to armed conflict

Just as the early Middle Ages had been marked by the sacking of Rome and the collapse of the Roman society and governance, it gave rise to petty rulers, unrest, and monasticism in the West. Widespread and radical changes occurred from the mid-Middle Ages to the late medieval period in Europe, leading to insecurity of Europe from the globalization of politics, power, and religion—as well as the formation of nation-states that organized the world into their own image. But at that time, Africa was already host to many nation-states. Moreover, other institutions existed that could have helped Africa to sustain her identity and cultures. For example, the dominance of the Catholic Church in the Middle Ages, which converted most of Africa to Christianity, could have helped Africa to retain her values if the Church had cared about the totality of Africa. As a major cultural influence capable of befriending African kingdoms and empires, and as unifier of Christian values, why did the Catholic Church fail to help Africa solidify her image and Africanness as a separate entity worthy of protection in the Christian world and tradition? By preserving Latin learning in monasteries something could have been done to help Africa retain her civilization. In like manner, the medieval period preserved and maintained the art of writing and of centralized administration through the strong network of Catholic bishops, with their vast influences throughout the Middle Ages. Why did those bishops, who also had influence in Africa, not do something to preserve Africanness and African identity for Africa's posterity? These missed opportunities for Africa need to be examined today, with a view to learning from past mistakes and ensuring that preventive measures for Africa are taken in the future.

Catholicism was particularly influential in Europe, especially after the conversion of the barbarian King Clovis I of the Franks. His conversion boosted the Catholic tradition, introduced orthodoxy and Catholic conservatism, and dealt a blow to Arianism, which disagreed with the Catholic Church on the nature of the Holy Trinity and was of great influence in Gaul. In this way, the Middle Ages became a factory of progressive forces in learning, religion, monasticism, Catholicism, governance (nation-states), as well as of the injustices of commercial globalization—the spread of disease such as the Bubonic Plague, which was called the "Black Death" in the 14th century—and continuing invasions by barbarians like those that ended the Roman Empire.

The events that shaped the world then were comparable to those that shape contemporary Africa today: the deadly pandemics of HIV/AIDS, Ebola, SARS, malaria, tuberculosis, etc. These illnesses remind one of the plagues of medieval times. Similarly, the information revolution of today, with its information and communication technologies (ICTs) such as the Internet and computer systems, etc., remind one of the commercial globalization, trade, and development efforts during the Middle Ages. The Dark Ages of medieval times that led to the collapse of whole societies in Europe, especially from the end of the 5th to the 8th centuries CE, remind one of the birth of new nations in the Third World and their leaders, who are confronted with countless challenges of governance, human rights abuses, and leadership deficiencies today in Africa. At the same time, the emergence of new generations of leaders today reminds one of the emergence of new peoples and powerful individuals who were constantly filling the political vacuum left by Rome's centralized governments. The parallels are striking.

The rivalries for hegemony in Europe by the Franks and German decentralized kingdoms, which created strong regionalism in European governance, is reminiscent of modern Majimboism (regionalism) in Africa, where ethnocentrism, tribalism, and cronyism have rocked every effort for unified governance and government, and thereby perpetuated the African paradox of poverty in plenty. Decentralization has been challenged in Africa, because decentralization often breeds tribalism, as it does not enhance economic integration of the African regions. However, European models, such as the European Union (EU), European Commission, and other regional arrangements, are effective, productive, beneficial to Europe as a whole, and can be effective for the general population. Thus, for example, European capitalism, if compared to American capitalism, seems to serve Europe better than American capitalism serves the American people. European capitalism is based upon socioliberal democracy that does not rely too heavily on borrowed funds and a credit card system that is overwhelming American capitalism by basing its success on borrowed money and capital, which can lead to excessive impoverishment.

Medieval times stretching mainly from 476 to 1453 CE were thus a great era between ancient and modern times that offer great lessons for Africa. In the Middle Ages, events came and went, diseases came and went, as did progressive and "dark" years. Europe went through them all and learned how to survive, recover from failures, and forge ahead on the basis of the lessons learned. Why did that not also happen in Africa? Why did the changes for worse and for better in Europe not help Africa to learn from past mistakes and map out strategies for the future? When the fall of Rome started with the invasions of the Germanic tribes, the consequences were the mushrooming of separate kingdoms in Europe. Similar invasions rocked Africa; why did they not help foster the creation of stronger and more self-reliant kingdoms in Africa? In fact, during the time that some things, such as structures and institutions collapsed in Europe, other things, such as trade, business, and organizations of state, that were stronger and more beneficial to European societies replaced them. The people of Europe emerged stronger than before as farmers, entrepreneurs, etc., and developed self-sufficiency in whatever they created as economies. Thereafter, a new system of feudalism was born, and thrived for centuries. Should the same not have been possible in Africa as well? If lessons learned from the misfortunes of the era known as the "Dark Ages" in Europe's early Middle Ages enabled the Europeans to improve their general condition, why did those lessons not reach Africa, which was next door to Europe, and, for that matter, much wealthier than Europe?

THE RENAISSANCE AND AFRICA

The term "Renaissance" stems from the French, meaning "rebirth," and is used to describe that period from the 13th to 17th centuries CE that marked the transition from medieval to modern times and was a time of enormous development in Western civilization. The Renaissance started in latter-day Middle Ages, and this rebirth, while not losing medieval culturalism in Europe, did nonetheless bring renewed interest in classical learning and values, first to Italy, and subsequently to the rest of Europe. The Renaissance triggered the spirit of adventurism, curiosity, and expansionism in Europeans, who later spread their values across the world. The question, then, that one has to ask again at this juncture is why Africa failed, even in the Renaissance period, to develop "immunity" to resist the subsequent European invasions of the African continent that presided over the demise of Africanism and African values? Why did Africa fail to resist European influences, given the strength of African cultures, civilizations, and institutions that flourished even as early as the Middle Ages? By then, Africa had hosted and witnessed the development and success of many kingdoms, empires, super empires and city-states.

After asking these questions, and giving answers to them, can Africa analyze her past with a view to establishing the Africa that Africans must want in the new millennium? In other words, can Africa reclaim her lost civilizations in the 21st century and redeem them for the future generations of Africans? With these questions and daunting challenges to Africa in mind, the present writer wishes that the 21st century be declared as the century for Africa's ownership of Africa through reclaiming and redemption of African civilizations.

The Renaissance grew from medieval times and flourished, especially between 1350 and 1450. The year 1453 marked the official collapse of Constantinople. What lessons should Africa have learned from those developments that shaped Europe in the medieval and Renaissance eras? Europe was confronted with challenges and impediments that Africa has suffered for centuries. Can Africa learn from European mistakes and successes? The answer to this question has to be given in the affirmative. For example, music is one of Africa's greatest values, and Africa could have used this value to her advantage. From 1300 CE, during the Renaissance, love for music in Europe formed an important part of European civilization. French, the diplomatic language, was used widely, and European cultures were promoted by the development of French music on a European scale. As the super mother of all kinds of music, Africa could have developed music and cultural diplomacy to eradicate some of the linguistic and cultural clashes that continue to haunt Africa today.

In like manner, African music could have played a major role if it had been used in Africa. In the Americas, for example, African music became a powerful tool for communication, tact, diplomacy, warning, and strategy for African slaves. American slaves used music for signaling the presence of enemies, danger, and rallying slaves against the enemies, getting food, protecting the wounded and the vulnerable, etc. Music was a means of fighting against slavery.

The Renaissance triggered many developments in Europe, including the following:

1. The rediscovery of Greek and Roman literature in the 12th century was an important catalyst for a humanistic movement in Europe of the 14th century. After all, the Renaissance was a great cultural movement in the late Middle Ages. That movement began in Italy and spread like wildfire across Europe.

2. The death of Roman emperor Frederick II in 1250 CE marked the beginning of the loss of power by secular rulers and the assumption of power by the popes of the period.

3. The period 1378–1415 CE witnessed the birth of small Italian republics, which arose with strong despotic forms of government. In 1415, the Portuguese established the first European contact with Africa in "modern" times. The Portuguese captured the enclave of Gibraltar called Ceuta from Morocco and claimed it for Portugal.

4. During the Renaissance, the city-state system was solidified, and at the height of the Renaissance, major city-states were born and many flourished in great regions in Europe. Italy saw great growth of Italian city-states such as Napoli, Venice, Florence, and Milan.

5. In like manner, advancements were made in Western Europe in the fields of music, arts, science, rhetoric, literature, and humanism. The great contributors to these works of art included Saint Albertus Magnus, Shakespeare, Francis Bacon, Averroes, and other writers. These included works on Aristotlean scholasticism; the humanism of St. Thomas More; the plays and sonnets of Shakespeare; the French Montaigne and Francois Rebelais; the Italians Petrarch, Giovanni

Boccaccio, Lorenzo Valla; and Desiderius Erasmus in northern Europe. Many of these writers stressed Christian humanism. Rebelais and Shakespeare produced works stressing the intricacies of the human character. They had been inspired by the advances of Ancient Greece and Ancient Rome and by the revelations of the Renaissance, which produced painters and sculptors like da Vinci, who used math, among other tools, to advance their talents.

6. Specifically in the field of science, and especially starting from the 15th century on, humanistic faith in classical scholarship led to the search for ancient texts to increase knowledge. Influential scientists of the Renaissance included Galileo, Copernicus, Johannes Kepler, Tycho Brahe, Isaac Newton, and others.

MOHAMED AND THE ISLAMIZATION OF AFRICA

Interestingly, the founder of Islam, Mohammed, the prophet and messenger of God (Allah), was also a mighty product of the Middle Ages. Born in Mecca, Saudi Arabia, in 570 CE, Muhammad, or Muhammad-ibn Abdullah, initiated a cultural heritage of Islam that reached North Africa as early as 622 CE. In fact, North Africa became one of the earliest places in the world to embrace Islam as a religion. By the time of his death on June 8, 632 CE, Muhammad had started a powerful religion. He used his skills as an active diplomat, philosopher, orator, legislator, merchant, reformer, and military general to spread his religion and advance his mission as an agent of "divine action." Mohammed had humble origins, having become an orphan quite early in his life when his parents died, and he was raised by his uncle. At 25, he married, and moved to live in a cave in nearby mountains for medication and reflection. At 40, he received, in the month of Ramadan, his first revelation from God. At 43, Mohammed started preaching these revelations publicly, proclaiming that "God is One." Mohammed had followers already in the early years of his ministry.

As a prominent figure in African culture, Mohammad is well remembered in African history because of the large portion of Africa that became Muslim. He has a large number of followers on the African continent, with a mixed history of culture, Arab slavery, and slave trade that Arabs conducted as a very lucrative illegitimate business for 12 centuries, from the 7th to 19th centuries! Later in his life, Mohammed had to move out of Saudi Arabia when he realized that he was not too much liked in Mecca. So he moved to Medina (Yathrib) in 622, and that event marked the beginning of the Hijra, which is the Islamic calendar. The Qur'an (or Koran) is "The Word of God."

THE RISE OF THE OTTOMAN EMPIRE

The Middle Ages also witnessed the rise of the Ottoman Empire. This empire flourished from 1299 to 1923 CE. That period could be divided into

three eras: the Old Ottoman/Turkish Empire era, the Late Turkish Ottoman era, and the Modern Turkish Ottoman era. The conquests of the
empire lasted from the 16th to 17th centuries and produced three powerful cultural influences on three continents—Africa, in the north; Asia, in
the Middle East; and Europe in the south. In 1533, the empire stretched
from the Straight of Gibraltar and the Atlantic Coast of Morocco beyond
Gibraltar in the west, to the Caspian Sea and Persia. It also extended from
Austria-Hungary and parts of Ukraine in the north to Sudan, Eritrea,
Somalia, and Yemen in the south. The empire comprised 29 provinces
and Moldavia, Transylvania, and Wallachia. The Ottoman Turks played a
major role in the interactions made between the East and West for almost
six centuries. This helps explain the wide spread of Islam—to Spain, the
former Slavic republics, and some parts of Eastern Europe.

Like Europe, the Ottoman Empire had its trials and tribulations during
the Middle Ages: rising between 1299 and 1453 CE; growing between 1453
and 1683; and experiencing serious revolts and reforms between 1699 and
1827. The empire, however, declined as it tried to keep pace with modernization between 1828 and 1908. It was finally dissolved in 1908–1922.
Mainly, it fell because of its economic structure, which failed to sustain
the required growth necessary for development at home. This burden
strained the political, social, and other aspects of people's lives. The outcome was an economic malaise that lead to disintegration in political
power and influence.

AFRICA: MISSING THE BOAT IN THE MIDDLE AGES, OR
RECLAIMING/REDEEMING HER CIVILIZATIONS
IN THE 21ST CENTURY

The overarching argument about Africa of the Middle Ages is that if
Europe was able to make it beyond the medieval times despite many
trials and tribulations, then reasons must be sought and lessons
learned as to why Africa did not make it. How did Europe, tiny as the
continent is in physical and population size, attain peace, prosperity,
stability, and dominance over the whole world. Furthermore, if Europe
and Africa had many areas of similarity, then we must explain what
went wrong with/in Africa.

After all, Africa underwent a long and grand evolutionary process,
and was first in many respects as has been established in previous
chapters, and hence could—and should—have done better or should at
least have prevented many of her hardships from rocking her as hard
as they have throughout history. Why should Africa have done better
than she has? Two aspects are worth exploring in this regard: (1) the
evolutionary process from nomadic, stateless, and ad hoc existence to
permanent settlements with well-established cultures, civilizations, and

institutions; and (2) the governance and democratic aspects of African life under city-state and modern statehood as well as across-border relations that gave rise to international relations, foreign policy, and diplomacy for Africa and her countries and populations.

HIGHLIGHTS FROM THE LONG AFRICAN PATH

Highlights of important events in Africa's past along the long path that has carried Africa from a prosperous past to its current condition include the following, among many others:

- A shift from permanent settlements in 5000 BCE after the rise of the Great Sahara Desert to the governance and statehoods that evolved over the millennia in various parts of Africa;
- Discovery of vast natural and human resources and endowments that Africa possesses—agricultural crops; minerals, water, and energy resources; and the African peoples and their cultural diversity;
- Great visionary and mighty rulers such as King Ghana of Ghana, Queen Sheba of Ethiopia, Queen Hatshepsut of Egypt, Queen Anna Nzinga of Angola, King Abubaker of the Mali Empire, King Nabongo Mumia of Wanga in Kenya, the Kabaka Mutesa and the other Kabakas of Buganda in Uganda, etc.;
- Decentralized and centralized forms and systems of government in Africa;
- Great African minds such as Saint Simon the Cyrene of Cyrenaica; Saint Monica and her Son, Saint Augustine of Hippo, Tunisia; Saints Cyril and Catherine of Alexandria, Egypt; Saint Cyprian of Carthage; General Hannibal of Carthage; Shaka Zulu of Zululand; and
- Astute political minds and leaders of Africa and of Pan-Africanism, such as W.E.B. DuBois, Marcus Garvey, George Padmore, Wilmot Blyden, Jomo Kenyatta, Nnamdi Azikiwe, Abu Baker Taafawa Balewa, Julius Nyerere, Gamal Abdel Nasser, Ahmed Sékou-Touré, Pattrice Emery Lumumba, Tom Joseph Mboya, Joseph Masinde Muliro, Kwame Nkrumah, Ahmed Ben Bella, Habib Bourguiba, Moamar Qadhafy, Kenneth Kaunda, Nelson Mandela, Kamuzu Hastings Banda, Simeon Kapwepwe, General Muhammad Murtala, Emperor Haile Selassie, and Ketema Yufru.

All of these leaders of Africa and of Pan-Africanism—as well as their talents and skills, the moral imperatives of Christianity and Islam, and the means and resources that existed in Africa—were more than enough to put Africa at the top of the world. They were more than enough to have prevented the slave trade, forced the introduction of empirical statehood in Africa, forced the reign of international law and norms and principles, solidified African diplomacy and foreign policy that would have emerged solidly, forced the retention of African values and heritage and resisted the adaptations of untenable values and practices to cope with contemporary life in the world; ensured the retention of trade practices for self-reliance and ownership of Africa by Africa; and promoted education that must be appropriate to the African Condition, etc.

Major milestones on the African path to independence were the Pan-African congresses and meetings of the 1900s held in London in 1900, 1905, 1911, and 1919, especially the First Pan-African Congress of 1919, which petitioned the Versailles Treaty powers to help in the decolonization process for Africa by agreeing to administer the former colonial territories for Africa and the Africans. The fifth of Woodrow Wilson's 14 points, which were points formulated for the advancement of world peace, solidarity, and cooperation, also played a major role in the decolonization process of Africa. The fifth point related to the need to grant self-rule to the colonized territories around the world. It argued that poverty and size should never deter peoples and countries from gaining self-government and political independence. In 1921, the Second Pan-African Congress in London, Brussels, and Paris focused on the issue of ending the British exploitation, enslavement, and impoverishment of African colonial natives, granted African natives some self-government, and condemned England for ignorance about the colonized African natives, their lack of training, education, and proper preparation for political liberation. The Third Congress, in 1923 in London, Lisbon, and New York, repeated the African demands for home- or self-rule, and majority rule in Africa to replace the system of minority white rule in Africa—especially in Southern Africa (South Africa and Rhodesia). The Fourth Pan-African Congress, in 1927 in New York, adopted resolutions similar to those of the Third Congress. However, it was the Fifth Pan-African Congress held at Manchester, England, in 1945, and organized by George Padmore that actually culminated in Africa's decolonization completion. By that time, Africa had produced a good number of Pan-Africanists, including Hastings Banda of Malawi; Kwame Nkrumah of Ghana; Jomo Kenyatta of Kenya; Chief Abafame Awolowo of Nigeria; as well as W.E.B. DuBois of the United States, the organizer of the first Pan-African Congress in 1919, who was 77 years old during the Fifth Congress; and Marcus Garvey, a Jamaican immigrant to New York. The Fifth Pan-African Congress, held in October 1945, was the most elaborate of all the five congresses and was attended by many scholars, intellectuals, and political activists. Its outcome included the following:

- Adoption of resolutions and propositions aimed at the colonial powers, African leaders, and people against racial discrimination;
- Promotion of economic, political, intellectual, and other forms of cooperation;
- Identification of the beginning of the end of imperialism and colonialism in Africa, and hence the need to mobilize all Africans displaced in the decolonization process.

Mobilization of those affected by the African Diaspora meant all Afro-Americans, Afro-Cubans, Afro-Brazilians, Afro-Jamaicans, Afro-Canadians, etc. would have to be mobilized for the common good of all the peoples of African extraction. The Manchester Congress thus put on the table all the colonial issues confronting Africa, and called upon the Africans in Africa, the Africans in the African Diaspora abroad, and the international community, including the donor community of the ex-colonial powers, to join their forces and help Africa to help herself toward political independence and multidimensional development.

CONCEPTUAL UNDERSTANDING: FOREIGN POLICY AND DIPLOMACY

The Middle Ages not only produced most of the concepts of sovereignty, statehood, international ethics and law, and the "civilization" of states, but served as the time period in which Europe herself acknowledged her past shortcomings and embarked upon processes and procedures to correct mistakes. Issues relating to foreign policy and diplomacy were defined in very clear terms, especially following the emergence and flourishing of city-states in Europe and in Africa, with the rapid growth of commercial, diplomatic, and political contacts almost unheard of in earlier times. No wonder then that the Renaissance was born during medieval times!

Foreign policy, like diplomacy and international relations, cannot and does not operate in a vacuum. Therefore, foreign policy can best be understood if defined in the context of states, which are the primary subjects of international law. This raises the question of the sine qua non conditions or requirements for a foreign policy to exist or function correctly and legitimately. So, there must be a state and since this is the 21st century, the state has to be modern (i.e., with civilized statehood, implying the need for sovereignty). There must be a state system that involves processes and procedures from within the state and an international or global state system that involves states as political units engaging in relations between and among themselves. Sovereignty, which grants authority or the power of ultimate operation and control to a relatively small group of individuals called "the government" and who are empowered, usually through general elections, to govern (i.e., to lead, protect, and defend the citizens of that state and its assets and endowments, both at home and abroad, and to provide citizens/nationals with the security and other necessaries for their existence—all of which are better known as *national interests* of the state) must be present.

An international or global system is basically a community or society of sovereign, independent nations that decide to collaborate and coexist as sovereign entities, and follow (public) international law, which is a body of international rules and principles designed or intended to govern the behavior of states in their relations with each other and one another. "Civilization" implies an advanced status of civility, as well as of progress in material, cultural, and intellectual development.

Modern States: International Law, Sovereignty, and the Civilization of States

An appropriate discussion of these topics must first begin by defining important terms. "International law" is used here to refer to the system of implicit and explicit agreements that bind together nation-states in adherence to recognized values and standards that can be used as an instrument for providing order among nation-states because the rules of international law can help mitigate destructive conflicts. International law developed through international agreements and treaties between states, customary practices that evolved over the centuries and became codified in law, general legal principles common to a significant number of states growing into a corpus legis internationalis, and sources of information created by a community of legal scholars expressing their views on technical issues. Foreign policy and diplomacy as managers of relations among nations can, and will, function only if these "necessities" and requirements for civilized international behavior are in place.

"Modern and civilized states" refers to those political units recognized by the principles of international law and created after the Treaty of Westphalia of 1648. Those that came into existence after the year 1800 are often referred to as "civilized states," mainly because these political units were created after the emergence of international law in the Middle Ages during the16th century as a universal tool for finding solutions to inter-state problems without resorting to violence, conflict, or war. In that regard, diplomacy was to be employed for the resolution of disputes between and among nations through peaceful means. As a civilized state, a modern nation is a complex society or culture, often referred to as a "civilization."

"Civilization" is characterized by dependence on agriculture and commerce for national economic development; the presence of a state form of government empowered by sovereignty or the authority, power, and control to manage the affairs of state for its inhabitants; and the assembly and dwelling of a population or inhabitants living together voluntarily in a given territory with demarcated borders and who share common services and engage themselves in organized labor and occupational specialization. Such civilized society enjoys a high degree of advancement in the arts and sciences and experiences progressive urbanism and class stratification. These tenets of civilization are closely associated here with the common criteria of city and state, as opposed to rural and primitive (not in the sense of "savage," but meaning "elemental," or "natural," as in close to tribal culture and practices of rural areas or agricultural communities not living in city dwellings).

Thus, the states of today, including the United States, Jamaica, Kenya, Myanmar, Singapore, and the States of Africa, are supposed to be civilized, meaning that they should adhere to principles of public international law, find ways of resolving their disputes or disagreements via peaceful solutions without resorting to armed conflict, advance multidimensional development, assure peaceful coexistence, and honor existing universal standards of civilized behavior that guarantee justice and sovereign equality among nations.

State Sovereignty and Hugo De Groot as Father of International Law

The founder of the modern natural law theory was the Dutch legal scholar Hugo De Groot (1583–1645). As explained previously in this chapter, the birth of international law in the Middle Ages, as solidified in subsequent years by the concept of empirical ("modern") statehood and the state system that was embodied for the first time in the Westphalian mode, triggered the birth of the modern state system. The Bodin Doctrine created the modern state system. Jean Bodin defined sovereignty as the supreme power over citizens and subjects, unrestricted by laws. He argued that the key to securing order and authority lay in recognition of the state's sovereignty. He also argued that lawmaking was the main function of sovereignty, and that treaties signed by sovereign states should be observed by the sovereign.[1] It was, however, the 1648 Treaty of Wetsphalia that, for the first time, recognized new states as the component units of the world's political organization.

Sovereignty

The concept of "sovereignty" refers to the exercise of full control and power/authority over the state by its government. It is noteworthy that international law and other international legal instruments—like the UN Charter and the General Act of the African Union (AU)—grant sovereign equality, but not equal sovereignty. This means recognition and endorsement of the equality of states in international relations as law gives every state, small or large, poor or rich, *equal* treatment under international law and the UN Charter. This also means that a country as rich and huge as the United States has equal treatment under international law and relations, with, say, a nation as tiny as Cuba or Djibouti. At the UN, for example, the United States and Cuba have one vote each, even though the United States owns and controls a larger area of assets, power, population, and wealth, etc. than Cuba or Djibouti. With sovereignty comes territorial integrity, a population voluntarily agreeing to be bonded and loyal to the country and its government and living within delimited borders, and a relatively small group of people who govern (i.e., the government of that state).

Statehood

"Statehood" is of two types: empirical statehood and juridical statehood. Whereas the Treaty of Westphalia of 1648 introduced empirical statehood, the 1885 Accord of the Berlin Conference, which decreed the partition of Africa, for example, introduced juridical statehood. This is because that the Accord of the Berlin Conference, also known as the Kongokonferenz, which was held from of November 15, 1884 to February 26, 1885, was negotiated and signed at Berlin by the European Powers, the United States, and the Ottoman Empire, without any participation of Africa in that conference. Empirical statehood introduced the modern state system as we know it today not only for Europe, but also for the entire world, including the principles of separation of powers and the modern democratic system of government.

The "International State System" is also known as the global system. The various regions of the world, including Africa, are members and sub-systems of the international system. Every sovereign state, including the United States, participates in and conducts its external relations from within the international relations of the global system. Foreign policy is a vital instrument for managing international relations for the members of the global system.

Foreign Policy, Diplomacy, and National Interest

As stressed studying Chapter 3 of this volume, the expressions "foreign policy," "diplomacy," and "national interest," although singular, actually are meant in the plural. This is why they are also described as pluralitantum expressions. Thus, every time one sees phrases such as national interest, diplomacy, and foreign policy, one needs to understand them as being meant in the plural as a collection of many. This is because the diversity of cultures and national interests of the world require that the United States and other states formulate and implement different foreign policies and pursue different national interests with other nations. Thus, it is not possible for the United States to adopt one foreign policy toward all of Africa, which comprises 53 separate countries, for example. Therefore "U.S. policy toward Africa" really means "U.S. policies toward Africa!"

Foreign Policy in American and African Contexts

If policies are plans or specific courses of action or inaction taken by states in order to protect national interests and to achieve certain goals and objectives, then it is evident that whatever may be defined as "national goals and objectives" must be that country's national interests. In this regard, foreign policies are state policies that elevate domestic policies to the international arena and aim both at serving and fulfilling certain principles and purposes, as well as attaining and securing the goals previously defined and decided upon by the government of the state concerned. Foreign policy of the United States or of Kenya is thus the extension of American or Kenyan domestic policy, respectively. Foreign policy begins where domestic policy ends, and they both aim at preserving national security, which is a vital national interest. A state's citizens are its most vital and fundamental national interest, and their protection is central to national security.

In short, then, both African and U.S. foreign policy comprises the contacts, interactions, proactions, actions, and inaction that the African or U.S. government decides to take, or not to take, in order to promote, project, protect, preserve, propagate, or promulgate and defend the national interests of the country concerned, as well as the image and prestige of the nation on the international stage. Therefore, the foreign policy of the United States or of an African nation, like that of any other sovereign country or region, is the totality of actions, reactions, proactions, non-actions, and contacts that the country decides to take as a sovereign state in pursuit or fulfillment of the dictates (goals and objectives, demands, requirements, situations, etc.), of safeguarding national interests, both at home and abroad (in global or foreign environments). These actions or non-actions are carried out by the government-based diplomats, who act on behalf of the country they represent as members of the international system.

Diplomacy: Origins and Development

The word "diploma" comes from the Greek and means "folded in two." In ancient Greece, a diploma was a folded paper or certificate, such as was used in early times for state papers, charters, etc. In ancient Rome, during the reign of the Roman Empire, "diploma" described official documents such as passports or passes for travel on imperial roads that were stamped on double metal plates. Hence, this diploma provided a privilege, license, or degree conferred upon an individual who was a diplomat, messenger, or envoy, who took or carried state papers on behalf of a state or sovereign to another state or sovereign. In academic circles in later years, the certificate or diploma represented a degree that was conferred on a person after the completion of a course of study and, likewise, typically folded in two.

Diplomacy is the art, practice, and management of international affairs or international relations by negotiation or by conducting negotiations between representatives of groups or states. Diplomacy is thus the method by which these relations or affairs are adjusted and managed by diplomats—ambassadors, national envoys, and representatives.

Generally, these individuals are professionals who are trained in handling matters of state.

Like politics, diplomacy is a way of doing things—the management of affairs by diplomats. This is why diplomacy, like politics, is an art, and not a science. For in diplomacy, it is not what you do, but how you do it. In diplomacy, diplomats aim at using peaceful means to resolve disputes, wars, and differences between and among a diplomat's country or institution, and the host state or international organization possessing an international legal personality, like the UN. The differences are thus to be resolved by peaceful means through negotiation or persuasion, that is, without resort to wars, violence, the use of brute force, or armed conflicts. The idea is for the diplomat to take or obtain the maximum national advantage of issues, events, etc., for his/her country without the use of violence, and without maximum friction or resentment, ensuring the minimum disadvantage to the sending state or organization. Normally, the expressions "sending" or "host" country and "receiving" country are employed.

Diplomacy started as an instrument of cooperation in antiquity. Peace through negotiation was employed in ancient times. For example, in 1050 to 256 BCE, the Zhou Dynasty in China used diplomacy as defined above. Since then, this art has been practiced as a vital tool for the conduct of day-to-day business, and for the promotion and implementation of foreign policy between and among sovereign states, their representatives, and the representatives of international law in the conduct of foreign policy. The key term is "implementation."

In U.S. practice, for example, there are three constituent and basic elements of foreign policy, (i.e., national goals or interests, national principles, and national actions or non-actions) that are conveyed to fruition through diplomacy. A particularly interesting definition of diplomacy was given by Sir Ernest Satow (1843–1929), who defined diplomacy as the "application of intelligence and tact to the conduct of official relations between governments of independent states, extending sometimes to their relations with vassal states, more briefly still, the conduct of relations between states by peaceful means."[2] In this regard, diplomacy is the art of adjusting the varying and often clashing interests of states to the advantage of the state the diplomat represents, but also with a view to preserving amicable relations with other states where possible. Diplomacy is also the greatest protector, projector, and defender of national interest and image.

NATIONAL INTEREST IN AFRICAN AND OTHER EXPERIENCES

The most important factors in diplomacy and foreign policy are the national interests of the represented state—the goals and objectives to be attained or secured by the state in its relations with other states or international legal persons, whose nature as organizations of sovereign states, enjoy international legal personality under international law, and which empowers them to deal with sovereign countries as international persons. Foremost among national interests is the maintenance and protection of national security and protection of citizens of the country concerned. The most important national interest of any state is its citizens, but national assets, endowments, prestige, image, territorial integrity, and economic and cultural interests are also vital for national survival and prosperity. Hence, there is a need to maintain and protect these interests as well. National interests are thus the reasons, dictates, and requirements for the formulation and execution of foreign policy.

In short, diplomacy is not a science, but an art. It is a tool, and a means to an end. It is the greatest protector, projector, and defender of national interest and image. It is a means of managing international relations and implementing foreign policy decisions. Foreign policy and diplomacy are the managers of international relations. The expressions "foreign policy," "diplomacy," "foreign service," and "international relations" are often used in a casual manner and, as such, they are often misunderstood. But all of these terms are used to refer to many situations of dealings, purposes, relations, and circumstances pertaining to external affairs of a state.

Furthermore, a diplomat is the one who is negotiator in international matters and manager of inter-state relations, who aims at accomplishing the purposes of diplomacy to acquire the national interests of his/her country through representation; information gathering and communication for his state; negotiation and search for common ground among the national interests of different states, and for short-term and long-term solutions to problems and issues at stake; reduction of disagreement among different states and parties to negotiations; pursuit of international peace and security; management and resolution of conflict. Diplomats fill administrative and advocacy roles, pursue regional arrangements for economic integration, and mobilize resources for development. They deal with international organizations for the creation and management of world order and avoidance of international disorder; protect and promote the interests of their own states, and search for ways of peaceful coexistence among different states.

Diplomacy has been defined and described in diverse ways by various practitioners and writers.[3–7] The analysis of diplomacy and foreign policy as presented in this study, however, is based upon its author's reflections, perceptions, and practical experiences resulting from more than 35 years in international diplomacy and foreign policy.

A NEW PROCESS OF RECLAIMING AFRICAN CIVILIZATIONS

In the case of African foreign policy and diplomacy, they basically refer to the totality of actions, interactions, contacts and non-actions that every sovereign state in Africa decides to conduct and maintain with other African states, as well as with foreign states or other international legal persons, such as the United Nations. As plans or courses of action or non-action, foreign policies are extension of domestic policies that are, in effect, national goals or interests, national principles, and national actions/non-actions through which the goals or national interests of an African country are pursued by that country in its efforts to protect, promote, project, promulgate, propagate, and defend its interests, image, and prestige on the international scene.

The sources, dictates, and determinants of African foreign policy are many and varied, but they can be grouped into three broad categories: those that are purely domestic, those that are purely or wholly external, and those that relate to domestic and external events and issues. In like manner, African foreign policies have been based on three major ideologies or dictates: the dictates of nonalignment (which does not mean neutrality, but constructive engagement in the discussions and resolution of various issues and challenges), capitalism, and communism/socialism. Communism and capitalism were the two determinants of the Cold War in the years between 1947 and 1990, when the communist ideology collapsed and made way for the birth of a new world order based on "Cold Peace." However, the main determinants of African foreign policies, including the cultism, personalities, and lifestyles of the African leaders and the colonial heritage, have not changed.

This is where the question of solidifying African foreign policy and diplomacy becomes important. The premise of this book is that Africa "missed the boat" in the Middle Ages, when kingdoms, empires, super empires, city-states, and super city-states grew quickly with clear sovereignty in Africa. The Middle Ages provided a significant historical divide between ancient and modern times in Africa; but one is bound to ask the question as to what would have happened, and what would Africa be today, if her foreign policy and diplomacy had been solidified in medieval times? The Middle Ages can be regarded as the dividing era between past and present/modern processes, procedures, issues, and challenges in African foreign policy and international relations. The present writer holds the strong conviction that some of the ills and burdens that confront Africa today could have been averted and even avoided if, in the Middle Ages, some concrete and practical actions or measures had been taken to maintain the sovereignty of African political units, and to avoid many of the injustices and burdens that Europe subsequently inflicted on Africa and the African people. Maybe the European colonization of Africa would have been prevented if illegitimate trade in captured Africans had been avoided. Maybe some of the lost civilizations of Africa might have been saved if European colonization of Africa had been prevented. Maybe the transformation of Africa would have been prevented if the destruction of

African values by European (Western) civilization had been avoided. Maybe self-reliance, absolute African nationalism and patriotism and resource nationalism in Africa would have been assured if the African leaders—kings, emperors, presidents, and premiers—had solidified their governance, collaboration, and coordination *the African way*, and also had solidified their relations at national, African continental, and external levels. Maybe African values would have been protected and promoted in a durable fashion from medieval times if Africa had been left to develop according to her own pace and timetable, so as to guarantee the prevalence of African civilizations and tenable customs, traditions, and cultures.

THE TEACHING OF AFRICAN FOREIGN POLICY AND DIPLOMACY

The teaching of African foreign policy and diplomacy is another area that requires sustained and improved undertaking both in Africa and abroad. Courses on African diplomacy and foreign policy in colleges, universities, and in other institutions of higher learning should be enhanced globally. Courses can and should be developed on African foreign service and diplomacy; African international relations; African development and security; African economic development; international business in Africa; regional integration in Africa, including the East Africa Community (EAC), the Intergovernmental Authority on Development (IGAD); Africa and the international development practicum; Africa's presence in the UN, the Americas, and the Third World; and other courses on African studies and international relations of the UN system. These courses address African foreign policy and diplomacy, the global economy, public international organization and administration, African international relations in theory and reality, and the like.

AFRICAN FOREIGN SERVICE AND DIPLOMACY

Foreign service and diplomacy are central in the management of African international relations and foreign policy. These disciplines deserve particular attention in the discussion of international affairs. The following need to be addressed:

- Conceptual understanding of general foreign policy, global diplomacy, foreign service, national interest, and international relations in historical perspective;
- Prioritization of the issues, challenges, and problems in African diplomacy and foreign policies;
- Outline of the practical aspects of African international relations, foreign policy, and diplomacy;

- Outline and explanation of the making and implementation of African foreign policy;
- Outline of the origins, nature, development, and function of African diplomacy from pre-colonial times to the present;
- Description of the essence of African foreign policy and diplomacy—goals, objectives, and advantages to Africa and the world;
- Understanding of Africa's foreign policy and bilateral/multilateral diplomacy as practiced in the UN and the Third World/non-aligned nations;
- Explanation of the new and emerging issues and challenges in African international relations;
- Understanding of Africa's diplomacy and foreign policy toward the Third World, Europe, and the United States in the new millennium; and
- Understanding of the future of African foreign policy and diplomacy—roles of public opinion, African leaders, and external determinants.

AFRICA-U.S. RELATIONS: ESSENCE, DIVERSITY, DICTATES, AND IMPERATIVES FOR THE NEW MILLENNIUM

Traditionally and for historical reasons, Africa has had special relationships with the countries of Europe, especially those Western powers that became colonial masters in Africa. But as a subsystem of the global system, Africa has maintained strong relations with the United States and the Third World/non-aligned countries. Africa's relations with the United States can also be regarded as special, in view of the large presence of African Americans in the United States. The African Diaspora in the United States, and in the Americas in general, is a huge boon to the Western Hemisphere. In more recent years, this relationship has been given a new impetus by recent developments and dictates, which are bound to enhance African-U.S. relations even further. For example, for the first time in the history of the United States, an African American who is of Kenyan extraction, is president—Barack Obama.

A comparative examination of Africa's relations with the United States reveals a considerable number of divergent and similar characteristics that are analyzed as significant foundations of U.S. and African foreign policies and diplomacy. These determinants can be clustered into the following broad areas, among many others:

- Physical environment;
- Traditional values as foundations of the foreign policies and diplomacy of the United States and Africa;
- Impact of colonization colonial policies and practices of Europe as applied to the United States and Africa, struggles against European colonialism and colonization, and paths to decolonization and aftermath (including kinds of statehood after decolonization);

- Schools of thought on continental union and unity;
- Political doctrines stemming from the decolonization processes and procedures; and
- Public opinion.

Physical Environment

The United States, which is about the size of the Sahara Desert in Africa, is a vast country stretching for 6,105,985 square miles (9,826,630 square kilometers), housing 50 states and the District of Columbia, with an estimated population of 320,768,086 (estimated October 12, 2009). The United States is the single Super Power in the world today and as such is the most powerful country of the world.

Africa is a vast continent, the second largest continent on Earth after Asia, and stretching for 11,725,385 square miles (30,368,609 square kilometers) that include the adjacent island states in the Atlantic (Cape Verde, São Tomé and Príncipe, and Guinea-Bissau).

Impact of Colonization on the United States and Africa

Similarities between the colonization of what is now the United States (but was once 13 colonies in the New World) and Africa are striking. The United States and Africa both were colonized by Europe—the American colonies by Great Britain; and Africa by Great Britain, France, Germany, Portugal, Italy, Belgium, the Netherlands, and Spain. Both the United States and Africa were subjected to colonial policies and practices that aimed at exploiting, humiliating, transforming, impoverishing, and dominating them. Both had to fight to gain their political freedom and independence from the colonial yoke and dominance.

Initially, colonies were granted royal charters to protect them as colonial possessions of their European masters. They were known as the Royal Chartered Colonies in America and the Royal Chartered Companies in Africa, which initially administered the African Colonies for the European mother countries. Thus, initially, colonial administrations were executed by colonial agents who acted in those capacities until the European colonial administrators—Governors—were sent from Europe to the colonies.

European value systems were imposed on the colonies in Africa just as they were in the New World. With colonization came the systems and institutions of government, education, democracy, etc., of the colonial power. America and Africa became by-products of Western civilization, meaning the progression of values and systems from ancient Greece and Rome that were handed down to later generations and formed the building blocks of European civilization. These Western values became predominant throughout the entire world. Acculturating happened in America and Africa when the major European languages (English, Spanish, French, and Portuguese) became the principal languages of communication in the colonies and globally.

The decolonization process for both started in America. For the United States, it started in 1775 with the decision to fight to expel the British from America. For Africa, it began in 1776, with the Back to Africa Movement, whose origins spread with the African Diaspora's spirit of linkages to Africa, the Mother Continent. The Back to Africa Movement also promoted the idea that people of African American extraction should fight to gain their ancestral origins and to help the Africans involved in the African Diaspora to fight against every possible colonial exploitation and dominance as demonstrated by some European individuals and countries. These sentiments and movements against European dominance in North American and African colonies were enhanced in subsequent years by demands for ending slavery and the slave trade, which was abolished in 1807 in Britain (thanks to the efforts of British member of Parliament William Wilberforce and his peers). The slave trade in the United States ended at approximately the same time that U.S. President Thomas Jefferson signed a decree that became effective in the United States from January 1, 1808. In the United States, President James Monroe, through the Monroe Doctrine, and President Abraham Lincoln, through the Emancipation Proclamation and Executive Orders of 1862 and 1863, made historic contributions to the decolonization of Africa in the 19th century even before Africa was colonized officially following the Berlin Conference of 1884–1885.

In like manner, the Back to Africa Movement of the 1900s not only originated in the United States and the West Indies, but was fostered by freed African Americans of various interests—religious, intellectual, business, and political—such as W.E.B. DuBois, Marcus Garvey, Sylvester Williams, George Padmore, and many others who supported the repatriation of freed African Americans to Africa, as supported by the Monroe Administration, and which saw the establishment of a free African state called Liberia (in Latin, "Liber" means "free"), with its capital named Monrovia in honor of U.S. President James Monroe.

Thus, dating back to the 1800s, passionate African Americans such as Paul Cuffe of Massachusetts, and into the 1900s, others witnessed and supported the birth of Pan-Africanism as the precursor of African independence and political identity, as well as the major source of African foreign policy, diplomacy, and international relations.

By contrast, the impact and influence of colonization in both the United States and Africa exhibits divergencies that include the following:

The United States is a country, as expressed in its motto—ex pluribus unum: "out of many, just one." Africa is a continent—ex pluribus multi: "out of many, still many." The United States gained political independence through fighting and managed to retain one official language, possibly because the main colonial power was Great Britain. Other Europeans who settled in the United States adopted English as their main language.

Africa gained political independence either through fighting, negotiation, or by surrender by the colonial powers. Fighting involved armed struggles, violence, and wars of independence. Negotiation took place between the would-be independent African country leaders, who secured dates and conditions of political independence, and the administering authorities based upon progress made toward independence of the former Colonial Territories that were taken away from Germany and Italy, the defeated World War I Axis powers. The victorious/allied powers, gave the administering authorities, who acted on behalf of the League of Nations (LON), the right to administer and prepare the colonies for political independence. Territories taken away from Germany were given for administration and preparation for independence to Britain, France, Belgium, and South Africa. Southwest Africa (now Namibia) was taken away from Germany and given to South Africa to administer; Tanganyika was taken from Germany and given to Britain to administer; Ruanda-Urundi was taken from Germany and given to Belgium to administer; and parts of German Togo and German Cameroon were given to France to prepare for political independence. All of these became known as Mandated Territories of the League of Nations.

When the United Nations was created on October 24, 1945, responsibility for the Mandated Territories passed to the UN, and they became Trust Territories under the UN, which, in turn, gave these colonial territories to the same authorities to administer and prepare for political independence. Both the LON and the UN created organizations to deal specifically with the affairs of these African colonial territories. In the UN system, the organization is called the Trusteeship Council of the United Nations. Over the years, all these territories gained independence and became African Republics.

The method of gaining political independence in Africa by surrender involved times when the colonial power weighed the benefits of continued colonization and concluded that the colonies were not worth retaining. This decision could have been reached because the expenses vis-à-vis the benefits accruing from continued colonization; the costs in human life that were being incurred when the populations of the colonial master were, in some cases, being slaughtered like chickens; and the tarnished image on the international scene of the continued colonization of Africa and elsewhere around the globe.

The policies and practices of divide and rule worked best in the vast continent of Africa. Unlike in the United States, many colonial languages emerged as official languages, replacing the mother tongues and African languages of the colonial possessions.

The United States inherited the Westphalia system of statehood, which is empirical, whereas in Africa, the colonial powers introduced a system of juridical statehood. Thus, for America, it was the 1648 Treaty of Westphalia that has been followed since 1776 in statehood issues. In Africa, it was the Accord of the Berlin Conference of 1884–1885 that has come to be followed in statehood affairs.

The American Revolution raged against Great Britain between 1775 and 1783. The causes of that revolution can be clustered into economic, social, and political changes that happened in the American colonies before 1750. These included the French and Indian War of 1754–1763, which changed the relationship between the American colonies and their mother country, and the decade of conflicts that existed between the British government and the colonies. In particular, there were the British parliamentary legislative acts that triggered revolution against the British by the Colonies. These British parliamentary acts exacting duties and responsibilities on the Colonies that were totally unacceptable to the American people included the Currency Act of 1764; the Quartering Act of 1765, which favored British troops in barracks in New York and elsewhere in America; the Stamp Act of 1765; the Townshend Acts of 1767, which exacted excessive taxes from the Colonies to pay for British government of the Colonies; and many others. The Colonies reacted by staging the Boston Tea Party in Boston Harbor in 1773, which inspired the colonists to demand the return of British tea ships to Great Britain with all the tea and without any tax payments whatsoever by the Colonies (at great expense to Great Britain). A group of American colonists disguised as Indians boarded the British ships on December 16, 1773, and dumped all of the tea into the harbor.

The fight against colonial occupation in Africa was waged through guerilla warfare, sabotage, and rebellion against colonial policies and practices. Also, in Africa, there was not just one revolution, as there was in the American colonies, but many wars of independence, since the European colonies in Africa gained their independence at different times. As explained previously in this chapter, some African colonies were granted independence by negotiation and others by surrender, but the majority gained independence rightly and properly by fighting for it.

First-Generation Leaders of the United States and Africa

The men (and, to a lesser extent, women) in the African and the American colonies who led their respective countries to political independence have been referred to in various ways and by different titles. They have been called first generation leaders, the founding fathers, the framers, the founders, the fathers of the nation, etc. These individuals either suffered because of colonization or lost their lives. Those who survived became the first rulers of their respective countries.

In the newly formed United States of America, the heroes of the revolution for independence became the first several presidents and vice presidents of the nation. In Africa, they became first prime minister and then president of the nation. In the United States, unlike in Africa, the founders of U.S. independence had been both in America and in Europe.

Most of the first leaders of the United States of America had been signers of the Declaration of Independence. That historic conference, the Constitutional Convention, held from May 25 to September 17, 1787, was attended by 57 delegates. These revolutionaries came from well-respected professional, academic, and business backgrounds:

- All were well-educated men in various trades,
- Many were prominent statesmen in national affairs,
- Four were governors,
- At least 29 served in the Continental Army of the United States,
- Thirty-five were lawyers,
- Many were judges,
- Thirteen were merchants,
- Six were land speculators and businessmen dealing in estate affairs,
- Eleven were business experts in securities,
- Two were small farmers,
- Eight were public officials,
- Twelve were slave owners,
- Three were retired economists, and
- Two were scientists.

Most were natives of the 13 original colonies, and some had religious affiliations, whereas others had no religion at all. Most were Protestants, but three were Catholic.

First-Generation Leaders of Africa

In Africa, the founding fathers of Pan-Africanism and of African liberation had been in Africa and/or in the United States. These included Edward Wilmot Blyden, W.E.B. DuBois, Marcus Garvey, Martin Delaney, Paul Cuffe Garnet, Henry Highland, George Padmore, Sylvester Williams, and Aimé Césaire of Martinique, among others.

The other founding fathers of African independence who were mostly based in Africa included Kwame Nkrumah of Ghana, Haile Selassie of Ethiopia, Jomo Kenyatta of Kenya, Hastings Banda of Malawi, Patrice Lumumba of Congo Leopoldville, Chief Hezekia Oladipo Davies of Nigeria, Nnamdi Azikiwe of Nigeria, Alhaji Abubakar Tafawa Balewa of

Nigeria, Gamal Abdel Nasser of Egypt, Ahmed Sékou-Touré of Guinea, Ben Bella of Algeria, Julius Nyerere of Tanganyika, Apollo Milton Obote of Uganda, J. Felix Houphouet-Boigny of Côte d'Ivoire, Leopold S. Senghor of Senegal, William Tubman of Liberia, Kenneth Kaunda of Northern Rhodesia (Zambia), Joshua Nkomo of Southern Rhodesia (Zimbabwe), and Chiefs Ndabaningi Sithole of Southern Rhodesia and Albert Luthuli of South Africa, as well as Nelson Mandela of South Africa, and others. These and other African leaders played major roles in the decolonization of the African continent.

Schools of Political Thought and Doctrines in the United States and Africa

In the United States, political philosophies were derived from earlier writers and thinkers such as John Locke Thomas Hobbes, René Descartes and other thinkers of the 17th and earlier centuries. Doctrines like the English Magna Carta of 1215, as well as the religions doctrines of earlier years (e.g., Lutherism, Protestantism, and Calvinism), also left their mark. In Africa, political doctrines and thoughts were based upon Pan-Africanism, a rejection of imperialism and colonialism, as well as African Socialism and identity. In the United States, it was democracy; but in Africa, it was unity.

In both the United States and Africa, these doctrines revealed themselves during the drafting of the documents of independence, the respective constitutions and charters. In both places, the main fears evolved around tyranny, domination, and injustice which were to be avoided and stopped. Likewise, fairness of all concerned was to be assured—at national, regional, and continental levels. In the United States, it was at the signing of the Declaration of Independence in 1776 and the U.S. Constitution in 1787 that doctrines collided and had to be sorted out. In Africa, it was in the charting of independence philosophies and unity that differences appeared, starting from the first Conference of Independent African States held at Accra, Ghana, in April 1958. In both cases, three schools of thought emerged. In America these schools of thought were known as Federalists, Anti-Federalists, and Loyalists. In Africa, they were known as Radicals, Moderates, and Minimalists. The main aim in the African case was to attain African unity in post-colonial times.

Political Doctrines in America

In 1776, Thomas Payne supported and advanced the cause of independence when he wrote a pamphlet entitled *Common Sense* that challenged the authority of the reigning monarch of England, George III, over the American colonies. *Common Sense* was against every monarchical form of government, but it was the first document to publicly suggest independence from colonial rule. The year 1776 also marked the start of the American Revolution, when on July 2, 1776, the Continental Congress voted in favor of independence, and on July 4, 1776, the Declaration of Independence was approved and circulated to all the 13 colonies for ratification.

War raged on between Great Britain and the United States until November 30, 1782, when the Treaty of Paris, negotiated at a peace conference held at Paris, was signed between Great Britain and the United States. This treaty demanded the withdrawal of all British troops from U.S. soil. On April 15, 1782, the Continental Congress ratified the treaty containing the preliminary articles of peace with Britain. The British had been defeated and lost the American Revolutionary War!

It was, however, at the signing of the U.S. Constitution, held at the Philadelphia Constitutional Convention of May 14 to September 18, 1787, that the struggle for political unionism was fought among the American leaders. There were 55 delegates to the Philadelphia Constitutional Convention, representing 12 states (Rhode Island did not send a delegation). What helped the 13 original states was that they held in common one enemy: Great Britain. However, fundamental differences occurred when the young nation's early leaders discussed the issues of sovereignty, federation, power sharing by the states, management of the affairs of the United States in such a way that there would be a system of checks and balances, size of the states, wealth and money, power, as well as slave trade and slavery (which, although hotly debated, was left unresolved).

General George Washington, who lead the army which defeated Great Britain in the American Revolutionary War, emerged quickly as the most respected leader and became the first president of the United States. There were other leaders who gained considerable respect, such as Roger Sherman of Connecticut, the author of a document called the Connecticut Compromise which merged the two main plans on the table: one for the big states, authored basically by James Madison; another called the New Jersey Plan, favoring the small states. Other suggestions for how to structure the new government were the Pinckney Plan proposed by South Carolina's Charles Cotesworth Pinckney, and the Hamilton Plan proposed by New York's Alexander Hamilton. Others such as Thomas Payne, Benjamin Franklin, James Madison (considered the "Father of the Constitution"), Thomas Jefferson (who drafted the Declaration of Independence), and George Mason (known as the "Father of the Bill of Rights") voiced their opinions and made their proposals.

Roger Sherman's Connecticut Compromise, dated June 11, 1787, blended the Virginia and New Jersey Plans and proposed the two-house national legislature that exists to this day and is composed of the Senate and the House of Representatives, which together form the U.S. Congress. His plan was endorsed on July 23, 1787. The thorny issues were the ones relating to slavery and the powers of the central government. George Mason was the architect of the Virginia Plan and of decentralized power to avoid the kind of tyranny that the British had imposed on the Colonies. Consequently Mason, together with Edmund Randolph, Elbridge Gerry, and Patrick McHenry, even though they remained at the Convention, refused to sign the Constitution unless it had a Bill of Rights attached to it. Thirteen other delegates also refused to sign the Constitution, and even left the convention before it was closed. Others who signed the Constitution did so with the full expression of the wish and understanding that a Bill of Rights would be drafted and attached. George Mason had drafted the state of Virginia's Bill of Rights and was instrumental in the creation of the U.S. Bill of Rights, which added the first 10 Amendments to the U.S. Constitution.

Of the Founding Fathers of the Constitution, seven are particularly remembered, and are often referred to as key. These are as follows:

- Benjamin Franklin, who signed both the American Declaration of Independence and the Constitution;
- George Washington, general of the Continental Army who became the first U.S. president;
- John Adams, who became the first U.S. vice president;
- Thomas Jefferson, who became the third U.S. president;
- John Jay, who became the first U.S. attorney general;
- James Madison, who became the fourth U.S. president; and
- Alexander Hamilton, who became the first U.S. secretary to the treasury.

However, others influential in shaping the new U.S. government have to be mentioned, such as James Monroe, George Mason, and Thomas Payne. Monroe was a member of the Continental Congress who became the fifth U.S. president. Payne was a bookseller and intellectual whose *Common Sense* was a pivotal document in the struggle for American independence and whose *Rights of Man* presented a powerful case for human and individual rights. Mason's influence is shown in the Bill of Rights to the U.S. Constitution.

Radicals

In the United States, the leaders who were Anti-Federalists wanted the States to have protection and to avoid any possible tyranny from the central government. Therefore, the central government should not be allowed to be tyrannical. There must be a system of checks and balances. In this regard, the Virginia delegation to the Constitutional Convention, led by George Mason, was instrumental in demanding that there be a number of rights attached to the Constitution. Mason became the architect of the Bill of Rights, having himself authored a Bill of Rights in his home state, Virginia. Mason was joined by 15 other radicals (Alexander Martin of North Carolina; Caleb Strong of Massachusetts; George Wythe of Virginia; James McClurg of Virginia; John Francis Mercer of Maryland; John Lansing Jr. of New York; Luther Martin of Maryland; Oliver Ellsworth of Connecticut; Robert Yates of New York; William Houston of New Jersey; William Houstoun of Georgia; William Pierce of Georgia; William R. Davie of North Carolina; and Patrick Henry of Virginia). Rhode Island was not represented.

Of the 16 radical delegates, 13 left the Convention before it closed. Those who remained at the Convention but refused to sign the Constitution were George Mason and Edmund Randolf of Virginia, and Elbridge Gerry of Massachusetts—these were the Anti-Federalists. Thomas Jefferson was a radical, but Washington was a moderate; both also came from Virginia.

In Africa, the radicals were the leaders who supported Kwame Nkrumah's call to "Seek Ye First the Political Kingdom," and called for the creation of a United States of Africa, in which the leaders of the individual states would be "small fish in a huge ocean." This call had been made by Nkrumah at the First Conference of Independent African States, which he convened at Accra in April 1958, in order to map out a strategy for the kind of political union that independent Africa might pursue. Nkrumah's doctrine did not get the unanimous support of all. Instead, serious differences emerged. The other groups were the Monrovia Group led by William Tubman of Liberia and Nigeria's N. Azikiwe and Alhaji Abubakar Tafawa Balewa, and was also known as the Group of Moderates. The other school was the Brazzaville Group.

The Radicals included the leaders of Egypt, Mali, Guinea, Tanganyika, Uganda, Libya, Morocco (moderate host), and Algeria. The foreign minister of Ethiopia, Ketema Yufru, also attended the Casablanca Group for Emperor Haile Selassie. The Casablanca Group met in June 1960 and January 1961 to discuss collective measures for dealing with the assassination of Premier Patrice Lumumba. They also met at Cairo in June 1962 to create Pan-African Advisory Political, Economic, and Cultural Committees.

The Moderates Were Africa's Federalists

In the United States after the end of colonial rule, the moderates such as George Washington, John Adams, and James Madison were called Federalists, and Anti-Federalists were considered radicals.

In Africa in 1960, the majority of leaders in the transition for independence were also moderates who called for a strong, central government. It was the Monrovia Group led by William Tubman (1895–1971) of Liberia, and the two leaders of Nigeria, Nnamdi Azikiwe (1904–1996) and Tafawa Belewa (1912-1966), that became known as the Group of Moderates seeking to observe international norms of independence and the dictates of the UN. They avoided too much extremity, as that fostered by the Casablanca Group, a group of radicals led by Kwame Nkrumah of Ghana and Ahmed Sékou-Touré of Guinea who were calling for a United States of Africa, and too much looseness as advocated by the Brazzaville Group, who wanted to remain closely allied with France. According to the Monrovia Group, therefore, it was necessary to "be a big fish in a small pond." The group included the leaders of Cameroon, Togo, Somalia, Chad, Mauritania, Sierra Leone, Tunisia, Congo Leopoldville (a Belgian colony, as opposed to Congo Brazzaville, a French colony), Liberia, Nigeria, Ethiopia, and Dahomey (now known as Benin).

The Brazzaville Group met in May 1960 in Monrovia to strongly oppose the Casablanca approach as being too harsh. The Casablanca Group dismissed the Brazzaville approach as being too loose and too minimalist. The second meeting of the Monrovia Group was in Monrovia in May 1961, and this served as the group's first summit. Soon thereafter, the Monrovia Group was joined by the Brazzaville Group, which had advocated strong ties with the ex-colonial powers for the purpose of engaging in diplomacy and keeping close to the former colonial powers. The Brazzaville Group's 12 countries included Cameroon, Congo Brazzaville, Côte d'Ivoire, Dahomey (Benin), Upper Volta (Burkina Faso), Gabon, Niger, Madagascar, Central African Republic, Senegal, Chad, and Mauritania.

The second summit of the Monrovia Group was held at Lagos, Nigeria, on January 25–30, 1961. In 1962, the summit set up charters and resolutions leading to the Organization of African Unity (OAU) Summit of May 1963 at Addis Ababa, Ethiopia.

The Brazzaville Group were the minimalists. They strongly supported the African and Malagasy Union (UAM), which they had created in 1960 at Brazzaville. They became known as the Group of UAM Countries, met at Yaoundé, Cameroon in March 1961, and adopted resolutions on African cooperation for French-speaking African states, and a resolution on convening a Pan-African conference at Yaoundé in 1961.

The Foreign Minister of Ethiopia attended the Brazzaville meetings as well. In order to bridge the gaps, the Foreign Minister of Ethiopia advised the Ethiopian emperor to convene a summit of the African states at Addis Ababa at which they should iron out their differences and adopt an African unity approach. Ethiopian Emperor Haile Selassie convened the summit which, on May 25, 1963, adopted the OAU Charter.

This charter created the OAU as an African unity organization that was a product of a compromise between African statesmen who wanted political union of all independent African States.

Thus, in the United States, the minimalists were the Loyalists, the moderates were Federalists, and radicals were Anti-Federalists. The Federalists were the radicals in Africa, and the Anti-Federalists were the moderates. Each was the opposite of the other.

In both cases, developments in the decolonization process laid important foundations that defined African and U.S. foreign policy, diplomacy, and international relations.

Public Opinion

Public opinion in the areas of foreign policy and international relations plays a more important role in the United States than in Africa. In fact, public opinion is a great shaper of U.S. foreign policy. As Africa's democratization matures, public opinion will have to be taken increasingly into account in the decision-making processes of African foreign policy establishments.

SUMMARY: FROM AMERICAN TERRITORIES TO AMERICAN BRITISH COLONIES TO UNITED STATES OF AMERICA

The colonization of America by the British started in the late 17th century, and reached its peak when the 13 original American colonies (Georgia, Delaware, North Carolina, South Carolina, Pennsylvania, Virginia, New Jersey, New York, Connecticut, Rhode Island, New Hampshire, Massachusetts, and Maryland) were established, and a protectorate—which was the Kingdom of Hawaii in the Pacific Ocean. The colonization process of America started with a small settlement of Europeans, initially from England, in Jamestown, Virginia, in 1607.

The 13 American colonies were chartered, meaning, they were founded as settlements of individuals from England, and then became royal colonies under British rule. The first English colonial settlement was in Jamestown in 1607. Others followed. At the beginning of the 18th century, the British were joined by the French. The English colony at Jamestown was followed just a few years later by the Pilgrims who arrived at Plymouth in Massachusetts in 1620, on a ship called the *Mayflower*. Other European-American colonies appeared in subsequent years under the reign of England's King George III. Many colonial settlers were escaping tyranny and religious persecution in England and Europe. Nonetheless, English rule in North America went on for 200 years, ending only with the Treaty of Paris of 1783. The Constitutional

Convention started on May 14 and lasted until September 18, when the Constitution was signed in Philadelphia, Pennsylvania.

THE AMERICAN EXPERIENCE IN BRIEF HISTORICAL OUTLINE

From the general comments that have been made so far in this chapter, the following is evident:

- Foreign policy is not an end in itself, but a means to an end.
- Foreign policy embraces a broad spectrum of aspects: political, economic, cultural, social, environmental, military, moral, ideological, psychological, diplomatic, and other aspects of a country's overall policy.
- Since foreign policy begins where domestic policy ends, both are aspects of national policy, which has to be taken as a whole. If, for example, we take the question of poverty in America, the United States cannot, and should not ignore the gravity of poverty in the United States. The years 1930–1980, for instance, were years of increasing governmental involvement in social welfare. That was because before the Great Depression of the 1930s, the poor of the United States had suffered gravely, mainly from weaknesses in the economy, not from moral flaws. In the early 1960s, poverty was a grave burden, but the scarcity of information and knowledge among most Americans about poverty in the United States was appalling. In the 1950s, very little help was extended to the more than 40 million poor in the United States, who were about one-fifth of the American population. Such neglect does have negative repercussions in a country's dealings with other nations. In Africa, the poverty syndrome has been haunting the majority of the African people for decades. The paradoxical connection to this is that Africa is very wealthy in natural resources, and yet it is still the poorest continent on Earth—poorer now than 25 to 50 years ago!
- Foundations of U.S. foreign policy were embedded in the American Dream of opportunity and self-reliance. The foundations of African policy have been embedded in hugely diverse determinants. For now, let us briefly examine the American situation.

Although the comments on the American condition in this study put emphasis on the American policies and diplomacy mainly toward Africa starting from the 1960s to the end of the first decade of the new millennium, it is worthwhile to recall the origins and limits of U.S. foreign policy and the origins of the American Dream—values, ideals, principles, customs, and traditions, as well as political and socioeconomic goals. In this regard, three legal instruments are particularly noteworthy:

1. The Mayflower Compact, alias the Covenant of New Plymouth, signed on November 20, 1620 by a group of English settlers that set sail for America on the *Mayflower* for various reasons, including the search for religious

freedom and economic betterment. The compact served as the basis of government for the Pilgrims' first privately built permanent colony in and around the seaports of Plymouth, Massachusetts.

2. The Declaration of Independence, which was drafted by Thomas Jefferson, and adopted by the Continental Congress on July 4, 1776.

3. The U.S. Constitution of September 17, 1787 (although it was actually signed in the morning of September18, 1787).

These first legal instruments solidified, for the United States, a system of government that would ensure democratic principles, among which was the separation of the branches of government; a clear and effective role of public opinion in government through free speech; and tolerance of contrasting laws in the various states, whose implementation could make it extremely difficult for the executive branch of the government to formulate and implement policies at the federal level that might be inconsistent with local and/or state interests as represented in the U.S. Congress. This American experiment with a system of "checks and balances" in government, is unique in the world. This writer has been to 68 nations around the globe and wanted to know how their systems of government function. The writer has not observed any government system that works like the American system—it is a remarkable separation of powers in a governmental process.

In the United States, however, as in any other nation, the doctrines, policies, and practices, of government depend basically on the kind of leader that one has has to deal with. A leader has the sole duty of assembling a team to be members of the ship that he or she captains. The leadership of George W. Bush is a memorable case in point. The Bush Administration was generally perceived as a government that decided to ignore the wishes of the nation and declared a war by choice on Iraq based upon erroneous principles, and with a stubbornness that was perceived to have ignored every kind of wise advice against the war. A situation like that puts an administration of the United States on a strong collision course in the system of checks and balances that characterizes U.S. governance and government, and the results in such circumstances can be enormously heavy losses to the nation both at home and abroad. That was the case, most unfortunately, with the war and conflicts in Iraq lasting for the entire two terms of the George W. Bush Administration. Whatever the motivations that may trigger the actions of a U.S. administration, be they an arrogance of power, ideology, and unilateralism, or a belief that as a single Super Power the United States can do things globally unchecked, contradictions and a tarnishing of the U.S. image on the global stage is inevitable, and the consequences and losses that arise are heavy and grave in human and material resources. It is only in a system of strong checks and balances that such blunders can be avoided and corrected. This is what makes the U.S. governmental system unique. The outcry is to see what lessons can be, and are, derived from such colossal political misjudgments. The defense of national interest is paramount, but national interests have to be defended correctly, and not via the dictatorship of dogma and arrogance of power. One big lesson is that a government should not decide to try something new just for the sake of it, or under the pretext that "it is in defense of national interest." The second fundamental lesson is that no one vis-à-vis the American political system can imagine a scenario where this system of separation of powers can be erased from the face and blood of the United States. Actually, it was King George III who facilitated and shaped this future spirit of America by his stubborn and exploitative attitudes toward the American colonies, his very heavy taxation, and ultimate aim of subjecting the American colonies and their inhabitants to his absolute control, which stirred the colonies to complete revolution, ending in the eradication of British colonialism in America.

Then came Thomas Jefferson's draft resolution of independence for the colonies that was debated, revised, rewritten, and finally adopted on July 4, 1776. The reaffirmation of those ideals in the Constitution of United States opened a Pandora's Box for future foreign policy bills of rights by governments around the globe, by intergovernmental organizations (e.g., the League of Nations and UN), and even by the legislative bodies of developing countries. From the foundation of U.S. democracy and government have emerged the following 10 traditional areas of U.S. foreign policy:

1. Europe: NATO, EU, etc.;
2. East Asia and the Pacific: relations with China, ASEAN, Indonesia-Indochina, etc.;
3. Near East and South Asia: Arab-Israel Dispute, Turkey, Egypt, Mediterranean Region, other Middle Eastern nations, etc.;
4. The Western Hemisphere: Latin America and the Caribbean, the inter-American system, the Monroe Doctrine, a unique position vis-à-vis Europe;
5. Africa: Liberia—a U.S. creation, unique political and economic developments, regionalization, regionalism, and regional integration: very poor performance of the United States except under the Kennedy Administration of the 1960s. It was a fascinating period during the creation of the Peace Corps and of the containment of the second scramble for Africa that was ideological. The challenge to the United States toward Africa has been boosted by the election of Barack Obama, the first African American to the United States presidency. For President Obama, the challenge is a double-edged sword: he is an American and not an African president. Therefore, his primary duty is to serve Americans, not Africans. However, he has to create a legacy that has to be unique toward Africa. In many African countries, including the country of his immediate extraction, Kenya, not only is

President Obama revered as an illustrious son of Kenya and Africa, but it is expected that he has to do something concrete and practical to help Africa. That expectation will be echoed among the people of the African Diaspora, especially the African Diaspora in the United States. Therefore, if President Obama does not develop a clear legacy toward Africa when he is president of the United States, history might not be kind to him. Moreover, other African American aspirants to the U.S. presidency will be judged, wrongly, on how the first African American governed while in office.

If President Obama does well during his presidency, then he will boost the chances of relatively ready support to future African American aspirants to the U.S. presidency. If not, then they will be reminded day and night, again wrongly, of the failures or lack of legacies of the first African American president of the United States. So, the opponents will argue for not putting another African American in the White House. Under these circumstances, it should be really difficult for one to envy President Obama. But all must help him to succeed. For his success will be their success in the future. If therefore one were to advise President Obama toward Africa, then one would have to remind the president of the need for him to develop a strategy toward Africa that will form a legacy for him. It could be just doing a simple thing for Africa. For example, helping Africans to build a Pan-African Hospital for HIV/AIDS in Africa; or requesting the African leaders/presidents and premiers to convene an African summit which President Obama would chair in Africa or the United States, as part of his U.S. policy toward Africa, and aim to get African leaders to agree to certain fundamentals for the common good of Africa. Examples of needed agreement in Africa include the following:

- Having African leaders agree to stop expatriations of capital via corruption practices, and invest the funds in and/or for the development of Africa;
- Eradicating poverty in Africa;
- Using African human and natural resources;
- Finding solutions to African problems using African means and methods, (especially to stop conflicts and wars, tribalism and ethnocentrism, the border and irredentism issues);
- Providing education appropriate to Africa;
- African Socialism, Ubuntu, and Amana;
- Eradicating leadership inefficiencies; and
- Eradicating most of Africa's paradoxes, especially that concerning acculturation, whereby Africa can reclaim her civilizations and redeem them in the 21st century.

If President Obama can help Africa to attain any or several of these goals and objectives for Africa, then he will be assured of a splendid legacy toward Africa that will be historically most significant;

6. Economic Affairs: not terribly impressive in the Third World, declining ODA performance, very frustrating to Africa and the rest of the developing world;

7. International Security: Reagan Administration "tear down this wall, Mr. Gorbachev," and the Strategic Arms Limitation Talks (SALT). Reagan and Gorbachev developed a unique working relationship. A new world order, better perhaps to be described as a new world disorder on the watch of a single Super Power, with a "big stick." Politics; Cold War politics, has been more of a frustration and failure than anything else;

8. International organizations and law: treaties and agreements, diplomacy, etc., and poor performance;

9. Social and scientific affairs: UN conferences on women; The U.S. delegation to the UN Conference on Women in Beijing in China in September 1997 was led by then First Lady Hillary Clinton. Too much lecturing on human rights in UN by U.S. delegations yet the human rights situation in the United States has not been the best! No solutions have been found, for example, on immigration problems posed by arrivals from Mexico, etc.; and

10. Management: Failed diplomacy in many aspects (e.g., on Bill Clinton's watch, there were many gross human rights violations and genocides in Rwanda and Somalia; under George W. Bush's watch there was unnecessary war in Iraq, conflicts in Sudan, etc.

The current global economic and financial crisis that started in the United States in 2008; global warming and climate change; the WTO stalled negotiations; protectionism and lack of debt relief for some developing country governments; international terrorism; disease and poverty; ignorance (illiteracy) in the Third World. The need to overhaul the education system in the United States at the primary and secondary levels to make them at par with the international system; implementation of the millennium development goals (MDGs), structural adjustment policies (SAPs), Highly Indebted Poor Countries (HIPC), and Small Island Developing States (SIDS); Washington Consensus; environment and development; Cold Peace and politics; Oil: what strategy? Food security; human rights, refugees, and displaced peoples; Economic insecurity and instability; disease and pandemics: HIV/AIDS; Ebola, Yellow Fever; Highland Fever; Onchocerciasis; TB; Malaria, etc. Empowerment of disadvantaged strata of society, especially in Africa.

President Abraham Lincoln's Emancipation Proclamations of September 22, 1862, and January 1, 1863; the Monroe Doctrine of December 2, 1823; Woodrow Wilson's 14 Points for the League of Nations, including Point 5 which was for self-rule for colonized peoples of the world; Some foreign policy blunders (e.g., at the UN when some U.S. diplomats get away with howlers during UN decision-making sessions); Failure to implement the Uniting for Peace Resolution of 1950 over the North Korean crisis; Failure to address genocides, poverty syndromes, debt and cancellation efforts of some countries; What strategy for the world by the United States as the only Super Power? Leadership deficiency for the free world.

The viewpoints of this writer are, however, that things in Africa would be quite different today if no foreign invasions of the continent had happened;

this is especially the case if the African path to the future would have been shaped by Africa and Africans in the Middle Ages—that is, if Africa's foreign policy and diplomacy would have been solidified in medieval times.

NATIONAL INTEREST AND FOREIGN POLICY—EXAMPLE OF AN AMERICAN PRACTICE: 2001–2008

The impact of U.S. foreign policy (formulation and implementation) depends on the personality and character of the president. An active president breeds effective foreign policy like John Kennedy, Richard Nixon, and Jimmy Carter did.

A remarkable practice in U.S. foreign policy was demonstrated when George W. Bush took office in 2001 and was president for two terms. The doctrine introduced by Vice President Dick Cheney and Secretary of Defense Donald Rumsfeld was noteworthy. Before becoming vice president, Cheney with colleagues formulated a strategy in 1997 called the Project for a New American Century (PNAC). The proponents of the project were Cheney, Rumsfeld, Richard Perle (Assistant Secretary of State in the George H. W. Bush administration), and Paul Wolfowitz (Secretary of Defense in the George W. Bush administration). They presented a neo-conservative approach in military and corporate networking.

In contrast, Kennedy's foreign policy was very popular in Africa because it stressed the Peace Corps and assistance to Africa, India, etc. in nation-building to prevent the spread of communism in Africa; to promote social and economic development of Africa and the Third World; to strengthen governments in those areas so that they could defend their security and win the support of their citizens. CIA aid went to foreign governments to help them attain internal security and enable them to cooperate in fighting insurgencies inspired and financed by the communists. To show his priority for Africa, Kennedy's first cabinet appointment was the assistant secretary of state for African affairs.

A CULTURAL COMPARISON BETWEEN AFRICA AND THE UNITED STATES

A brief cultural comparison between Africa and America reveals the following value systems, assuming that a value is something of worth, whether tangible (material), or intangible (non material).

Africa

African values include the following: human life; home; living and offering help or material things; truth; land; the supernatural; goodness;

beauty; religion; ancestors; worship (ancestral in African culture); age; honor; respect for African custom, tradition, culture and civilization; respect for the aged, parents and grandparents; moral values and morality; music, dance, hospitality, love for/practice of the extended family; loyalty to ethnicity but not necessarily embracing ethnocentrism and Majimboism and other inward-looking tendencies that are against African traditional values; nature, events and oral stories, rituals; love for the community; children, marriage and traditional forms of dowry; justice, economic fairness, and barter; African Socialism, Nationalism, and Pan-Africanism; Ubuntu, Ujamaa, and Harambee (Swahili for pulling together); village and village parenthood; Negritude, consensus in decision-making; agriculture and African heritage, and the like. These traditional values of Africa have been expanded by later and new values such as Christianity and Islam; and the new value systems of/in urban areas, such as money and other economic imperatives that traditionally did not constitute African values. Self-determination and self-sufficiency tending to stress individualism have been added to the African value system. Cultural identity and personality to humankind and the urge to make contributions to the community, society, and even globally have been parts of the African history and civilization which, when translated into global knowledge, become important tenets of alliances and coalitions as embedded in African foreign policy, diplomacy, and international relations.

United States

American values are basically Western values that include the stipulations of the U.S. Constitution, Bill of Rights, and Declaration of Independence of 1776: liberty, inalienable rights; freedom of expression; democracy—government for, with, and by the people; equality of rights and opportunity; freedom and the right of ownership; (formal) education; individualism; money speaks; capitalism; freedom and the right of worship; different political cultures; equality of sexes; patriotism; protection of the country first, and not regionalism or parochialism; no racial or ethnic superiority complex; and protection of laws and the rule of law and basic freedom.

THE MONROE DOCTRINE AND THE 21ST CENTURY

The significance of the Monroe Doctrine lay in it being a body of principles for acceptance or a belief statement of official U.S. government policy, especially in foreign affairs, which President Monroe entrusted to his secretary of state, John Quincy Adams, to draft for the president's delivery as what is known today as a State of the Union Address to a joint session of the U.S. Congress on December 2, 1823. Monroe was one of the Founding Fathers of the United States. The essence of Monroe's message was that the European powers were no longer to colonize, or no longer to interfere with the affairs of the newly independent states of America. The United States, which had not supported the European colonization policies and practices, planned to stay neutral in wars between European powers and their colonies. However, if in the Americas, such wars would be viewed by the United States as hostile.

The implications of the Monroe Doctrine revealed themselves in a number of actions. These include the support of the president to the Back to Africa Movement of the 1800s that eventually produced Liberia in West Africa. No wonder then, that Liberia's capital, Monrovia, got its name from James Monroe, the fifth U.S. president (1817–1825). Apart from that moral opposition to colonialism, the United States was fighting with Spain to buy Florida, and began to recognize Argentina, Chile, Colombia, and Mexico in 1822. This American tradition of recognizing subjugated colonial countries for self-rule was advocated later by U.S. presidents, including Woodrow Wilson and John F. Kennedy (the 28th and 35th).

THE CULTURAL FRONT

The diversity of cultures on the African continent leads to many cultural clashes. Africans and Americans differ in perceptions of each other, as well as having leaders' with differences of ideology (communism and capitalism). Africans follow customs, traditions, and cultures, which are the soul of every African nation or group of people. African values are quite different from American values, as we have established.

Whereas the diversity of cultures in the United States has made the United States become a melting pot, in Africa, the diversity of cultures and individuality is stronger than it is in the United States. The common features between Americans and Africans include their colonial past; problems of "roots"; political culture based upon European culture; and many paradoxes that are common (e.g., in the United States, there is poverty in wealth, whereas in Africa, there is wealth in poverty). The United States and Africa both acknowledge good and bad policies and practices, corruption and their consequences. America and Africa support the UN Charter and its principles and purposes. Africans and African Americans share many viewpoints and African Diasporism. Both the United States and Africa are, in principle, opposed to tyranny, exploitation, and international terrorism. African values include Negritude, customs, and traditions. The U.S. struggle for independence produced a movement and a revolution against Great Britain that prevailed in the years 1775–1781, until the drafting of the U.S. Constitution. The American colonies fought against the alleged tyranny of the British government, just as Africans fought against colonialism and imperialism. In Africa, the independence struggles also led to the pouring of blood to get rid of colonialism and subjugation. In Africa, as in America, three schools of thought emerged on unity (in Africa) and union (in America). Both America and Africa became by-products of Western civilization.

Of the divergent features, the following are noteworthy: Africa is a continent, whereas America is a country. Education and money are important values in American culture; conditionality and arrogance of power could be guiding tenets in U.S. foreign policy, depending on the type of administration that may be in place. Humiliation, exploitation, and state weakness are, on the other hand, African facts that weaken African dignity and Africanism as the foundation for identity in Africa. Democracy means one thing for Americans and completely another for Africans. In like manner, the Cold War politics meant one thing for Africans and another for Americans. Also, the United States developed a "hands off" foreign policy in the Monroe Doctrine of 1823. Nothing like that has existed for Africa. In fact, it has not been successful for African leaders to form a united states of Africa, whereas in the United States, American strength has been embedded in their unionism.

NOTES

1. Jean Bodin (1530–1596) was a French political theorist, economist, lawyer, natural philosopher, and historian of the Renaissance era. Bodin is often described as the Father of International Law. He expounded on the doctrine of sovereignty in his book *Les Six Livres de la République* [Six Books of the Commonwealth] (1576). See chapter 8.

2. Ernest Satow, *Guide to Diplomatic Practice*, 6th ed. (Oxford University Press, 2009).

3. Thomas C. Schelling, "The Diplomacy of Violence," in *International Politics*, eds. Robert J. Art and Robert Jervis (Boston and Toronto: Little, Brown and Company, 1984) 171–185.

4. Joseph Frankel, *International Politics, Conflict and Harmony* (London: Penguin Books Press Ltd., 1973) 145–150.

5. John A. Vasquez, ed., "War," in *The Classic of International Relations*, 3rd ed. (Englewood, Cliffs, NJ: Prentice Hall, Inc., 1995) 204–243.

6. John G. Stoessinger, "Diplomacy and Political Order" in *The Might of Nations, Part III, The International Struggle for Order* (New York: Random House, 1979) 261–278.

7. Henry A. Kissinger, *Diplomacy* (New York: Simon Schuster Paperbacks, 1994).

CHAPTER 8

Slave Trade and the Effects of African Slavery on Geopolitics

Slavery and the slave trade combined are an institution, process, and practice of forced or unpaid labor in which labor mistreatment and dehumanization are practiced. Slavery predates written records and has existed for millennia and in practically all continents and cultures throughout the world. In some societies, slavery was a vital socioeconomic system.

The expression "slave" is derived from the Medieval term "slavic," meaning a people of Central and Eastern Europe and Southern Russia, many of whom were sold into slavery after the conquest of their lands by the Holy Roman Empire. In Latin a slave is called "servus." The Slavs did not enjoy rich lives. So they used to travel to the Mediterranean Region from Eastern Europe, looking for what one today might call "summer jobs," that would enable them to earn some food and other goods in kind, such as used clothes, shoes, and similar items for daily use. The Slavs would buy or get these necessities from their temporary employers, and would take them back to their families. Such labor was cheap for the people for whom the jobs were done. Given that slavery has always been linked to the exploitation of the majority of society by the few rich and well-to-do, exploitation was prevalent in slavery and slave work. Wherever the slave trade became a lucrative business, it became very hard to abolish. That is why slavery still exists in the 21st century in places such as Sudan, even though it is illegal and done in a smaller scope than it was in the past.

MUSLIM AND ARAB SLAVE TRADE IN AFRICA

Slavery, however, can be traced to early records such as the Bible and the ca. 1760 BCE Code of Hammurabi, which refers to slavery as an established institution. Historically, slavery thrived in ancient cultures that had highly developed civilization—like in ancient Egypt, Assyria, ancient Greece, Rome, and the Islamic Caliphate. Even the Roman Catholics approved slavery and slave trade when Pope Nicholas V issued his Papal Bull in 1452. The Dum Diversas granted Afonso V of Portugal the right to reduce any Saracens, pagans, and any other unbelievers to hereditary slavery. This papal action against the Saracen Muslims legitimized slave trade, and these papal bulls justified the subsequent practice of slave trade and of European colonialism.

In Africa, slavery and the slave trade were practiced, and causes for the trade varied from captures in wars to greed and conduct of business in human beings. When the Portuguese started to conduct legitimate trade with African chiefs and kings, the business was limited to coastal areas, as it was risky for Europeans to venture into the interior where weather conditions, disease, and even African hostility were harsh. Trade was in goods and services. But when the Portuguese came to learn that the chiefs and their agents were conducting illegitimate trade in captured Africans, the Europeans started to buy those precious commodities and shipped and sold them to Europe. That was around the 1440s. That trade became lucrative and lasted for 400 years until its abolition at the beginning of the 19th century. Even so, the slave trade continued until the 1860s.

But before the start of European-led slavery and slave trade in Africa, Arabs had been dealing in the slave trade from Africa since the 9th century CE.

THE ATLANTIC SLAVE TRADE

From 1400 CE, slave labor was used to mine gold and diamonds from the forest kingdoms of West Africa—Ghana, Mali, Benin. The mines needed workers, and slaves were sold to supply free/cheap labor. When the Portuguese determined that Arabs had been trading with West Africa across the Sahara Desert long before Europeans/Portuguese "discoveries" of Africa, the Portuguese began to undertake voyages in 1470s along the West African Coast toward the Cape of Good Hope in South Africa to try to reach India to gain access to spices and other goods that they could sell in Europe.

As the Portuguese advanced southward along the Atlantic Coast of Africa from the 1440s and encountered the slave trade, the Portuguese captured Africans, began to sell them as slaves, and thereby began a very lucrative business. In the 1480s, the Portuguese established trading bases on the African Coast and began buying Akan gold in exchange for slaves from Benin (forest areas) and cassava and maize, which the Portuguese had brought from Brazil.

Portuguese commercial interest grew in Africa with passing time. If the Portuguese could control that trade, then European coinage from the African gold would fall into Portuguese hands. So, it was vital for them to reach India and to gain control over those territories through the Cape that would facilitate Portugal's access to India's spices, perfumes, silks, and other luxuries that provided lucrative profits to the Portuguese.

The Portuguese capitalized Atlantic islands from Madeira southward to São Tomé and extended their plantation system for growing sugarcane to the tropical São Tomé Islands, which became the largest single producer of sugar for the European market, using African slave labor, but owned and run by Europeans.

From Africa, the success of slave trade and slavery was exported to the Americas and the Caribbean plantations. After the 1480s, the Portuguese relied on plantations on islands in the Atlantic such as islands of the Americas for sugar, cotton, and tobacco to trade. The Portuguese also had settlements in São Tomé and Príncipe in the Gulf of Guinea where sugarcane plantations were run with slave labor brought from mainland North Africa.

The plantation system for growing sugarcane originally was developed on various Mediterranean islands and in Southern Spain and Portugal during the 14th and early 15th centuries. The slave labor for these plantations was drawn from North Africa and from among the slaves of southern Russia (the Slavs).

From the early 1500s, the Portuguese added shells and luxury cloth from the Indian Ocean trade to the range of goods they offered in exchange for West African gold, salt, and ornaments. They traded southward, away from Songhai and the trans-Saharan trade, toward European trading parts along the African Coast.

Origins and development of trans-Atlantic slave trade can be traced back to the 15th and early 16th centuries. Slaves were captured from chieftains with the help of chiefs. African chiefs and forest kings had agents who helped to capture and sell Africans as slaves. The agents of the chiefs and kings included Arabs who captured Africans and sold them into slavery. The original slave captives came from Gambia and Senegal, and were transported to Portuguese and Spanish plantations for slave labor. The captives from the Niger Delta and Congo River went mostly to São Tomé.

As the Portuguese traded with West Africans and sought trade routes to India and a route to the Americas and the Caribbean, European colonization of the New World followed Christopher Columbus's voyage of 1492 that discovered America. In 1532, the first African captives were taken directly across the Atlantic and sold into slavery. Thereafter, small cargo loads of slaves went to America in the 1500s, but from 1630s the Dutch, French, and English, questioned the Europeans involved in the rapidly growing sugar plantations.

CAPTURED AFRICANS IN THE MIDDLE EAST AND SOUTHWEST ASIA

The Arabs practiced slavery in North Africa and East Africa. The markets for African slaves were in the Middle East and North Africa. They traded in East Africa and North Africa. They traded and captured Africans for 10 centuries (9th–19th centuries), concentrating on north and northwest Africa across the Sahara to Ghana and Senegambia, for example. The Islamic Caliphate emerged in the 8th century CE and grew strong in the 9th century. It can be stated that the Arab slave trade in Africa actually started in the 8th century.

Writers are divided as to how many Africans were taken as slaves to the Americas, the Middle East, and Far East. It is possible that more than 30 to 50 million slaves were shipped to the Americas, whereas between 11 and 18 million Africans slaves were shipped to the Orient via the Red Sea and the Indian Ocean. This was a very lucrative business, especially between 650 and 1900 CE.

In both cases, the main routine of the slave trade was to make money. The methods of capturing and treating the Africans were cruel and the reasons for enslavement of the Africans include political, economic, military war, taxes, confiscation, and punishment for "trespassing" and other unwelcome behavior.

When Africans were considered dangerous or posed political and other competing acts, this led to their enslavement. Generally, those enslaved whether as war prisoners or for other reasons, were men, but women and children could also be taken as slaves for the trans-Atlantic trade. It was the Dutch, Danes, British, Portuguese, Icelanders, and Spaniards who carried out the trade.

The slave trade had a large negative impact on Africans throughout the continent. Because of the long distances to their destinations, the slave trade took away "the producers," those in the prime age brackets—just like HIV/AIDS does today in Africa. This loss of brainpower, muscle, and skills, resulted in the draining of the veins of the African nations. This introduced an inferiority complex in many. The African psyche toward Europeans and Arabs and the hatred and repulsive attitudes that prevail in some quarters of Africa can trace their roots to the realities of African life during centuries of slave trade.

Often called the Islamic slave trade, the Arabs took Africans from Kenya, Tanzania, Sudan, Eretria, and Ethiopia across the Red Sea and the Indian Ocean, mainly to Iraq, Iran, Kuwait, and Turkey, as well as to India and Pakistan. In this way, the African was transported, mostly to the New World and the Muslim world, beginning from the 7th century CE, and spread to embrace the Mediterranean, North Africa, and the Liberian Peninsula, as well as parts of the Byzantine Empire (Western Asia and Persia).

The slave trade in Africa replaced the legitimate trade that had existed between African kingdoms and Arab traders. Before the slave trade, goods traded were gold, salt, cloth, and agricultural commodities.

The Sudanese Belt consisted of Arab states and kingdoms stretching east and west from Sudan to the Empires of Ghana, Mali, and Kanem–Bornu, as well as Nubia, Axim, and the Barbary states of the Mediterranean—where pirates captured African slaves. From Zanzibar were the Bantu-speaking Africans who were captured as slaves on the East African Coast[1] from Tanzania, Mozambique, and Malawi. Those Africans were shipped to the Orient as slaves starting from around 696 CE, and often were bartered for objects of various different types: cloth in the Sudan; horses in the North; lengths of cloth, pottery, Venetian glass, beads, dye stuffs, and jewels. At that time throughout black Africa, gold coins, cowrie shells from the Indian Ocean or the Atlantic Ocean, canaries, and Launder, were used as money. Sacks of cowries fetched money.

In western North Africa the slave markets included Tangier, Marrakesh, Algiers, Tripoli, Cairo, and Aswani. In West Africa Aoudoghost (Mauritania), Timbuktu, and Gao in Mali held slave markets. In East Africa slave markets could be found in Bagamoyo, Zanzibar, and Kihua (in Sofala/Veira in Mozambique) as well as in the Horn of Africa and Mogadishu in Somalia and Zeila.

From the foregoing, it can be concluded that the African Diaspora, even though it did not spring full-blown from the African slave trade, did nonetheless have slavery and the slave trade as its most elaborate factory. In like manner, it can be affirmed that the transformation of Africa by European colonization started mainly during the era of the illegitimate trade in captured Africans.

EUROPEAN CHRISTIANS AND SLAVE TRADE IN AFRICA

Thus, in the early years of the slave trade in Africa, the Islamic states of the western Sudan did very well. They included Ghana (750–1076 BCE) and Songhai (1275–1591 CE). In these states more than one-third of their populations was slaves. Between 1300 and 1900 CE, about one-third of the population in Senegambia was slaves, and by the beginning of the 19th century the slave trade was a lucrative business practically everywhere in Africa.

It is the slavery and slave trade that used the trans-Atlantic passage however, that is remembered most vividly. There are several reasons for this including the following:

- The Atlantic slave trade was the most brutal, the most dehumanizing, and the most bestial of all the slave trades. this was especially true of the British practices and treatment of the slaves. Human beings, often naked, were bundled in the decks of ships and tied with chains. The sanitary conditions were deplorable.

- "Triangular" trade (from Europe to Africa, the Americas, and then back to Europe) involved enormous wealth in gold, diamonds, and other minerals as well. Experts in agriculture thought slaves improved the production of the soil and crops on the plantations. The slave traders in Africa and slave owners in America experienced a lot of lucrative business. They could not be stopped even after the abolition of slavery in 1807 in the United States.

- The trans-Atlantic slave trade was known globally and condemned globally by all races of the earth. In England, political leaders and humanists like William Wilberforce spread the gospel against the slave trade and tirelessly worked for its abolition both from within and outside the British Parliament.

- Perhaps more importantly, the slave trade was a very hot political issue. It divided and weakened the United States, resulted in the American Civil War, and caused the assassination of President Abraham Lincoln.

Once the Portuguese discovered the "black gold" being traded in the forest kingdoms of the African interior, they started to buy African slaves and sold them in Europe and in the Americas. It was slaves, pepper, cotton, salt, ivory, gold, and other commodities. The African slave became the most valuable commodity that was taken from West Africa. They were taken to Lisbon in small numbers starting in the 1440s. The first slaves landed in Lisbon, Portugal, from the Guinea Coast in 1460.

From Lisbon, the slaves were taken to the islands of São Tomé and Fernando Po. In 1500, Pedro Cabral "discovered" Brazil. Soon after, the African slaves were transported from Portugal and Spain to the Caribbean. It took about a month to get to the Americans from Portugal and Spain. The 16th century saw a huge influx of slaves from Africa to the Americas, especially to the West Indian island of Hispaniola from Spain as sanctioned by Spanish kings.

In 1618, a British ship captained by George Thompson sailed 400 miles up the Gambia River, where the captain was killed. Thereafter, British ships challenged the Portuguese monopoly of the West African slave trade. The British added African slaves to their trade in African cotton, gold, and ivory. By 1620, the British assumed control of the West African Coast and in that very year, the *Mayflower* set sail from England to Plymouth in the present-day U.S. state of Massachussets, thereby marking the beginning of the British colonization in America. Slaves started flowing into the English colonies in North America. In subsequent years, the Danes, Dutch, and other Europeans increased their interest in Africa.

THE CHARTERED COMPANIES

The Europeans formed companies for trading in Europe and overseas. The idea was to avoid unnecessary competition in Europe and to do business overseas. That approach prompted the newly created trading companies to seek protection from their royal leaders. Consequently, the businesses known as the East Indies Company and West Indies Company received protection form the kings through charters that gave the companies the right to fly their nation's flag. The Dutch East Indies Company had received similar protection from the monarchy. This enabled the companies to do business and make profit from which the royal masters also benefit.

The chartered companies were thus associated with exploration, foreign trade, and colonization that came into existence with the formation of the European nation-states and their overseas expansion. The granting of a charter to such a company signified support from the state. A chartered company was a corporation. This was a group of individual investors and traders operating with their own capital and bound only by the general rules of the company charter. The main purposes of the corporation were trade, exploration, and colonization.

The company exercised law-making and treaty-making functions that were subject to the approval of the home government. The chartered companies were granted other privileges. Each chartered company received a monopoly of trade or a monopoly for a specific type of trade.

Among the European chartered companies were the Dutch East Indies Company (1602), Dutch West Indies Company (1621), French Royal West Indian Company (1664–1674), German East Africa Company (1885), the Royal Niger Company (1886), British South Africa Company (1888), and others. These companies traded and made lots of profit for themselves and for their sovereigns. Later, the chartered companies were replaced by modern companies that had limited liabilities.

NOTE

1. W.H. Schoff, trans., *Periplus of the Erythraean Sea: Travel and Trade in the Indian Ocean by a Merchant in the First Century*, (New York: Longmans, Green, and Co., 1912).

CHAPTER 9

Conclusion: African Geopolitics before the "Scramble for Africa" Patterns Set

HISTORICAL BACKGROUND

The year 1800 marked the end of the beginning of a new but significant era in African history. Some writers have suggested that that year marked the beginning of modern Africa. In the view of the present writer, however, there is no single date on which all are agreed that marks the beginning of "modern" Africa history. What is necessarily "universally modern" for everybody in the modernity of Africa?

Nonetheless, significant milestones occurred along the path to political independence in Africa.[1] If the whole African road to independence is considered, then a big number of historical posts need to be highlighted at the beginning of the narrative of Africa from the Cradle of Humankind to the present, as served from the perspectives of the foreign policy, diplomacy, and international relations of Africa.

Thus, in looking at Africa in a nutshell, it is not hard to see the important milestones in Africa's condition from the start to the present: the creation of the universe and the appearance of Pangaea and Gondwana; the evolutionary process of humankind; the gathering and hunting skills acquired for human survival; the domestication of crops and animals for human use; the ages in human history, including the Stone, Iron, Copper, Silver, and Gold Ages, and the use of metallurgy; agriculture and the roots of the African person; the Bantu-speaking expansions in central, southern and eastern Africa's antiquity and its fascinating discoveries; the appearance of the Sahara Desert around 5000 BCE, marking new natural and human orders up to the fall of Rome in 476 CE; the first foreign invasions and colonization of Africa in antiquity; proliferation of new political entities in Africa, better known as kingdoms, empires, super empires, and city-state systems; the events shaping Africa between 1 CE and the 16th century CE, including the globalization of two religions (Christianity and Islam) and the first "modern" (CE) contacts with Europeans when the Portuguese arrived in 1415 CE; and the spread of trade broadly in Africa, encompassing legitimate goods and services (salt, ivory, gold, diamonds, etc.) and illegitimate goods—the "African black gold"—the African slaves taken for illegitimate trade.

With the advent of strong rejection of and opposition to slavery and the slave trade, the value of European trade in Africa, and Africans moved from the slave trade to the urge for "exploration and discovery" of nature in Africa. That era was a precursor of the imposition of European, alien rule in Africa.

The first individual Europeans in "modern" Africa served as agents of the gathering storms of Europeans everywhere in Africa: in West, North, East, Central, and Southern Africa. They began to explore and discover, as if there had not been any existence at all of the "things of nature" that they set out to discover.

But more importantly, the advent of the Back to Africa Movement in the 1800s, especially between 1800 and 1945, produced important seeds for Africa's international relations, foreign policy, and diplomacy as we know them today. Imperialism and neo-imperialism prompted a wide expansionist life in Western Europe leading from the first European settlement in the African interior by the Dutch in the Cape region of South Africa in 1652, to the eventual colonization and transformation of the African continent. As will be shown in Volume II, this is why the year 1885 is known in history as the "Annus Horribilis" for Africa—it was the beginning of Africa's colonial enslavement. It can be stated that the process of decolonization in Africa actually started in earnest at the Pan-African Congress in Manchester, England, in 1945. As years passed, the pressure for political liberation of Africa intensified. But whose Africa was being created? Was it Europe's Africa or Africa's Africa? This rhetorical question was answered as the years advanced from the earliest part of the 20th century to 1960. This is why the year 1960 is also known as the "Annus Mirabilis"—a wonderful and joyful year that marked the beginning of political independence in Africa.

Then came the inter-bellum years for Africa, between the two global wars of 1914–1918 and 1939–1945, followed by the post-colonial era. During these years and "mini eras," Europe prepared itself for invading and conquering all five regions of Africa—North, Southern, West, East, and Central Africa. This reminds one of Julius Caesar's maxim of "veni, vidi, vinci" ("I came, I saw, I conquered"). That was why African geopolitics were set up in Africa before the "scramble for Africa."

In endeavoring to trace the origins and development (i.e., the foundations and dictates) of African international relations, foreign policy, and diplomacy, it is quickly established that their roots date back to remotest antiquity. Therefore, it is in geography and topography; it is in the skills of governance and government, and in human security and safety in Africa; and in observing the rule of law, diplomacy, democratization, and democracy, as well as in rights, duties of mankind, and the eradication of slavery and the slave trade that the genuine foundations of African international relations, foreign policy, and diplomacy can be found. It is also in correcting the evils of colonization that we must trace the dictates and determinants of African international relations, foreign policy, and diplomacy.

The analysis of the African Condition has revealed that the events, themes, issues, and dictates that have shaped Africa from time immemorial are best understood if clustered into three eras: the pre-colonial, colonial, and post-colonial periods of time, with mini eras falling in between the major periods.

The first volume of this book has addressed Africa's condition from more than 10 million years ago to the end of the 18th century, more or less up to the year 1800. Slavery and the slave trade in captured Africans was one of the most durable of all of the injustices done to the African people. No race has suffered the kind and extent of dehumanization and humiliation that were accorded to the African person through slavery and the slave trade.

The slave trade in Africa took two major tracks, as described in the previous chapter. First was the Arab slave trade, which started in the 7th century CE following the globalization of Islam but became more pronounced from the 9th century. The Arab slave trade through the Indian Ocean and the Red Sea took captured Africans as slaves to the Middle East and beyond to the Orient. At its height, this cruel business lasted for at least 10 centuries.

Second was the European slave trade, better known by several titles such as the "Trans-Atlantic Slave Trade," the "Middle Passage," and "Triangular Trade" (triangular, meaning from Europe, to Africa, the Americas, and back to Europe). First, the European slave traders would come to Africa with items like pieces of cloth and use these to buy slaves from Africa. Then, the Europeans shipped the African slaves across the Atlantic Ocean to the Americas. This journey took about four weeks to cross the Atlantic, but the cargo could also be unloaded along the way—especially on the Atlantic Ocean islands of São Tomé and Príncipe, Guinea-Bissau, and Cape Verde. These slave trading posts became Portuguese properties even before the scramble for Africa started. Of particular observation is that slavery and the slave trade, as institutions, have always been linked to civilization, exploration, and wealth. In the triangular European trade, for example, the relationship was always that of the "haves" exploiting the "have-nots," and in each case the exploiters have always been smaller in number than the exploited. Thus, slavery has always been dictated by affluence.

Slavery and the slave trade have been business practices in Africa and elsewhere in the world because wealth and civilization create class societies with superior and inferior characteristics. The superiority complexes prompt the haves to look down on the have-nots and to exploit and dominate the have-nots, who, are generally the lowest strata of society.

ABOLITION OF THE SLAVE TRADE

In Western Europe, the slave system aroused little protest until the 18th century when rational thinkers of the Enlightenment criticized it for violating the rights of man, and many Christian groups, such as the Quakers, criticized it as un-Christian.

This resulted in the banning of imported African slaves into the Americas according to the following timetable:

- British colonies: 1807;
- United States: 1808;
- British West Indies: 1833; and
- French colonies: 1848.

In Great Britain, the slave trade was abolished by an act of Parliament on March 25, 1807, that was engineered by Prime Minister William Wilberforce. On August 28, 1833, the Slavery Abolition Act received royal assent. By August 1, 1834, all slaves in the British Empire and in Europe were freed.

In the United States, the issue of slavery was contentious from the nation's beginning, and emancipation was gradual. In 1775, Thomas Paine (1737–1805) wrote *Slavery in America*, which was the first published U.S. work that advocated abolishing slavery and freeing the slaves. In 1785, John Jay (1745–1824), the first attorney general of United States, founded the New York Mission Society. At the Constitutional Convention of 1787, agreement allowed the federal government to abolish the international slave trade, but not prior to 1808. In 1821–1822, Liberia, which gained political independence in July 1847, was founded in Africa by the American Colonization Society. This group supported the repatriation of freed African Americans to Liberia and its supporters and founders included Abraham Lincoln, James Monroe, and Henry Clay.

The abolition of slavery in the United Stated was advanced in 1860 with the election of Abraham Lincoln to the U.S. presidency. He opposed the spread of slavery to the country's western frontier and its continuation in the South. In 1863, President Lincoln issued an Emancipation Proclamation that freed all slaves. The conclusion of the Civil War and 1865 passage of the 13th Amendment to the U.S. Constitution prohibited slavery throughout the United States.

Thus, the new global order necessitated by the actions of nations to abolish the slave trade was an important milestone in African and world history, for from those actions emerged the African Diaspora that not only played a major role in the formation and establishment of foreign policy, diplomacy, and international relations, but also established patterns for inter-African and international relations between Africans and other peoples and countries.

One can thus state with certainty that the scramble for Africa at the end of the 19th century was set up by the events that shaped Africa prior to the meetings of Europeans that fixed the partitioning of Africa among the various European colonial powers. The events leading to, and determining, the actual scramble for Africa are analyzed in Volume II of this study.

NOTE

1. Roland Oliver and Anthony Atmore, *Africa Since 1800*, 5th ed (New York: Cambridge University Press, 2005).